FORGOTTEN VOICES

OF THE HOLOCAUST

LYN SMITH

ISIS
LARGE PRINT
Oxford

First published in Great Britain 2005
by
Ebury Press

Published in Large Print 2007 by ISIS Publishing Ltd.,
7 Centremead, Osney Mead, Oxford OX2 0ES
by arrangement with
Ebury Press

British Library Cataloguing in Publication Data
Smith, Lyn, 1934–
   Forgotten voices of the Holocaust. – Large print ed.
   1. Holocaust, Jewish (1939–1945) – Personal
   narratives
   2. Large type books
   I. Title
   940.5'318'0922

ISBN 978–0–7531–5669–8 (hb)
ISBN 978–0–7531–5670–4 (pb)

Printed and bound in Great Britain by
T. J. International Ltd., Padstow, Cornwall

Contents

The struggle of men against power is the struggle of memory against forgetting.

Milan Kundera

Author's Preface

I first became aware of the Holocaust sixty years ago as World War II ended. In particular it was the newspaper and newsreel images of the emaciated bodies being bulldozed into mass graves in Bergen-Belsen concentration camp that shocked me into an entirely different perspective of the war which I had spent in relatively sheltered circumstances as a child evacuee in the Sussex countryside. Yet, although thousands of inmates — Jews and non-Jews — perished there of starvation and disease in the most terrible conditions, Bergen-Belsen did not reveal the full horror of the Holocaust because it was not a Nazi death camp as such. There were no planned massed killings, gassings or crematoria. The "Final Solution" — the mass extermination of Jews and gypsies — took place farther east in the six designated death camps situated in occupied Poland, Auschwitz being the most infamous.

Working as a freelance interviewer for the Imperial War Museum's Sound Archive in 1978 gave me the opportunity and privilege of recording testimonies of men and women who had been directly affected by the Nazi Holocaust. This was a pioneering project on the topic; it covered refugees who had fled Nazi Germany in the 1930s and who had been interned as "enemy aliens" during the invasion scare of 1940, as well as their pre-war lives and experiences of the rise of Hitler.

Over the next two decades, along with other interviewers, I continued recording the Holocaust story. By then "Holocaust" was interpreted by the Sound Archive to include not only the millions murdered or imprisoned by the Nazis during the period 1933–45, but also those whose lives were affected by Hitler's policies, or who were witnesses to the persecution and atrocities. Therefore, refugees, families of the murdered and of survivors, aid workers and troops who liberated the camps were included. It was due to this broad definition that I came full circle when meeting and recording the late Bill Essex — the soldier who had the gruesome task of bulldozing the piles of bodies into the mass graves of Bergen-Belsen in April 1945.

When planning for the permanent Holocaust Exhibition started in the mid 1990s, the recording programme was expanded. Survivor testimony was to have a key role in the exhibition which was opened by HM The Queen in the Millennium year. Today there are 785 Holocaust-related recordings in the Sound Archive. It is from this extensive, rich and varied archive that over a hundred voices have been selected for this book. In order to give as full a picture as possible, these have been supplemented with a small, complementary range from the United States Holocaust Memorial Museum in Washington, DC.

Throughout my interviewing and transcribing work, I have been impressed with the unique nature of each survivor's experience. Every man, woman and child experienced and coped with their ordeal in their own way — Roman Halter, for instance, who summoned his murdered family to his bedside each evening to give account of his survival for yet another day; or George Hartman, whose desire to experience love and sex gave him the will to live. Different reactions are given to wearing the Star of David: the pride expressed by Janice Ingram and Anna Bergman compared with the shame and humiliation felt by Jan Hartman and Harry Lowit. Each person experienced their own particular portion of Holocaust history and not one had a complete overview of the monstrous system in its entirety.

Gathered together, I hope this mosaic of voices gives access to the complexity and human reality behind the abstract statistics of extermination and allows readers to see beyond the stereotypes of what constitutes a "victim". We can read and see films about the violence of *Kristallnacht* in November 1938, but how much more vivid and real this becomes when we hear Susan Sinclair describe the terror and distress she and her parents suffered when Nazi louts broke into their apartment, engaged in an orgy of destruction, attacking her and ripping her nightgown to shreds. There are numerous historical accounts of deportations to Auschwitz and other camps, but listening to Trude Levi or Barbara Stimler describing their journey in locked, airless cattle wagons to Auschwitz, we get a vivid sense of the overcrowding, stench and fear, as well as the bewilderment and shock at the hellish scene that awaited them when the wagon doors were flung open.

Talking about their traumatic experiences has not come easily to the majority of people in this book, which is why so many remained silent for so long, their voices truly forgotten. During interview sessions, I experienced first-hand the enormous effort required, as well as the distress which occurred when survivors related their ordeals, many for the first time. Details were often too painful to recall and many have explained the inadequacy of language to convey the sights, sounds, smells, humiliation, degradation and sheer terror endured. Also, given the challenge of building new lives in the austerity of the post-war world, they were usually too busy to dwell on the past; and if survivors wanted to talk — and many, like Kitty Hart-Moxon, did — then few were willing to listen: the mood of the time was to put the war behind and get on with life. Although the International Military Tribunal in Nuremberg 1945/46 had revealed for the first time the full horror of Nazi rule, the genocide against the Jews was not distinguished from the general Nazi barbarity nor recognised for what it was — the greatest human rights' crime of the twentieth century. It was only after the Adolf Eichmann trial in Israel in 1961 that the situation changed and the world began to pay serious attention. The fiftieth and sixtieth commemorations of the liberations of Auschwitz and Bergen-Belsen opened up the subject still wider. Today the Holocaust is one of the most documented historical events with personal testimony at its very heart.

Despite the brutality and degradation endured, these testimonies are far from being unrelieved images of darkness and despair. Although, as Alfred Huberman explains, the law of the jungle prevailed in the camps, many instances of mutual support, goodness and little acts of reciprocity are recalled: the precious — even life-saving — gift of a needle and thread Jan Hartman received from another prisoner to patch his threadbare, torn clothes. There are countless examples of how, even in the most deprived, degrading and cruel circumstances, people held firm to their humanity and steadfastly clung to the values that their parents and communities had bequeathed them; and there was resistance to the Nazi order in both overt and more spiritual ways.

Jewish humour persisted; although often of a gallows nature, jokes were made in the grimmest of circumstances. Little episodes of cultural life were clawed out to ease the pain and uncertainty of daily existence and precious moments of love were snatched by couples whenever possible. There are even cases of small gestures of kindness and humanity from individual Nazis and their functionaries — the Hitler Youth who saved Halina Kahn's life as she returned from a smuggling trip outside the Lodz Ghetto, or the SS who took pity on Jan Imich who had collapsed with exhaustion while working in Dora concentration camp. Most remarkable is the tolerance and lack of vengeance shown by many survivors towards their former tormentors, although justice has been vigorously sought and indignation and anger persists. This is not to imply that survivors emerged unscathed. As the late Rabbi Albert Friedlander has explained:

We are still maimed sufferers with injuries that will not heal. We have lost members of our families. We have lost the great community of Eastern Jewry. We have lost the most special warmth and gaiety of Sephardic Jewry along the Mediterranean Sea. We have lost our scholars and our simple people. And we hate the evil of the world which has overwhelmed us, the Sinti-Roma, the homosexuals and the anti-Nazis who were wiped out by that evil in the camps. We mourn the million of children and we wonder what the world would be like if their lives had been permitted to flower.

This book is dedicated to all victims of the Nazi Holocaust: those who were murdered and those who survived.

Lyn Smith, May 2005

Acknowledgements

One of the pleasures of completing a book is being able to acknowledge and thank those who have helped bring the work to fruition. Within the Imperial War Museum I should like to thank the Director General, Robert Crawford, for allowing full use of the Museum's resources. The Sound Archive has provided the bulk of services and material and I thank the Keeper, Margaret Brooks, and Peter Hart, Richard McDonough, John Stopford-Pickering and Richard Hughes for their enthusiastic and unstinting support throughout. In the photographic department, I am very appreciative of the help Rose Gerrard, Claudia Condry and Yvonne Oliver have given. The Holocaust Exhibitions Office has given its support for the project and I would like to thank Suzanne Bardgett and Steve Slack for their advice and assistance. Terry Charman, the Museum's historian, deserves a very special vote of thanks for editing the text with meticulous care and for the advice and help he has given. In her role as agent for the IWM as well as for myself, Barbara Levy helped initiate the project and has proved to be a strong and valued support throughout — thank you Barbara. Last, but certainly not least, Elizabeth Bowers, the Publications Manager, could not have been more helpful; ably assisted by Gemma Maclagan and Kay Trew, she has guided the book through all stages to publication. My thanks to them all.

I am indebted to Dr Joan Ringelheim, Director of the Department of Oral History, in the United States Holocaust Memorial Museum (USHMM), for the use of the archive and wish also to thank Ina Navazelskis, Michlean Amir and Maren Read for the help they have given me in selecting a small, but vital range of interviews and photographs with which to complement the IWM's collection. I am also very grateful for the excellent translations provided by Edita Jodonyte, Andrew Visnevski, Anita Andreasian and Nina Assauer.

I could not have been more fortunate in having Jake Lingwood as my editor and publisher. My thanks to Jake and his dynamic "can-do" team at Ebury Publishing, with special thanks to Claire Kingston, and to Rachel Rayner, Caroline Newbury and Katherine Norman-Butler.

Laurence Rees's outstanding documentary series *Auschwitz*, broadcast earlier this year on BBC2, was truly inspirational. I am honoured and very grateful that he agreed to write such a splendid Foreword.

I very much appreciate the enthusiasm my husband, Peter, and children have shown for the book and give special thanks to Alison for her perceptive comments on both script and photographs.

My greatest debt is to the survivors and witnesses who have given their testimony and allowed the use of tapes and photographs. To survivors in particular, I'd like to say what a privilege it has been to record and present your voices. I realise that each voice deserves its own book, and for every voice presented here, there are hundreds of others of equal worth and interest. The good thing is that they are all preserved for posterity in the Sound Archive, potent evidence against Holocaust denial. Finally, I hope that all survivors will accept the simple dedication of this book as an indication of the respect and affection I feel for them, as well as my sympathy for their losses.

Lyn Smith, May 2005

Foreword

This book will trouble you deeply. You will hear stories that will haunt and disturb you. And yet I wholeheartedly recommend it. That's not as strange as it may first appear, because the very point of this book is that it should upset you. It must make you so upset that you will determine never to forget this history.

The first-hand testimony gathered here, of those who suffered during the Nazi genocide, is a significant contribution to our emotional understanding of the Holocaust. Its effect is cumulative. There's not one single piece of testimony here that is so wholly distinctive that it will alter the consensus historical view that has grown up around the subject. But taken together — as desperate story builds upon desperate story — this material constitutes a devastating hammer-blow of a read. It is another fine example of the important work of the Imperial War Museum in chronicling the effects of conflict.

There is a lot we can learn from this book about the nature of human behaviour in crisis. It confirms me in my belief — which I expressed in the introduction to my own recent book on Auschwitz — that mostly what we learn from a study of the Holocaust is "not good". Not good because we face head-on the easy malleability of the human spirit. Not good because we learn — what we always suspected and hoped was not so — how the majority of people most often act in their own narrow self-interest. For instance, John Silberman recollects how in the face of Nazi persecution "my parents' gentile friends did not stand by them. The average German did not care." And Hedy Epstein remembers her experience at school, directly after the Nazi attacks on the Jews at *Kristallnacht* in 1938, when her own head teacher suddenly pointed at her and said "Get out, you dirty Jew!"

The depressing view of human nature that emerges from this testimony is not confined to the so-called "bystanders"; it also spreads amongst the persecuted themselves. One of the most revealing recollections in the book is that of Susan Sinclair who recalls how her father found, when he was imprisoned in the concentration camp of Dachau, that the prisoners became so desperate that they fought over a dead man's toothbrush. In the camps, just as amongst the rest of the German population, self interest was key.

But not everyone acted for themselves. There are also a number of testimonies which point to the possibility of virtuous actions in the face of danger. In one case — that of Denmark — a whole society acted together to save the Jews. More common were the extraordinary acts of individuals. Halina Kahn survived only because, when she was on a dangerous excursion outside the Lodz ghetto, a member of the Hitler Youth unexpectedly hid her Jewish star when it fell into view. And in Austria, John Lawrence was saved when a senior SS officer said to the louts who were assaulting him that they must stop hurting him at once, since the Germans wanted "law and order" not "thugs like you".

Why did a small minority of people act with kindness and courage? Well, one of the important lessons we learn from this testimony is that we can't ever really know. Moreover, circumstances were so extreme that we can't extrapolate from this material and know for sure how each of us would behave if — God forbid — a similar situation were ever to arise again. I remember Toivi Blatt, a survivor of the death camp of Sobibor, telling me that the one lesson he had learnt from his own horrific experiences was that "nobody knows themselves". He believed, and he should know, that it's impossible to predict human behaviour in extreme conditions. We cannot know how we would act; not, that is, until we are called upon to be tested.

What we also learn from this book is the fragility of the world around us. In Germany, in Hungary, in Czechoslovakia, the minority Jewish populations found that their comfortable lives were ripped apart in a matter of moments. Testimony after testimony of Jewish people who were children when the Nazis came to power, registers one emotion above all in the face of sudden and unexpected persecution — bewilderment. Edith Baneth, for example, was abruptly turned away by her ice skating teacher because she was a Jew. "I couldn't understand," she says, "what had my Jewishness got to do with my ice skating?" In attempting to make sense of this kind of ultimately senseless persecution many people looked inside themselves. What had they done to deserve such treatment? Thus we learn a little known, insidious, consequence of the Nazi actions against the Jews in the 1930s. Tragically, some Jewish children began to blame themselves for their own suffering.

On a more uplifting note, we can marvel at the sheer variety of reasons people found to try and come through this horror. For some it was the thought of staying together and supporting each other as a family, for others it was the dream that one day they could return home, and for the young Czech Jew George Hartman it was the desire not to die before he had lost his virginity.

But there is an important caveat to all this. Not just the obvious one that oral testimony can on occasion by its very nature be partial and fragmentary, but that the stories we should most listen to cannot be present in this book because they belong to people the Nazis murdered. We must bear in mind when reading the testimony contained here that it belongs to the minority, who for whatever reason, managed to survive. No one came back from the gas chambers of Treblinka or from the makeshift graves on the Eastern Front or from the mountains of disease-ridden corpses in the ghettos in Poland to tell us of their experience — the experience that was the norm, not the exception. We must use our own imagination — however inadequate it may be — to try and fill that gap when we read this book.

There is something else that you will search fruitlessly for in this book — any profound explanation of why some people survived and others did not. What you learn instead is the essential capriciousness of life. Some people, for instance, were chosen to live rather than die in the camps simply because they were "lucky". Imagine a work of fiction being constructed around such a plot. The hero is beaten around by a fate he cannot control and survives or dies through chance. Scarcely the recipe for a bestseller, is it? Yet time and again in this book you will see how people have to take the horrific circumstances that are thrust upon them — through no fault of their own — and cope as best they can. And it's this terrible reality that makes this book more important than any popular work of fiction. In this book the good people — the ones the reader should be rooting for — are often killed arbitrarily and unjustly. Such things, as a rule, do not occur in fiction, which is why history can be so much more important.

There's one final reason, of course, why the world is a better place for this book being in it; which is that there are still those who want to pretend none of this ever happened. Recently, at a talk I gave about my Auschwitz book, I was confronted by a Holocaust denier who started screaming at me. He would not listen to argument and was high on insane conspiracy theories. Such people really do exist. And there is always the chance that once everyone personally involved in this terrible history has died, more attempts will be made to diminish or deny what really happened. Each of the people who agreed to give their testimony to this project fights back personally against such a calumny. Each of them bears witness to the truth that there existed in Europe in the middle of the twentieth

century a criminal regime like no other in history. Each
of them preserves the memory of their suffering forever.

Laurence Rees
May 2005

Prologue

The life was very good and we lived like one of the Germans.

Rudi Bamber
German Jewish schoolboy, Nuremberg
My family had lived in Germany for several generations and regarded themselves as Germans mainly. My parents had married in 1919 after my father came back from World War I; I was born in 1920. We usually went to the synagogue on High Holy Days and my parents attempted to inform me about Jewish festivals, but we were not a very religious family. It was a quiet, pleasant sort of childhood on the outskirts of Nuremberg where my uncle had built a large house and we lived in the ground floor with other relatives on the upper floor. My sister was five years younger than me, very Germanic looking, with long fair hair, blue eyes and fair skinned. I was also fair-haired and blue-eyed and got known as having an "Aryan" appearance.

Nuremberg was a beautiful old town with many old buildings. There was a huge market square where, at Christmas, they used to have stalls with toys and sweets; I found it quite exciting to trail around and look at all the different things which were being sold. It was quite a cosmopolitan town with lots of shops and restaurants and there was a big castle. And of course it was the home of Dürer and eventually of the Meistersingers which Wagner wrote an opera about. Bavaria was very right-wing with lots of underlying anti-Semitic attitudes, mainly fostered by the Catholic Church. The Jews had been very prominent in the liberal and progressive left-wing movements; this was disliked by what was largely an agrarian community with very strong right-wing influences. So there was always an undercurrent of anti-Semitism — no coincidence that Hitler started an armed uprising in Munich in the early twenties which was suppressed.

John Fink
German Jewish schoolboy, Berlin
I come from Berlin. I was born on 12 August 1920. My father had a dry-goods store in a suburb of the city and he lost everything during the Depression in 1923/24 when rampant inflation meant that money was worthless. He found employment in a big warehouse in Berlin ... I remember in 1928 there was a terrible winter and my father was out of work for many years. He peddled foodstuff — margarine and sausages — from house to house. During the evenings my father and mother worked for a mail-order house, addressing envelopes. Very, very tough times.

Ruth Foster

German Jewish schoolgirl, Lingen

I was born in 1923 in Lingen, a small provincial town not far from the Dutch border. My father's family had lived in the area since 1670. My mother originated from Holland. Lingen at that time had about 25,000 inhabitants and roughly twenty Jewish families. I was an only child; my parents were fairly comfortable: my father was a cattle dealer as most of the Jews in that area were. We had a Jewish orthodox household; my mother was just a housewife, she loved singing and going to the theatre in the nearest towns of Osnabruck and Münster. We were a very close family: my uncles, aunts and cousins all lived in the province. In the summer we used to go to the forest to pick berries, on a horse and cart my father arranged for us. The life was very good and we lived like one of the Germans; even so we were very Jewish at heart and at home. My father belonged to the local male choir and to the rifle shooting club; he was very outgoing. He was a soldier in the First World War and was quite proud of it. He served with the Hussars and won the decorations of the Iron Cross First Class and Second Class for valour.

I went first of all to kindergarten then an ordinary school in Lingen. At eleven I went to the high school, to the gymnasium in Lingen. I had lots of friends, lots of neighbours, I was very, very popular. I was in the school choir and in the local sports club. I was one of *them*.

(Sir) Hans Krebs
German Jewish biochemist, Freiburg
When I went to Freiburg I was developing my own line of research and I was extremely lucky that what I attempted was a great success. I chose a simple problem: the mechanism by which the end product of nitrogen metabolism is formed in the body, and I made what turned out to be a major discovery which was immediately recognised internationally and nationally. It established me as an independent and original research worker internationally. I published first in '32.

Stephen Dale
German Jewish youth, Berlin
I got involved in the youth movement in 1927 at the age of ten. It was a Jewish youth group called *Kameraden* (Comrades). Youth movements were a very important feature in Germany after the First World War. With the advent of the Weimar Republic young people felt they could do their own thing, they dressed differently and behaved differently. They wanted to expand their spheres of interests and activities because previously they had been terribly regimented. So it was accepted that young people joined these groups which were either to the right or left of the political spectrum; later on they were used by the political parties as catchment areas for future members. The Nazis created their own Hitler Youth movement, separate movements for boys and girls. As a Jew, I couldn't be a Nazi, so it was natural for me to be involved on the political left. I

must say, though, that among my many non-Jewish friends, there weren't any Nazis and the majority of them not only disregarded Nazi concepts but worked desperately against them.

Else Baker
Part gypsy German child, Hamburg
I was living with my foster parents. I thought they were my real parents and I lived in what was their own house with a large garden. I remember sun-filled days playing in the garden and having a friend and getting things from Father Christmas and looking forward to Christmas, getting Easter eggs at Easter. In the winter I had a beautiful sledge and I remember riding on that with my friends. My foster parents' children were older than me and it was quite an idyllic early childhood on the outskirts of Hamburg.

Magdalena Kusserow Reuter
German Jehovah's Witness child, Bad Lippspringe
I came from a large family, a happy family, and I was the eighth of eleven children. We had much fun. We went on excursions, everyone had to learn an instrument and we made much music. My father taught us the Bible; it was joyful, we loved it so much. We all went swimming with my father. We had a garden with apple trees and when the apples were ripe we sat around the table and prepared the apples and made apple cake. We had some animals: geese and ducks and sometimes a goat for milk. I started school in 1930 and the first years were good.

John Lawrence
Austrian Jewish schoolboy, Vienna

I was born in Vienna, in the Ninth District on 29 May 1922. Both my parents were Austrian by nationality but were not born in Vienna, my father was born near Krakow in Poland and my mother was born in a place known as Oswiecim — Auschwitz now. I lived in Vienna until we were able to get out on 29 June 1938. We lived in a nice apartment and I went to very good schools. I was very fond — as we all were as youngsters — of art, music and the theatre and we went to all the leading theatres and concert halls. At school there were not many Jewish people — I think we were six in the whole school of almost a thousand. Time was spent like any other youngster: we had *marvellous* holidays, skiing and going to the Mediterranean area. Fortunately I was not short of anything. I had a great deal of love for my parents and they looked after us well. We were good middle class. My father was a modest man in the sense that he didn't like to show off; although he could have afforded a private motor car, he bought two taxis and used the taxis with the flag down all the time. He didn't want to arouse jealousy, you see — this is one of the principal traits of the Austrians — jealousy.

Jan Hartman
Czech Jewish schoolboy, Prague

My name tells you part of my story; this is Jan, which is Czech for John. As a little boy and a young man I always thought I was a Czech like all the others, brought up in the midst of a Czech family. But it wasn't as simple as that. My father was a lawyer and a sportsman and someone devoted to art. He was of Jewish origin but nobody ever told me about that. He had married my mother who was also of Jewish origin. Again, nobody told me about it . . . Our upbringing was very liberal. If you asked me about the religion of my mother, I think her religion would be her two children, that is my brother Jerzy (George) and I. She was devoted to the two of us. Materially we were affluent and had an easy life so that when war came we were in no way ready to face the difficulties that were coming.

Edith Baneth
Czech Jewish schoolgirl, Opava
We lived a very nice family life in a very big family. We owned a very nice flat in the suburbs of Opava, Silesia, and we had a car and were pretty well off. The Jewish community was well integrated, there was no anti-Semitism and we were just citizens like anybody else. My parents had Jewish and non-Jewish friends and the idea that we should be different never entered my mind. In school we had a few Jewish girls in my class and when there was religious education, we just left the classroom. We had our own religious education on a Sunday morning — that was the only difference between Jews and non-Jews in our town.

Jacob Pesate
Romanian Jewish student, Czernowitz, Bukovina
Czernowitz was a multi-ethnic city, about 120,000 inhabitants with half the population Jewish and the

other half a mix of Germans, Ukrainians and Romanians. My parents were never well off; my father had a small store where he sold textile goods. I was the eldest of three children. My parents paid for a private school where I passed the exam into the Orthodox *Real Lycée*, sponsored by the Orthodox Church; in that school Jewish boys felt quite a lot of anti-Semitism. The boys came from various nationalistic-inclined parents and some of the professors were members of the fascist parties, but they behaved very correctly in school. I was in the year when Jewish children were still admitted. During the following year, 1932, the rule set by the Church was introduced, announcing that no more Jewish children were to be admitted. We Jewish boys had a difficult time; the children of Orthodox Christian parents, who knew less, got better marks in exams. We were often called, pejoratively, "Jewboy". Because we were quite a substantial number, we fought back and many times it was not pleasant at all.

Roman Halter
Polish Jewish schoolboy, Chodecz
I was born in Chodecz, a small town which in Yiddish would be called a *shtetl*. The Jewish community of 800 people consisted of poor and very poor people. I thought we were very well off and we belonged to the three or four families who were considered rich. My father was a timber merchant and he also dealt in coal and building materials.

Our synagogue was built with an outer wall and inner compound and it had a wooden structure. In addition, as a precaution, it had metal grilles over the windows. They were so beautiful that the Jewish community decided to put them on the inside, not the outside. One of our people was a glazier and he undertook to glaze the windows when they were smashed by catapults from outside. To us children the synagogue was beautiful. It was like a musical instrument inside: you felt that you sat inside a violin and prayed. It was built so that the *bimah* (raised platform for the reading desk) was in the centre, and the ark was slightly elevated and was attended by the *kohanim* (Hebrew priests).

The rabbi sat on the right side with the elders close to him. My father was on the Rabbinic Council and the Town Council, so he sat close to the rabbi. I had to sit next to my father and grandfather and not fidget because I was in this prominent position. Sitting there facing the gallery, I had a very good view of my mother and the ladies up on top; they all had lovely veils and looked like Goya's paintings of Spanish ladies. To dress up and then veil yourself was quite a thing and everybody attended *Shabbat* service. I used to love sitting inside the synagogue and watch the ladies and look at the grilles and the lovely *bimah* of carved wood. And to me it was a sense of security, a sense of well-being, and to hear the lovely singing and think: perhaps next year my voice will be right and I can participate.

People who didn't have baths or hot water used to go to the ritual baths which were warmed on Thursday and Friday mornings — one session for women, one session for men. The bath was attended by the same man who read the Torah on Saturday. When I went with my father and grandfather to the ritual bath — called the *mikvah* — the *shamus* (attendant) was given a coin, a bit like a tip, before entering, and we undressed there and were scrubbed by him and some of the men were beaten with twigs and for that he earned a little bit more. Then, after being washed again over the head, we were allowed to go downstairs and submerge ourselves in the ritual bath. This had to be kept clean so no one was allowed to go down without either washing himself, or being washed by the *shamus*. Everyone who went down submerged three times in the steaming water and came out. And after this some people poured cold water over themselves and then sang songs. Because of the metal drum which held the water for the ritual bath down below, like a well, the acoustics were wonderful. And they would sing and then they started telling jokes. I was then removed to the front, and I was so sorry that I couldn't participate, hearing these ditties and dirty jokes. All I heard were muffled sounds of laughter and sounds coming through the walls. And there I waited for them to come out and we'd walk home bundled up. The significance was to cleanse yourself before *Shabbat* so that at least once a week everyone was clean.

On Friday one took the *cholent* to the baker. This was the big pot which was closed like a pressure cooker with the lid wrapped up with various rags. And in that would be potatoes, barley, beans and meat — usually brisket which was considered the best. Within that was another pot set in with carrots and raisins, sultanas and sometimes apples, and that was the dessert. That was all sealed up and on the pot the instructions were given whether it should be put in the middle, right-hand side, left-hand side — every woman knew which was the hot part of the baker's oven. And the youngest children used to take that, and during the winter my sleigh was adapted with guards on the side so I could pull the pot to the baker. In addition to the instructions, I would have to poke him and say, "Make sure it's on the left-hand side and not far from the end", because when put in the middle it became too burnt. This had to be collected on Saturday when everybody came from *Shabbat*. It was a heavy meal, so heavy that after the meal everybody disappeared for a siesta. You had to find a corner to snooze for a couple of hours afterwards. But we thought it delicious and because the winters were so cold that sort of meal was wonderful.

If I compare life then with today's existence, there is no comparison really because life was *very* hard. The diet was really one main meal a day. But it didn't do people any harm — to be slim and having bones showing was fine — we're all too fat today. The air was fresh, there was no pollution and the life in a little place like Chodecz was wonderful: there were forests, there was the lake and after this heavy *Shabbat* meal and our little snooze, because one was not allowed to do anything else on the Sabbath, one went for a walk to the lake and came back again to town and one's home. In our house we were fortunate, there was a big oven and the place was warm in winter. My aunt was musical and she would play the mandolin and my uncle who was the conductor of the fire brigade orchestra, would play the flute and there was music and singing and they played chess and had discussions, and I loved it all.

The rabbi decided there must be a library so there was a library full of Jewish books, and there were so many gifted Jewish writers of short stories. My father took a paper and on Friday after the meal he would read many of the interesting articles in Yiddish, we would all sit there and there was a wonderful sense of intellectual richness. There was also the custom that when travellers were coming through the town, after the service on Friday they lined up next to the rabbi, and certain families were obliged to invite them to a meal and stay overnight. So one shook hands with them, and my father would say, "Come with us", and they would come and bring news of other places. And this was reciprocated when people travelled to other places. In this way we heard of the world outside Chodecz.

Lili Stern-Pohlmann
Polish Jewish child, Krakow

I was born in Lvov which was then in Poland — now it is part of the Ukraine — but I spent all my young years in Krakow until the outbreak of war, apart from yearly visits to my grandparents in Lvov. Krakow was a little Florence, a beautiful medieval city, very old with the architecture all intact. We lived at first near the Jewish area, called Kazimierz; then we moved to Pijarska Street, opposite the Florian Gate, in the historic area.

Our apartment was on the third floor which meant that we overlooked the Barbican. There were all sorts of fascinating things going on there — very colourful historical events, entertainments and suchlike. I was a vivacious, independently minded child, very much like my father who often took me with him on his travels. We had a great time together: we went for walks, to coffee houses, we both loved music, and he would take me to the five o'clock dances and dance with me perched on his shoes. We had a lot of fun. My family was very assimilated and did not experience what maybe the people in the Jewish sector of the town would have experienced. My father was a very intelligent, handsome man, very sporty, and he spoke beautiful Polish.

Stanley Faull
Polish Jewish schoolboy, Warsaw
My family lived in a street in Warsaw called Twarda Street. There was my father, my mother, my brother and sister older than I. In the summer the weather was very hot and it was usual for the family to go away to a place where there was a river and woods and where the children could play. There were about twelve of us, including my aunts and uncles, and we had a wonderful time. My father came from a religious family but he was a modern Jew and had no beard; my mother's family was similar — Jewish, but not orthodox. We were a middle-class family, we had a resident maid and we lived in a very large apartment. My father inherited a factory and foundry from his father and I used to be

fascinated watching the workmen taking an ingot of metal, melting it down, pouring it into a form and making something of beauty and usefulness. We were speaking mainly Polish, but our second, mother tongue was Yiddish. I liked school very much because I liked the teachers and the people there.

Maria Ossowski
Young Polish schoolgirl, Warsaw

I must stress very strongly that we had friends from Jewish families, nobody really knew any difference. The people who did not belong to our religion just didn't come into the classroom for prayers. That was the only difference. We played with each other, visited each other in our homes.

Kitty Hart-Moxon
Polish Jewish schoolgirl, Bielsko-Biala

I lived in Bielsko-Biala, a town very close to the Czechoslovakian-German border. And because of this people spoke three languages: German, Polish and Czech. My recollection of childhood? A very, *very* happy time indeed. The emphasis of the town was on sport and so I knew absolutely nothing about politics, war or anti-Semitism. I was purely interested in sport. We had athletics clubs, we had gymnastic clubs, we had swimming clubs. We were very close to the mountains so we skied in the winter, we skated on skating rinks, we hiked in the mountains. As a matter of fact at weekends the whole population took to the mountains. My first recollection of my life at home is possibly being on my father's back, hiking in the mountains. I was sent to a very strict Catholic school. This was incredibly difficult for me, but I think it stood me in good stead. I learned a lot from the nuns, not just because of the discipline, but because I learnt to *resist* discipline and any attempt to obey.

Marsha Segall
Lithuanian Jewish schoolgirl, Siauliai

I was born on 16 January 1922 to a well-to-do Jewish family, traditional but not religious, in Siauliai, Lithuania. It was a small Jewish community, in proportion about seven per cent because the whole population of the country was small. I had a very happy childhood, a very happy home. I had two sisters, one two and a half years older than me, and one about five years younger. My father was an industrialist and he also represented American Oil for Lithuania. Mummy was a very happy woman, loved entertaining, loved people, always used to sing, and it was a very happy atmosphere — we had everything we wanted.

Leon Greenman
British Jewish businessman, Rotterdam

My family left England for Holland two months after I was born in 1910. That's how I came to live in Rotterdam. My father was in the cigar-making trade, then in the diamond polishing trade, later on he became a salesman of new clothing for sailors. As a youngster I went to Hebrew school until I was thirteen. My grandfather was a very orthodox Jew. I also

21

remember that my father used to say the Hebrew prayers before and after food, and we children were not allowed to leave the table until the prayer was finished — to us it seemed a *very* long prayer. Later, I went back to the East End of London to work as a hairdresser, but I returned to Holland after I married my wife, Else van Dam, in 1935. I was then in the antiquarian book business and went backwards and forwards to London on business buying and selling first-class books. That is how the business grew.

Steven Frank
Dutch Jewish schoolboy, Amsterdam

We lived in a lovely part of Amsterdam, the southern part. Our house was a large house, three storeys high. It must have had about four or five bedrooms and a garage. And in the loft there was actually a swing so you could play there. Opposite our house there was a school, outside of which was a statue of Erasmus and often we used to climb all over it. It was a free-and-easy neighbourhood, we had our friends we played with in the street, religion didn't occur to any of us. We had a brand new park in a new development. I learnt to skate almost before I could walk: in winter, I can remember being taken onto the ice with skates tied on my shoes and with a little chair with which I pushed myself over the ice. Sometimes there would be a hot drink — they were really lovely, happy times. We weren't religious, not one bit. In fact we had a Christmas tree in our house; my mother, who was born in England, always had one in her house and so did we. I had no conception at all of Judaism, of being Jewish. We three boys were all circumcised by a *mohel* (specialist circumciser), but that's about as far as it went. There were no Jewish festivities or ideology at all in the household, no *Menorah* (eight-branched candelabrum) or anything really to indicate that we were Jewish. My father was a very successful lawyer in Holland, a very humanitarian man involved in many organisations related to mental health.

Janine Ingram
Greek Jewish schoolgirl, Thessaloniki

I was born in 1923 of Jewish parents of Spanish descent; both my parents' families had migrated from the Spanish Inquisition 500 years before and established themselves in Greece. We were a tight community, a small town of about 200,000 people then, and 60,000 of these were Jews. I never felt that I was different, that I was Jewish; no, I always felt that I was Greek. I had a French education at the *lycée* and I met my friends at the yachting club and the tennis club and felt that we were one. I was never aware of any anti-Semitism. I never went to synagogue, except for weddings, and my parents were not religious although, oddly enough, they kept the feast of *Pesach* — the Passover. There was a big difference within the Jewish society of the time; there were people like us who were comfortably off — we had a large rambling house and all we wanted — and then there were the extremely poor Jews who lived on the outskirts of town, and they were totally uneducated and spoke only Spanish.

John Dobai

Hungarian Jewish/Catholic schoolboy, Budapest

Well, the life we lived — shall we say in British terms — was a comfortable, middle-class existence. We lived in the Third District of Budapest, a very good one, high up on the western side of Budapest. My father worked in a bank with British connections and my mother was an excellent weaver; she made textiles and looked after children and we lived a very comfortable sort of life governed by the seasons: in the autumn we went on excursions to the woods and walked a lot. In winter, if we were lucky enough to get snow, we went skiing — I was skiing by the age of four. In the spring more walks followed and when school ended in June, then came the long summer vacation when we went down to Lake Balaton and we spent maybe a month there with my father coming down for a week or two.

I was born in 1934 and my parents had converted to Catholicism in 1931 and some time before then the family name was changed to Dobai, it was made more Hungarian; before then it had been Kupferstein — Copperstone. By 1931, those who were perceptive could see that the events in Germany, which reflected themselves in Austria and to some extent in Hungary, boded ill for the Jewish people. My parents and many others thought that by converting to Catholicism, it would be useful later. But sadly it didn't happen that way.

1933–1936

PERSECUTION

After 1933 it was just accepted that if you were a Jewish child you were liable to be beaten up, bullied, or whatever else they chose to do with you. It was no use appealing to policemen or teachers because they're not supposed to interfere or even be interested in helping you because you are perceived to be an enemy of the state.

Hitler's racism and hatred against the Jews and other groups began well before the National Socialist Workers Party — the Nazi Party — came to power on 30 January 1933. Nazi ideology outlining the worldwide conflict between "Aryans" and Jews was a major theme of Hitler's *Mein Kampf* (My Struggle, published in two volumes in 1925 and 1926 respectively). Jews, along with Communists, with whom they were closely identified, were regarded as threatening the very basis of German and "Aryan" (Caucasian of non-Jewish descent) culture, and Hitler's stated mission was to alert Germany and the world to this threat, and to destroy it.

Although the first fatal Jewish victims of the Nazi era can be dated as early as 1 January 1930, when eight Jews were killed by Nazi storm troopers (*Sturmabteilungen*, SA), it was not until the *Machtergreifung* — Hitler's seizure of power

— in January 1933 that the impact of anti-Jewish measures was felt. German Jews, increasingly isolated by Nazi anti-Semitic propaganda and segregated by the various laws, were the main victims during the years 1933–1936. There was, however, a certain amount of spillover of anti-Semitism into neighbouring countries.

During this period, the increasing violence against German Jewry was of a relatively sporadic character compared with the mass campaigns which came later, although there were indications of what was to come. For instance, on Saturday, 1 April 1933, a one-day boycott of Jewish shops occurred, when windows were daubed with anti-Jewish slogans and armed SA guards prevented Aryan customers from entering Jewish shops. A purge of German Jewish, Communist and other books considered to be "disruptive influences" was also undertaken, culminating in the mass book burnings of 10 May 1933 — both events organised by Joseph Goebbels and his Nazi cohorts.

One of the first tasks the Nazi Party set itself on achieving power was to establish the concentration camp system. Dachau concentration camp was opened in March 1933, the first prisoners consisting mainly of Communists, Social Democrats and other political enemies of the Nazis. In 1934, an Inspectorate of Concentration Camps was created by the *Schutzstaffel* (SS) chief, Heinrich Himmler, under the command of Theodor Eicke, the SS *Lagerführer* of Dachau. The aim was to restructure the camp system. All units henceforth operated uniformly under a central command with strict training of guards who were organised into the *Totenkopfverbände* — an SS unit. Total organisation of prisoners' lives, backed up with a brutal regime of punishment, was the order of the day.

It was during this phase that legislation was formulated and implemented restricting economic and professional activity as well as social contact with "Aryans". On 11 April 1933, the publication of the Law for the Restoration of the Professional Civil Service and the law establishing a *numerus clauses* on Jews for admission into the legal profession was published. More than fifty other decrees were enacted between this date and September 1935, each of which covered a different profession. On 15 September, the so-called Nuremberg Laws, passed by a special sitting of the Reichstag during the massive, dramatic Nazi Rally held in the city, brought shockwaves to German and European Jewry. The Nuremberg Laws defined who was considered a Jew and revoked what few rights Jews still possessed. All these measures were backed up with an increasing vitriolic anti-Jewish and racial propaganda campaign by the Nazi-controlled media, led by Julius Streicher's (Gauleiter of Franconia) rabid anti-Semitic paper, *Der Stürmer*. Throughout this time, Jews were encouraged to emigrate and, despite all the problems of gaining admission to safe havens, just over 35,000 Jews left for Palestine, Western Europe, Britain and the United States in 1933.

Ludwig Baruch
German Jewish schoolboy living in London
My father had come to England in 1928 to manage a German firm in Liverpool; I left Hamburg in September 1930 to join my parents there. When the Nazis came to power in 1933, it was a traumatic event in our family; my mother completely broke down. She cried for days on end, she feared both war and what it meant for the Jewish people and for the Germans as well. She was very much an established German intellectual and was completely overwhelmed by Hitler's seizure of power. At that time the resistance to Nazis in Germany and elsewhere were the Communists. I was most impressed, especially as a Jew; I felt the only people who could really oppose and contain the Nazis were the Communists.

John Fink
German Jewish youth, electrician's apprentice, Berlin
When Hitler came to power I had to leave my school. I went to a Jewish school for one year then my parents decided, as there was no sense in continuing education, I should learn a trade. They found me a position as an apprentice in a small Jewish outfit, just the boss and me. I was fourteen years old. We had a motorcycle with a sidecar and we did gas and water installations as well

as electrics. In 1936 the boss, who was married to an "Aryan" woman, had to flee Germany. He went to South Africa and I lost my job. I was lucky enough to find another job in Berlin near the Kurfurstendamm, again a small electrical contractor where I finished the four years' apprenticeship.

Ruth Foster
German Jewish schoolgirl, Lingen

When Hitler came to power things changed. We had teachers at school who were very pro-Nazi — they went to the Nuremberg rally each year — and I was the only Jewish girl in this high school. One particular teacher made my life a misery; she told the girls not to talk to me, and the girls with whom I used to go to school in the mornings and met afterwards suddenly ignored me because of the fear of this one teacher. And she arranged that I would sit right at the back of the class, two rows were left vacant and I sat against the wall. Then there came a law — more or less at the same time as the Nuremberg Laws came out — that all the Jewish children had to leave German schools and universities.

At one time there was a boycott when the SA put big slogans, "*Deutsche, kauft nicht von Juden, die Juden sind unser Unglück!*" — "Germans, don't buy from Jews, the Jews are our misfortune." This was quite soon after Hitler came to power. They smashed the windows and they looted the shops. The farmers didn't dare deal with Jewish people any more, even though they were quite sympathetic, and so it became very hard. My mother had quite a bit of jewellery which she had to sell in order to raise some money and times were, well . . . tough.

Gudrun Kübler
German woman, Berlin
You had to be very careful. I always had to be because of my husband's job (on the General Staff of the *Luftwaffe*). It would have been a catastrophe if I had shopped in that Jewish store, for example.

Magdalena Kusserow Reuter
German Jehovah's Witness schoolgirl, Bad Lippspringe
When the times of Hitler started, they observed us not saying "Heil Hitler" and every year it became more difficult when we didn't say this. My father wanted to teach us religion and he took us out of the religion lesson. And this one teacher said, "These Kusserow children, they are not for Hitler, they have to go to Moscow, they are Communists." Then the children made fun of us and said, "You go to Moscow, you are not our people, you are not for Hitler." My father taught us that saying "Heil Hitler" meant that salvation came from Hitler, but the Bible tells us that salvation comes from Jesus Christ. He told us that we must choose, that real Christians would be persecuted, and that one day maybe they would persecute us also, because the Bible says some will be killed because of faith, the belief in Christ. I never thought this would be in our own family, never thought about it until it came.

Dr Edith Bulbring

German part-Jewish (Mischling) doctor, Berlin

I qualified as a doctor in 1928 and had a position in the Virchow *Krankenhaus* (hospital) in Berlin at the time when Hitler came to power. There was a well-known Jewish professor there, Dr Friedmann. He was an expert on infectious diseases. After 1933 Dr Friedmann and his Jewish staff were dismissed. I was the only one left because I wasn't fully Jewish. I was in charge of three hundred beds and perhaps thirty turnovers a day. So the conditions in this hospital were now quite unimaginable.

At that time there was a very severe diphtheria epidemic; one of the children got to the stage where his throat was blocked by a diphtheria membrane and needed a tracheotomy. We were told there was no doctor left to do this. The nurse asked me if I had ever done this operation. I said, "No, but have you ever assisted in such an operation?"

"Oh, many times," she said.

"Well then, that's fine, we'll do it. I know how it's done."

And I did it and the boy got better. I was very pleased. The telephone rung when I got back to my room: would I please come to the administration. The administrator said, "Miss Bulbring, we gather from your questionnaire that you are of part-Jewish origin. Therefore we no longer have any use for your services." There were no other doctors left in that hospital.

(Sir) Hans Krebs
German Jewish biochemist, Freiburg

The first really great change which affected everybody when Hitler came to power was in early April 1933. A number of us, including myself, were temporarily relieved of our posts, allegedly in order to comply with the furious wishes of the people who wouldn't tolerate the presence of Jewish people in these positions. So I was personally directly affected: I was paid but was not allowed to deal with my patients nor was I allowed to go into my laboratory. In fact that was to be the end: I left right in the middle of the experiments — had to leave right in the middle of these — from one day to another.

Beate "Bea" Green
German Jewish schoolgirl, Munich

One day in 1933 I had a bad cold — I was eight at the time. My mother said, "You stay in bed." So I was in bed when the front door opened. Now normally when my father came in, he would open the door briskly and whistle and my brother and I would rush down the corridor to see who would get there first to embrace him. Now, first of all this wasn't the right time for him to come back, so I assumed that it was either my mother or the maid, neither of whom were in the flat as far as I knew. But nobody came into my room which is what I would have expected. After a while I got out of bed and went to the corridor where, outside the bathroom, I saw my father's tattered and blood-soaked clothes.

For an eight year old it was a shock, but there wasn't an adult around that I could ask, "What's happened?" So I wandered along the corridor to where my parents' bedroom was. The door was closed and I did something I'd never done in my life before — I knocked on the door and then opened it. I saw my father pull the bedclothes right up to his eyes. Obviously, with hindsight, I know that it was so I shouldn't see his bashed up face. He simply said to me, "Wait until your mother comes home." That was odd because he would never have talked about "mother", he would say "*Mutti*" — Mum. And of course in due course my mother did come home. From then on I felt I was being protected from the truth. They thought that by not telling me about what really happened, I wouldn't worry, when of course as a child you worry much more if you don't know than if you know, however hard it is to know the truth.

Later I heard that my father, who was a lawyer, had on this day — 10 March 1933 — gone to the police headquarters in order to lay a complaint on behalf of one of his Jewish clients who owned one of the big stores in Munich and who had been arrested. When he got to the police headquarters, somebody said to him, "Dr Siegel, you're wanted in room so and so," which happened to be in the basement. When he got there he saw it was full of brownshirt thugs who proceeded to beat him up. They knocked his teeth in and burst his eardrums. The one thing my father was worried about was that they would damage his kidneys. So he held his arms against his back and of course that meant that his head was unprotected which is why he had all the injuries that he had. But fortunately, our family has thick heads, lots of bone and in fact apart from the fact that he was beaten, bloodied, had his teeth knocked out, his skull was not broken.

They then cut off his trouser legs and took off his shoes and socks and hung a placard around his neck with the notice, "I'm a Jew and I will never complain to the Nazis again." They led him around Munich like that. They got tired of it after about an hour and let him go near the railway station. As he got into a taxi, he told us that a man came up to him and said with a slight American accent, "I have just taken a picture of you, do you mind if it is published?" My father said, "Do as you like." I mean this is not something he would have worried about at that time. That picture appeared in the world's press, published by Hearst (William Randolph Hearst, American newspaper magnate).

Rudi Bamber

German Jewish schoolboy, Nuremberg

When the huge Nazi rallies were held in our town, I had very conflicting emotions. It was very exciting, even attractive: the razzmatazz, the marching columns and the colours. The Nazis were very good at organising these and they were very impressive and spectacular and one could not but — I suppose "admire" may be the wrong word — but they certainly impressed me; the power and the force and ability were all very evident. Everything was decorated in Nazi flags, everywhere, every window — it was an absolute riot of colour.

And the Party leaders used to go on a motorcade through the town, and people would mass and shout as they stood or sat in their cars, clearly visible. I admit, very foolishly, joining the throng, standing there to watch this spectacle. I saw Hitler, Goebbels, Goering, Hess — they all went by in their cars. Of course my parents would have been appalled to think what I was doing. In a way I was slightly tainted by the Nazi propaganda. People used to say to me, "Well, you are Jewish but you're all right, it's the other Jews, the international Jewry which are evil and out to destroy Germany." So I had this sort of dichotomy, that on the one hand I knew that I was hated and despised, and yet felt that when it came to an individual approach, people said, "Oh well, you're all right, you're not like them."

Else Baker
Part-gypsy German child, Hamburg
Hitler? You couldn't *escape* Hitler, even a two-year-old would have picked up Hitler then. On his birthday and certain other days everyone had to fly his flag, and when he spoke on the radio, everyone had to listen attentively. I never had contact with gypsies or Jewish people. I think I led a very sheltered, rural life — racial and ethnic differences wouldn't have meant anything to me. I had heard about gypsies because there was a song about them in German and it describes how they lived in forests and didn't pay taxes and had a jolly life of it. I also heard stories of gypsies stealing washing off washing lines but I never came across any; just a sort of folklore about them

37

which had rubbed off slightly on me. I loved my adoptive parents as my mother and father — that's all the parenting I knew.

Sergei Hackel
German Jewish schoolboy, Berlin

I remember at the beginning of the school day we had to stand up and raise our arms in the Hitler salute; and instead of a prayer, we had to thank the *Führer* for giving us such a nice day. Loyalty was expected, loyalty was instilled, there was nothing *other* than loyalty. I remember the schoolbooks; because the Nazi designers were so good at their job, the indoctrination didn't strike one as aggressive, or abrasive, or alien. You opened your first alphabet book, or school book, and the very first picture would be of the *Führer*, a very nice *Führer*, kindly, in civilian clothes. I think he could have been in *Alpenhosen* standing on a flower-strewn mountainside holding two children, a boy and a girl, by the hand. And the inscription on the frontispiece, as I remember it, was, "Two things the *Führer* loves best: children and flowers." At the time it seemed a very pleasant thing for the *Führer* to be busy with, so that put one at ease.

On their part my parents kept quiet, a sort of *dull* silence. When I brought home cheerful reverberations of Nazism they didn't say, "Nonsense, don't you ever talk like that in this home of ours," but nor did they say, "Lovely that you learnt all these marvellous things at school." There was some sort of in-between, neutral position which they adopted for fear of repercussions; and repercussions could have been severe.

John Silberman
German Jewish schoolboy, Berlin

I was only seven years of age in 1933 and I had just started school a year before. There were warnings from parents and others not to get mixed up in fights with the *Hitler Jugend* (Hitler Youth). The *Hitler Jugend*, if you want to give it its kindest interpretation, was a sort of Boy Scouts. Of course the Jews were not wanted, Jews were to be chased and beaten up. After 1933 it was just accepted that if you were a Jewish child you were liable to be beaten up, bullied or whatever else they chose to do with you. It was no use appealing to policemen or teachers because they're not supposed to interfere or even be interested in helping you because you are perceived as an enemy of the state. That was fed into my mind as a matter of self-preservation. One took care; travelling to the Jewish school on the public trains, we used to travel in groups of twos and threes together, which gave a certain amount of protection. However, one stayed clear of travelling in large groups as that would be seen as provocative, and as we didn't wear swastika badges or *Hitler Jugend* uniforms, we were clearly identifiable. The bullying and verbal assault was not confined to German children: it was quite common if some adult, who was nothing more than an ignorant thug, called you names, or kicked you. It was bullying all down the line and that was totally accepted.

John Lawrence
Austrian Jewish schoolboy, Vienna

From six years old I began to hear about socialists and the Nazis, oh yes. I must say that although we had a lot of fun in the family, we had no youth. We had literally to fight almost daily — in the school, in the streets. Anti-semitism in Vienna was rampant and had always been. Even before Hitler came on the Austrian stage, we knew what was coming. I had to fight almost daily. My mother was a very astute woman and she engaged an expert boxing champion to train me in self-defence — ju jitsu and boxing. When I returned to school after the summer holiday, this six foot something chap, who used to bully me, came up again, and I floored him. His name was Bum!

Stephen Dale
German Jewish youth, Berlin

After Hitler came to power, I got involved in political work. It wasn't very important, but I took it seriously and with my friends did some illegal work — this was mainly printing leaflets and sticking these little notices on lamp-posts proclaiming anti-Nazi views. It wasn't anything organised or in any depth, rather it was a spontaneous reaction to prevailing circumstances and the expression of the need to do something active. In January 1934 I was picked up by the *Gestapo* and taken first to the *Gestapo* headquarters in Berlin and later in a prison for political offenders where I spent a week in solitary confinement — quite an experience at the age of sixteen.

Jan Hartman
Czech Jewish schoolboy, Prague
About 1933/34 we were going skiing because we were sports people, and there, at the highest mountain in Czechoslovakia, we looked into Germany. That was already a dangerous, hostile country from which something bad could come. That was the first time I had to face a political question.

Lili Stern-Pohlmann
Polish Jewish child, Krakow
We were not discriminated against in any obvious way, but occasionally my father had difficulty in changing his job because he was Jewish — he was as qualified in his profession as anybody else. Apart from that, what I remember distinctly is that when Pilsudski died in 1935, from our third floor window we could see the funeral procession passing, and after it passed, I noticed policemen were beating people with truncheons. I asked my father, "Why are they beating those people?" And my father said, "My dear child, they didn't do anything wrong, it's only because they're Jewish."

Roman Halter
Polish Jewish schoolboy, Chodecz
Anti-Semitism existed in Poland simply because the teaching of the Catholic Church was so bad. What

41

happened was that all Jews, including children, were accused — especially at Easter and Christmas — of killing Christ. So, at Easter, I was a "Christ-killer" and my grandfather taught me how, when I came out of my religion class, to take off my belt and stand against the wall and swing it from side to side so that children should not beat me up. Then, if there was an opening, to run quickly through that.

Gertrud "Trude" Levi
Hungarian Jewish child, Szombathely

On Sundays my father usually took me for a walk; he knew a lot about plants and insects and it was always fascinating to go with him. On this Sunday I remember, I was wearing a beautiful red coat, white socks and black shoes and he said he wanted to stop off to see a woman who had given birth the previous night. He took me to a part of town which was very poor and left me in the middle of this large courtyard while he went inside to see his patient. Doors were suddenly opened, and children started to come out, and the bigger boys started to throw stones at me and call me a "dirty Jewish pig". By the time my father came out, I was bleeding and crying. I said to my father, "I am not a pig because that's an animal, and I'm not dirty because I had a bath, and what does *Jewish* mean?" I hadn't heard that word. He explained about minorities and about how Jews are sometimes ill-treated. And I said, "Right, from now on I'm going to be a Jew."

Jacob Pesate
Romanian Jewish student, Czernowitz, Bukovina
There was a native fascist party in Romania; it was the Iron Guard, and from a very small unit, it became a threat to democracy. They were going around in Nazi-style uniforms and they attacked meetings of the parties who were in power. So the Iron Guard was all over the place, in small numbers but active, aggressive and mimicking the German Nazis. The leaders were sent for training in Germany and they returned with programmes which were no different from *Mein Kampf* under Hitler.

Gisela Eisner
German Jewish schoolgirl, Berlin
One saw these displays of the newspaper, *Der Stürmer*, full of anti-Semitic things and they were always done in display cabinets — you had no excuse for not seeing them. We used to stand there and read all these things and look at the pictures (caricatures of Jews). That was really quite extraordinary too because we didn't know anyone who looked like that, or had a nose, or ears, or lips like that. I remember reading that Jews also smelled of onions and garlic — I mean, we didn't *know* people like that.

Peter Kronberg
Austrian youth part-Jewish (Mischling), Berlin
I remember one curious incident was in a biology class; we had learned about the "Aryan" head form, and the teacher picked me as an example. I think he may have

43

done this on purpose; it was the only time I remember being singled out like this. I was very, very conscious of being part Jewish, and I looked at myself in the mirror to see if I had a "Jewish profile". You know, the typical, comic appearance that was constantly in the papers. I was very concerned.

Peter Bielenberg
German lawyer, Hamburg
One evening I came from a party with the son of the mayor of Hamburg who was a quarter Jewish, but in fact looked Jewish. We were standing outside his father's house and from behind me came three Nazi Storm Troopers. One of them went straight at my Jewish friend and before we knew what was happening he hit him in the face and said, "Another bloody Jewboy." I reacted by punching him without any great aim — it was a physical reaction of surprise and I hit him in the solar plexus. He was hit hard enough that he went breathless to his knees. This Jewish-looking friend of mine was a good sportsman and I was unusually strong and we gave the other two a really good hammering. When we thought they had had enough I told them to get lost and take this little heap on the ground with them.

Eva Mitchell
German Jewish schoolgirl, Münster
My father had a very nice chauffeur whose great ambition it was to become a flyer. He once went to my father and said, "Would you mind if I joined the SA

(*Sturmabeitlungen*, Storm Troopers) on a three-days-a-week basis — they said they'd teach me to fly?" My father said, "Of course I don't mind" — what else *could* he say. This man joined the evening SA group and was immediately told that he couldn't work for a Jewish employer any more. He was heartbroken and said to my father, "You're the best employer I've ever had, but I can't do it any more." And from that day onwards he drove the SS *Gruppenführer* (high-ranking officer) in the town in his dirty big car with a swastika on it.

Gerda Williams
German schoolgirl, Berlin
I don't remember being told much about the Jews in the school. And of course we had many Jewish friends. It was pretty early on when those who could afford to go came to say goodbye. And of course those who didn't have the money had to remain. But when they came to say goodbye and said, "We're going to Shanghai", "We're going to America," "We're going to . . ." wherever they managed to go, well, you knew it wasn't because they *wanted* to go, it was because they were forced to go.

(Sir) Hans Krebs
German Jewish biochemist, Freiburg
I was somewhat surprised when I got a letter from a German colleague who worked in Cambridge, England telling me that people had heard that I was in difficulties. He told me that if I was interested in

coming to Cambridge I should write to Hopkins (Sir Frederick Gowland Hopkins, OM, English biochemist) and I would be sure of a sympathetic response. So I wrote to Hopkins and got a reply which I found very touching because it began with the sentence, "I admire your work so much that I am anxious to help you . . ." I decided to emigrate and I left Germany on 19 June 1933, and there was one very fortunate circumstance: I could take with me a lot of the immediate equipment which I needed, twenty boxes actually . . . And so I arrived very well equipped and it was very reassuring to me that I had not to make any claims on the somewhat limited resources of the department in Cambridge.

Christabel Bielenberg
Anglo-Irish woman, Hamburg

This doctor was usually a very busy man and one time my boy, Nicky, was sick. And he came round and we sat through the night together and in the morning the baby was better. I was so surprised that he had time to sit with the child and myself. When he left — I'd like to point out that he was a Jew — he said, "I would like to tell you, Mrs Bielenberg, that I can't look after your child any more, you'll have to take a new doctor." That, I remember, was the first huge shock. I said, "A new doctor, for goodness sake why?" And he said, "As you know, I was head of the clinic here in which I invested a lot of my earnings. I have been banned from that; it's been taken away from me and I have had a letter which said that I am not allowed to lay my hands on 'Aryan' children ever again."

Magdalena Kusserow Reuter

German Jehovah's Witness schoolgirl, Bad Lippspringe

About 1936, the police started searching the house; my father had much literature from the Society about the Kingdom of God, and the *Watchtower* and *Golden Age* which we now call *Awake*. About sixteen or eighteen times the police and *Gestapo* came to search our house; the *Gestapo* did not wear uniform but my brother Siegfried would always recognise them and call, "The *Gestapo* comes, the *Gestapo* comes!" Then we hid the Bible in the cupboard and the literature under the floorboards because my mother said, "They are too lazy, they don't like to bow down."

My father was arrested many times. The first time was in 1936; my mother was also arrested. They were taken to Paderborn, but my mother was there only one week because she had so many children.

John Silberman

German Jewish schoolboy, Berlin

As time went on I became aware that business for my father seemed to be getting difficult. I didn't fully understand why, but there were pressures on customers not to buy from a Jewish manufacturer, and pressures from suppliers to get higher prices, or not supply Jews. My father's situation was not unique, it went on all over the place. It wasn't so much a rule or requirement from the Government to trade and industry, it was the taking of advantage by individuals: right, he's a Jew so we can squeeze him, and what can he do about it? There was this perpetual threat that if you didn't comply with non-Jewish requests, you'd be reported to the *Gestapo* and be arrested. One always heard of people disappearing, or being arrested then coming back after a week or so having been beaten up or given hard labour or, occasionally, being killed — although the latter was much more common from 1937. But even in those early days, talk of the *Gestapo* was always rife.

1937–1939

THE SEARCH FOR REFUGE

Everyone understood that they ought to be emigrating, but it was only when the watershed of Kristallnacht occurred in November 1938 that my parents, in common with ninety per cent of other German Jews, thought: it's no good staying, they're going to kill us. Survival in the life-threatening sense was the only thing that mattered.

After 1938, the campaign to create a *Judenrein* — Jewish-cleansed — economy started in earnest; further laws and decrees published between 1937 and 1939 led to an ever-increasing spiral of anti-Semitic violence, suffering and desperation among all sections of the Jewish community, destroying the very foundations of Jewish life in Germany. As a result of the strident anti-Semitic rhetoric spilling over the German borders, Jews in Germany's borderlands were growing increasingly uneasy. The Nazi takeover (*Anschluss*) of Austria on 13 March 1938 intensified these fears. Whereas the process of discrimination and violence against the German Jews had been relatively gradual, the persecution of the Austrian Jews was immediate and devastating; overnight, they were deprived of civil rights and subjected to extreme violence and humiliation, especially in Vienna.

In the autumn of 1938, thousands of Polish Jews were forcibly expelled from Germany to the border areas between Germany and Poland. On 28 October of that year, for instance, some 17,000 German-Jewish citizens of Polish origin were stripped of their citizenship and dumped in no-man's-land on the border near the town of Zbaszyn. This outrage provoked Herschel Grynspan, the son of one of the displaced, to assassinate Ernst vom Rath, the first secretary of the German embassy in Paris, which resulted in a wave of Nazi anti-Semitic attacks throughout Germany, Austria and the Sudetenland. This is known as *Kristallnacht* — the night of broken glass — when more than 7,500 Jewish shops were wrecked and many synagogues and precious religious artefacts desecrated or destroyed. Following *Kristallnacht* 30,000 German Jews were rounded up and imprisoned in concentration camps. As the camp population changed from "undesirables" and "criminals" to Jews, living conditions deteriorated to subhuman levels. *Kristallnacht* had enormous international repercussions and helped swing public opinion against the policy of appeasement. The violation of the Munich Agreement in March 1939 spurred Britain and France to react with their guarantees to Poland, Hitler's next likely target.

As war approached, Jews desperately sought refuge from what was now a very obvious threat. Jewish parents were particularly anxious to find safe refuge for their children. This is when, in late 1938 after *Kristallnacht*, Britain agreed to take 10,000 Jewish children. In the event just over

9,000 arrived under the *Kindertransport* plan, the last group coming on the eve of war.

Despite the stringent immigration policies of potential host nations, emigration from the *Grossdeutsches Reich* (greater Germany) increased dramatically throughout the autumn and winter of 1938/39. Adolf Eichmann's Central Office for Jewish Emigration, based at first in Vienna and later in Berlin, began to drop its previous policy of persuasion for a new policy of intimidation, with Jews being subjected to humiliations, beatings, confinement in concentration camps and even death. These tough methods, along with the anti-Jewish laws, were extended to Czechoslovakia after the occupation of March 1939. By September 1939 about half of Germany's 500,000 Jews had left the country, along with 125,000 from Austria and 20,000 from the newly occupied Czech lands. Many thousands more were trapped.

John Silberman
German Jewish schoolboy, Berlin
My father's business simply died. Nobody would trade with Jews: you couldn't get supplies, customers, and you couldn't get staff to work for you. If you did you were at their mercy; they could do as they liked — they could steal, they could rob and there was no remedy. A Jew had no rights. I remember that my parents' gentile friends did not stand by them. The average German didn't care: the more Jews that were got rid of, the more of their assets were available for

them to take. The mass of the German population was entirely happy with what was going on and was fully supportive of Hitler so long as they were on the winning side.

John Fink
German Jewish electrician, Berlin
The Nazis knew how to torture us, to put the screws on. Every few weeks, months and years, other laws came. We had, for instance, to move from the west of Berlin to where the Jewish people were congregated in a poorer neighbourhood. We lived in two rooms in a so-called "Jewish House" which the Nazis controlled.

Fritz Moses
German child, Strehlen, Silesia, Germany
We were not Jews and other relatives changed our name (Moses); but my father didn't want to give our name up. I had problems with the name in elementary school and in the first two grades of high school. They would frequently call me "Pinkus" or "Abraham". In addition I was not adept at sports which was considered a big drawback in the Third *Reich*.

Anna Bergman
Czech Jewish university student, Prague
That Hitler was in Germany locking up Jews was something that didn't concern me at all. I was so young, I had boyfriends and nobody talked about

politics; life was marvellous. In 1938, I was with a group skiing in Austria when the *Anschluss* happened. But we were Czechs with Czech passports so we were not concerned. Then I saw that they didn't really *occupy* Austria: they were *welcomed* with flowers and open arms and shouting; and suddenly Nazi flags were all over the place. That was the first sign. I was then twenty-one. It is unimaginable that we didn't take some precautions and do something.

John Lawrence
Austrian Jewish youth, Vienna
I was arrested on Easter Monday, 1938, and taken to the local barracks. I was butted with a rifle and made to lie beneath a mattress on the springs of a bed and four of them jumped on the mattress. I was then taken up to the top floor — by which time they had stripped me to my underpants. They held me out of the window. "Shall we let him go now?" I was *sixteen* for heaven's sake, not even that! Then they took me downstairs. "We've forgotten something, the lavatories need cleaning." So three of them held me, and the lavatories were cleaned with my head, with my hair. It was dreadful, dreadful. I couldn't defend myself. If I told you in detail what happened in that barrack you wouldn't believe it! And they were all Austrians. A German high-ranking SS officer came and saved me from certain death. He told the Austrians that they wanted law and order, "Not louts like you." I owe him my life, there is no question about it.

Herbert Elliott
Austrian Jewish youth, Vienna

Within days of Hitler walking in, the janitor in the building where you lived would give you a mop bucket and say, "Clean the stairs." You were wanting to go to work, but you couldn't do anything about it. It was not physically difficult, but it was humiliating. I was amazed that you had no redress against it, but I was told that if you did try and he called in a policeman or Storm Trooper, you could be sent to a concentration camp or they would beat you up and there would be no questions asked.

Gertrud "Trude" Levi
Hungarian Jewish schoolgirl, Szombathely

In school, some of our teachers were very, very viciously anti-Semitic. In Hungary Jews liked to keep a low profile and tried not to speak of it, but I was a Jew and on occasions I made certain that everyone knew I was a Jew. Therefore I was picked on, especially by my history teacher. Our town was on the border of Austria; the *Anschluss* of 1938 affected us very much because we thought we'd be the next taken. And from that time we had refugees coming to Hungary as one country after another was occupied.

Roman Halter
Polish Jewish schoolboy, Chodecz

By 1937 and 1938 the screeching from Nazi Germany had got quite bad and ever louder. It was then that the traders who went to other markets to trade used to travel in convoys with the butcher's sons at the back and the strongest man in front. There were many stories of how people were robbed, the goods taken away and the women raped. There were reports from Jewish papers which made the community very sad and worried. But they felt trapped because they had no money, no means; they couldn't sell out and get passports. In fact the doors were shut for them and all they could do was hope and pray, believe in God and trust that one day this was going to stop. In my family the discussion was going on from 1934. My father was sixty when I was nine, my mother was his second wife, twenty years younger; he had not enough get-up-and-go to leave all he had built up and emigrate to Palestine as some of the family had. Also we heard that since my uncle in Palestine had died, the family there were living in great poverty. People from large cities with means managed somehow to get out, but no one from our community.

Jan Hartman
Czech schoolboy, Prague
After Hitler occupied Austria, my father brought strange people to our home who looked very funny because they were dressed in black and had black hair. I had never seen a person of that type in Prague. I understood that they were Jews fleeing from Austria; I think my father was trying to help them.

Janine Ingram
Young Greek woman, Thessaloniki
My parents were very much aware of what was going on in Europe and I often wondered why they had such sombre faces; but I am sorry to say that I was not interested. I was fourteen, fifteen and all I thought about was my schooling and a boyfriend. It's very difficult to imagine that one day you will become a non-citizen and that you will be so frightened that you will go into hiding or they will get you and kill you — it was beyond belief.

Marsha Segall
Lithuanian Jewish schoolgirl, Siauliai, Lithuania
There was no anti-Semitism expressed in childhood, not in early teens; but later in 1937 and 1938, there were a lot of Lithuanian youths who would say, "Why don't you go to Palestine!" but generally it didn't worry us. From 1933, one would regularly hear Hitler's speeches attacking the Jews, but one got used to it and thought it was just political speech, a local evil in Germany. We didn't think it would spread or that we would be *occupied* by Germany.

Josef Perl
Czech Jewish schoolboy, Veliky Bochkov
When the Hungarians came in after they annexed our part of Czechoslovakia in late 1938, they immediately got rid of our teachers and put in German trained anti-Semitic Hungarian teachers. The first day we went to school. After that, they told the Christian children

not to associate with us any more; even they couldn't understand why one moment we were playing together and friendly, and all of a sudden, we were different. I didn't realise how easy it was to turn somebody's mind, because within days, a friend I used to play with, kick balls with, eat with in each other's houses, all of a sudden called me "Dirty Jew". My pony was confiscated when the Hungarians came in, and one day I was walking home from school and saw there were lots of soldiers resting in the gutter. As a religious Jewish child I used to have ringlets hanging down over my shoulders, and one of these soldiers got up, came over to me, took out his bayonet and cut off my ringlets. I came home, I was shaking; I felt that I had lost part of my body. I refused to go to school after that — under the age of nine years, my education stopped, finished.

Hugo Gryn
Ruthenian-Slovak Jewish schoolboy, Berehovo, Ruthenia
I have very vivid recollections of the events of 1938 when Czechoslovakia was dismantled and we had been "liberated" by the Hungarians. It was in November, virtually everyone in our town was lined up along the road that led in from Hungary. It was really a military entry, not a civilian one, and suddenly people were pulling out Hungarian flags. The thing that haunts me was that the senior rabbi of our community — a very dignified man with a lovely posture — was wearing his World War I uniform as an officer of the Austro-Hungarian army, with all his decorations. An uncle of

mine and several others, who also had been officers in that war, did likewise. In a curious way they were greeting their old comrades-in-arms. At the age of eight years, I think I was one of the very few people who cried. I thought it was so sad.

KRISTALLNACHT

Susan Sinclair
German Jewish schoolgirl, Nuremberg
A number of men, somewhere between seven and ten, came bursting into our house and started smashing up everything. They locked my parents in the bathroom and they were desperate to know what was happening to their girls. There were only two of us at home at the time, my older sister was away at college and my younger sister and I shared a big room and I saw that her bed was full of glass and that everything had been smashed and the furniture was turned upside down. Then they pulled me out of bed and tore my nightdress to shreds and I was so self-conscious as a fifteen-year-old. There were roars of laughter from these young men, who seemed as if they were drunk, and they said to me, "Well, get your clothes on, where are they?" And I said, "In that wardrobe" — this was heavy continental furniture. "OK, go and get them." So I went to get them and as I went up to it they got behind it and threw it over. In fact it certainly would have killed me if they hadn't turned quite a large table upside down first; for a short time the table held the wardrobe and I

crawled out underneath. Then they started smashing up the rest of the place. My parents were screaming and shouting because they didn't know what was happening to us, it really was awful. Then they left to smash up somebody else's house. It was then that life as I had known it, stopped.

Freddie Knoller
Austrian Jewish schoolboy, Vienna
On 9 November, we received a telephone call from a very close friend of ours, who lived in the street opposite our synagogue, to say that the synagogue was in flames and the SA (Storm Troopers) wouldn't let the fire engine put out the fire, only making sure that it sprayed water on the adjoining houses. We were very anxious and worried and when I looked at the ceiling, this was quite red from the flames of the synagogue which was only in the next street. Somewhere around eleven o'clock that night, we heard a noise in our courtyard, and looking down we saw the Storm Troopers talking to our caretaker. He took them into the building. My mother became quite hysterical: "What are they going to do? Where are they going? Are they coming up to us?" My father turned off the light so that the apartment was in darkness. Suddenly we heard a woman's shrill voice, a screaming voice, and we heard the glass of a window breaking. We heard a thud in the courtyard. We looked down and saw a body lying there. We didn't know who it was until the woman, Mrs Epstein from the first floor, came running into the courtyard, screaming and going to her husband's body.

61

Gudrun Kübler

German woman, Berlin

You were shocked that something like that could happen, and *why*? These were also human beings; you can't do that to somebody, just destroy everything rather than let them have synagogues and keep their own religion. The houses and the shops! Some of them were attacked, windows smashed. In other words, you could plainly see it; also the oppressed people, later with their Stars (the Star of David that Jews were ordered to wear) and suchlike. It was very noticeable.

Hedy Epstein

German Jewish schoolgirl, Kippenheim

I remember on the Wednesday night, 9 November 1938, before I went to bed my father said to me, "If you hear some strange noises during the night, get out of bed immediately and get into the wardrobe in the hallway." I said, "What are you talking about? Why? What kind of noise?" He said, "Don't ask any questions, just do as you're told," which was totally unlike my father — I was always encouraged to ask questions and received answers. So I went to bed and was probably lying awake for quite a while before I was able to sleep, listening for something, I didn't know what. Finally I went to sleep and got up the next morning and forgot all about it, getting ready to go to school.

I left for school at ten minutes after seven just like I did every other day, on my bicycle, together with this one other Jewish child from Kippenheim who was at the school. As we approached the school we had to pass a house where a Jewish dentist had his home and his practice and I noticed every window in that building was broken and although I didn't know why, I assumed it was because he was Jewish. As we entered the school yard and parked our bicycles I could sense something was different but I didn't know what it was and I was afraid to ask; and so I proceeded to my classroom and this other boy proceeded to his. Classes started as they did every day and then about half an hour later, the principal walked in and he gave a long talk — even later that day I couldn't remember what he actually said, but at some point while he was talking he pointed his finger at me and he said, "Get out, you dirty Jew."

I heard what he said but I could not believe it. How could this nice man, this gentle man whose daughter was one of my classmates, how could he have said that? So I asked him, "Please would you repeat what you said, I didn't hear." And not only did he repeat it but came over, took me by the elbow and pushed me out of the door. I stood in the hallway and all kinds of thoughts were racing through my head: What did I do? Did I not listen? Did I yawn? What am I going to tell my parents? And the kind of searching questions I was asking myself, I heard later on, is typical of how victims think: what have I done? Rather than realising it is an outside force that has caused the problem.

Hannah Hyde
German non-Jewish schoolgirl, Uelzen

On my way to school, I used to pass a very large, villa-type house that belonged to Jews. And from this house they ran a business which sold bedding. In the front garden beside the entrance gate, they had a showcase, showing samples of their bedding: feather duvets, pillow, and the quality of the feathers — different grades. And I remember the morning after this *Kristallnacht* — the most direct way for me to get to school was past this Jewish house — and the whole showcase had been smashed up. There was glass all over the pavement. The feathers and contents were strewn all over the place. My mind's eye shows me a wan-looking girl standing in the front garden. She was probably a couple of years older because she looked taller — very slim, dark hair, a fine sort of face. And I can see this lonely, sad-looking girl standing in the front garden . . .

John Richards
Austrian Jewish schoolboy, Vienna

Although our local friends wore the swastika, they weren't too bad; some were good friends of ours until the 9 November when things changed drastically. On this day, my father asked me to meet my uncle. On my way I saw all these books being burned in the streets and then saw the synagogue on fire. I heard this man calling out and saw that he was being beaten up by these young lads and a couple of men dressed in black uniforms. Now my uncle had a particular walking stick

— bone handled and the bottom of it was polished — I saw this stick on the ground and when I ran forward, I saw that it was my uncle who was being beaten. I was only eleven years of age and not a brave person — I used to run away from fights — but I kicked one or two people with my boots and tried to help my uncle up; but unfortunately I got beaten as well. Anyway, I managed to help my uncle to his feet and we both managed to get away somehow. I knew the area pretty well and although we were chased, some people nearby, who could see what was happening, took us in.

John Fink
German Jewish electrician, Berlin
The German name *"Kristallnacht"* — the night of the broken glass — was so clean and nice, but it was an inaccurate description of what happened. Actually it was a *pogrom* because so many people got arrested and killed, and synagogues and shops were set on fire all over Germany (and Austria). It was a well-planned destruction of Jewish property. After that things got very, very serious.

Stephen Dale
Young German Jewish seaman, Hamburg
After the night called *Kristallnacht*, I was picked up in the Jewish hostel in Hamburg, taken to a prison complex outside Hamburg and eventually to Sachsenhausen concentration camp, just north of Berlin. I was there until just before Christmas with thousands of other Jews rounded up at the same time.

65

It was no picnic in Sachsenhausen. This was the third time I was in the hands of the *Gestapo* since 1934 and I wasn't totally surprised by what was happening. We were made to stand for twenty-four hours if not more, and gradually we were kitted out: our clothing was taken and carefully marked with names; then you were given a striped uniform and marched off to a block. This had straw on the floor, tables to eat from and a washroom. When we slept on the floor, each with a blanket, we couldn't lie on our backs, only sideways because there wasn't enough room. It was all organised. Each block had a block leader, in our case it was a political prisoner — a very powerful personality, he helped to keep morale up tremendously by his sheer presence. We were marched out to work, such as it was; it wasn't very constructive work, we were digging. Then, to occupy us, they made us run between two points in relays. There was one man, older than us, he was terribly upset by it and kept shouting. "I was an officer in the last war!" — it was an affront to his dignity, as well as being exhausting for him.

There were two roll calls a day and in that cold weather you had to stand for ages. The guards also had inmates to take over certain duties. Jews had yellow triangles on our jackets; politicals, red; criminals, green; and homosexuals, pink. The foremen were either criminals or politicals, so within the camp there was a grading of degrading of inmates — extraordinary! That was the end of 1938. I think they were concerned with organising us and learning lessons for future reference.

Susan Sinclair
German Jewish schoolgirl, Nuremberg

After *Kristallnacht*, my father was imprisoned in Dachau. Eventually, my mother with a lawyer's help got him released. He spoke to us about some of his experiences. They were told, "You can commit suicide if you want — there's the electric fence, but if you attempt it and you don't succeed, your punishment will be very heavy." He spoke of an evening when there was an opera singer in his hut who sang most beautifully. My father, who was particularly musical, was deeply touched by this. But it was awful and the details of the awfulness he didn't tell us. But he said that people became a lower kind of person quickly. Someone had died and two or three fought over his toothbrush. He found this unbelievable because they were cultured, professional men. He couldn't believe that human beings could so quickly become lesser people. The experience certainly had an effect on him. Now he was a changed man: he had a lot of nice wavy dark brown hair when he went in and when they shaved his head it came through as a grey stubble. He was also a very angry man. Normally German men in those days wore hats in the winter and he was walking around in December without a hat on; I was a bit embarrassed because of the way he looked. I mean nowadays people shave their heads, but they didn't in those days and I kept saying, "Oh do put your hat on, Daddy," and he'd say, "No, *I'm* not ashamed, they have to be ashamed at what they've done to me; I've done nothing wrong, let them see."

I heard later that my mother had marched into a police station with my father's wartime medals and said, "If you can stick him into a concentration camp, you know what you can do with these." And she just dumped them.

Fritz Moses
German child, Strehlen, Silesia, Germany
My parents had problems with our name, Moses, in 1938 when kids from our town marched through the streets and dumped excrement in front of our store, thinking it was owned by Jews. As for my father, it really bothered him. First of all he was very proud to be a member of the Nazi Party, and I still remember when I was a child, all kinds of people came to our house in the evenings and he gave them vouchers to spend for food and things. So he was interested in social welfare. He thought that what Hitler did was good. It is false to presume that everybody who was in the Party was involved in murders, that they wanted to start a war.

Leon Greenman
British Jewish businessman, Rotterdam
So I went to and from London. In 1938 I remember seeing people digging dugouts in the streets. They were also queuing up for gas masks. I didn't quite understand, but I got my gas mask. I became panicky and went back to Holland with the idea of getting my wife out of Holland and probably her grandmother too. Then I heard Chamberlain announcing that he

had seen Hitler and there wouldn't be a war between England and Germany. So I must have fallen asleep again because I said, "All right, we won't go tomorrow, we'll go in six months' time." Life went on again.

KINDERTRANSPORT

John Silberman
German Jewish schoolboy, Berlin

Over the years since 1933, my parents were changing from hoping that the Nazi era would only be short-lived, that life was going to be hard and we needed to lower our standards and our sights for a while, withdrawing to the inner family and survive as best we can economically. But with the Nuremberg Laws it became quite evident that there was no future for Jews in Germany and that's when people seriously started to consider emigration. But even then it was half-hearted.

Putting it in today's comparable terms: if you're in your forties or fifties age group, with children at school, with a home and no serious economic difficulty, and if somebody says to you: look there's a threat on the horizon and you may not be able to carry on this lifestyle, why don't you emigrate to Uruguay, or Iceland? You say: yes, that sounds sensible, I'll think about it. That was just about the atmosphere: Jews realised that it wasn't sensible to stay where they were but the likely points of immigration were not attractive;

added to which there was a language problem and an economic problem because already the Nazis had laws in place forbidding Jews to take assets and capital out. So if you left you were going to be poor in a world which was just clawing its way out of the 1929/30 recession.

So wherever you went from 1935 to 1938, you were going to be fighting the local population for an income, for work or setting up business. Everyone understood that they *ought* to be emigrating, but it was only when the watershed of *Kristallnacht* occurred in November 1938 that my parents, in common with ninety per cent of other German Jews, thought: it's no good staying, they're going to kill us. Survival in the life-threatening sense was the only thing that mattered. Even then nobody understood what the Germans had in mind for the Jews — the mass genocide — it was only perceived to be the mass takeover of Jewish assets and driving the Jews out.

Margareta Burkill
British non-Jewish civilian, Cambridge
When *Kristallnacht* happened in November '38, it went through Great Britain like an electric current: in every little town, every village in England they said, "We must save the children." It was quite a *fantastic* thing. People who'd never thought about the Nazis, when they heard about this murder and burning, *that* was the reaction. We were very early on the scene in Cambridge; I started it and I got Sybil Hutton to join me. We were responsible for quite a lot of children in other places, in

the small villages around Cambridge. Within nine months before the beginning of war, the *Kindertransport* had brought out just under 10,000 unaccompanied children and we would have made the full allowance of 10,000 if one trainload from Czechoslovakia hadn't been stopped in Germany just as war was declared. They were the Czech orphanage children and of course they disappeared.

John Richards
Austrian Jewish schoolboy, Vienna

I went up to my father before I got on the train and put my arms around him and I said, "I'm sorry about the (torn) trousers, I don't want to go, I love you so much." He kissed me and said, "I forgive you, try and behave and be a good boy." I went up to my mother and she kissed me; although she was my stepmother I could see tears in her eyes and she told me she loved me. I then went to my stepbrother Heini and he came into my arms and we knelt down; we had those long socks on, you don't see them in England, and he kissed me and hugged me and *begged* me not to go. Little Zilla was there, I kissed her and said my farewells and we got on the train.

I held my sister's hand. We found a compartment. As we got on the train they shut the door, we tried to open the windows and all of a sudden these black uniforms appeared and they pushed our parents back, they weren't allowed to come near us. Father tried to shout something, but with all the commotion, we couldn't hear. The younger children started to cry then. I had a sense of relief; I felt a sense of sadness; I felt a sense of anger. I thought: was I such a bad lad to be torn away from my father and mother? Will I ever be lucky enough to see them again? The emotions that were going through me! Tears. For some reason, I don't know what, my sister didn't cry. Later on in life, she told me that from the day we left Nordbahnhof in Vienna, she cut the past out of her life.

Hedy Epstein
German Jewish schoolgirl, Kippenheim

My parents were trying to paint a wonderful picture for me of England: I'm going to a big city, I'm going to school, "You'll be learning a new language, you'll make new friends, and we'll all be together again soon, if not in England, then in the United States. This is just temporary." I wanted to believe this but I had all these mixed feelings about it and then I got the notion into my head that my parents wanted to get rid of me. I told them that, and it must have been very painful for them because, although they never showed their pain, they must have felt it. Plus, there were also Jewish people telling them: at times like this you don't separate the family, the family stays together.

As they put me on the train, they were still smiling about this wonderful thing I'm going to. The window was open and we chit-chatted, last minute admonitions: always be polite, always say please and thank you — two words of my very limited vocabularly. Then someone called, "*Alles einsteigen!*" — "all aboard". Then the tug and groan of the train, then a whistle and it started to move very slowly. And my parents, who had this almost artificial smile on their faces, started to move with the train as it moved out of the station, and as it moved faster and faster, they ran faster and faster, tears streaming down their faces, waving goodbye with their handkerchiefs.

Then I knew: they really *did* love me, this was a great act of love. I watched and saw them getting smaller and smaller until they were two dots and then they were gone. I didn't know at that point that I would never see them again. But I immediately sat down and wrote a letter apologising and telling them that I knew they loved me very much and that's why they sent me away. Later they mailed me that they had got that letter.

John Silberman
German Jewish schoolboy, Berlin
I remember in my carriage there was a baby of two or three years old, and this child was given to a teenage girl who was told, "Look after her until you get to England." What courage that took for those parents! We travelled from Berlin for several hours until we came to the Dutch border. It made a *huge* impression on me: here I'd been in an ever-deepening situation of bad treatment, bullying, vulnerability, victimisation and here comes the Dutch border. Trains used to stop on one side of the border while the German officials did their stuff, then the train shunted over to the Dutch side and the same thing happened all over again. But, with one difference: accompanying the Dutch officials came a load of ladies in grey uniforms and I think it

was the first time for years that non-Jewish people said something kind to us. They brought chocolate, soft drinks; they gave us postcards to mail home to our parents that we had crossed the border. Somebody had gone to a lot of trouble there to understand what kids would need. We hadn't expected it and to this day I have a great fondness for the Dutch.

Bertha Leverton
German Jewish child, Munich
Of course what your parents put into your cases were your best clothes and they left all the rubbish behind because you couldn't bring very much. This was later on a minus point against us in England because we didn't look like refugees, like how English people expected refugees to look: refugees look bedraggled, they look very sad and we didn't look like that at all. In fact in many instances we had nicer clothes than the people we came to and it didn't endear us to our foster parents.

Warren Mitchell
Jewish schoolboy, London
My father showed me the pictures of *Kristallnacht*, of the smashing of Jewish shops, and there was a picture of a Jew being beaten by passers-by outside his shop; my father had sheer blind hatred that such crimes could be committed. I suppose that *Kristallnacht* was the beginning of the realisation of what a monster was being spawned on the Continent.

My main involvement with it came when Jewish families in Britain were asked to take Jewish children. Jewish organisations were collecting and giving money and getting boatloads out. My father had responded to an article in the *Jewish Chronicle* and I went with him one Sunday morning, in 1939, to Liverpool Street Station to meet this train. Something like five or six hundred children came off that train. They were so frightened, so traumatised by what had happened to them. It was bad enough for kids in this country who were evacuated, but some of these children had been persecuted for months, like the case of Ilse, the girl who came to us. She hadn't been out of her house for six months, just frightened to go out.

Ilse came to live with us; she didn't speak for about a week, she was so traumatised by what had happened to her. Her father was in a concentration camp. She learnt to speak English very quickly. She began to tell us what had happened and the appalling thing was that it wasn't the Nazis — the *Gestapo* or the SS — it was the neighbours, the ordinary people who behaved so abominably towards the Jews in their community. Ilse and her sister Lotte got out. She was very tearful, she didn't think she'd see her parents again. She did get two letters via the International Red Cross and in a very short space of time she was speaking English and doing tremendously well at school. Ilse was my second sister; we played Monopoly together and we argued and fought just like brother and sister.

(Sir) Hans Krebs
German Jewish refugee, Cambridge
There were quite a few German refugees working in Cambridge. One of the Cambridge professors, J. B. S. Haldane, a very famous national figure, offered his house free of charge to refugees — one gesture of the general generosity. But we decided it would be wrong for us to live together, it was important to mix and learn something of English life and not form an isolated group. Although it would have been of financial advantage, we thought we should integrate as quickly and effectively as possible, and living together would interfere with integration.

Stephen Dale
Young German Jewish seaman, Hamburg
When I got out of Sachsenhausen, I knew I would go to England. What I didn't know was the timing so I was hanging around. Eventually, I arrived in England in a ship from Hamburg. I had sailed from there quite often and the stevedores knew me. They gave me the most rousing send-off — it was really marvellous, quite, quite touching. They knew I was a Jew but it was never a talking point. I have this abiding memory of the people connected with the sea in Germany: they were tolerant and understanding people.

Martin Parker
Polish Jewish electrical engineer, Warsaw
There was no way of going abroad and staying there. Couldn't go. Some people did it, two friends of mine,

but it wasn't easy with a child of three years. There was no option. My younger brother-in-law, a chemistry student, just finished university, told me, "Go to Russia," but I didn't want this. Where could I go? To Argentina? They would accept us; or Brazil? But they were primitive countries; we didn't have many luxuries in Warsaw, but compared with those . . . And besides, we didn't have enough money to go so far abroad.

Edith Baneth
Czech Jewish schoolgirl, Opava
I remember the thing which gave me the first shock. I belonged to an ice-skating club in the town. I loved ice-skating and was pretty good at it. Then one day, I came to my ice-skating teacher and was told, "I'm sorry, this is the last time, we don't accept Jewish people as members any more." I couldn't possibly understand: what has my *Jewishness* got to do with my ice-skating? After this shock my parents' friends, who were leaving, said, "Come with us." My father couldn't possibly believe that things would get so bad. "Nobody could possibly harm me, I've done nothing wrong, I've paid all my pension rights and I would lose all that."

Harry Lowit
Czech Jewish child, Olcška
When the Germans walked in, in 1939, we left Prague and went to live with our grandmother in this place called Oleška where we had this little house opposite my grandma's shop. Yes, life changed then: the Jews were very much restricted, and a lot of people showed

they were anti-Semitic — it came into the open. The children were quite cruel, I remember cat-calls about being Jews, quite derogatory. The Czechs flow where the water flows, they go with whoever is in charge. I must say that I resent that very much. I don't think they behaved well at all. In this particular village of Oleška, though, there were some very nice people who sided with us.

At the age of eight, I didn't fully comprehend what was going on; it was just inconvenient to be driven out of your own home and beautiful standards and to live in this small house in Oleška in more humble surroundings. Then later, of course, the rule of Jews wearing the Star of David was introduced, which I resented. Nobody likes to be humiliated. I remember the invasion of Poland. My father was apprehensive about it. He had a visa to go to Bogota; eventually he decided against it and it probably cost him his life and my mother's life as well.

Zdenka Ehrlich
Czech Jewish child, Rokycany

It was a Wednesday in March 1939, about six o'clock in the morning — we were three children and parents, a family of five. My father came to wake us up and he said, "Quick, quick, children, come to the window, there are columns of German army motor-cyclists trundling through the town." Of course a child is curious. We all rushed to the window and had a look. It looked very menacing; they were helmeted and drrrrrrr, drrrrrrr, one after another in long columns like black ants. And of course we didn't quite know what the consequences would be, but the feeling was very menacing. Then we listened to the radio which had a feeling of urgency and they were repeating, "Stand by, stand by." When we heard they'd reached Prague and occupied the castle and there was a big upheaval, we knew that was the beginning of the end.

Jan Hartman
Czech Jewish schoolboy, Prague
My father had exclusively non-Jewish friends. I just didn't know what a Jew was. The first time I made the connection was when the Germans came on 15 March 1939, occupying Prague. Then it went very quickly because within two or three weeks they came and arrested my father. In June 1939 our French school was abolished. Children of Jewish origins came under the Nuremberg Laws. Not to go to school was a big blow. I was thirteen, so I finished the school year and then no more school. One after the other, things were taken away from you: radios, dogs, jewels, you had to declare everything. You were completely stripped of everything.

Edith Baneth
Czech Jewish schoolgirl, Postejov
We moved to Postejov, Moravia, for my father's work in the garment industry, but when the whole of Czechoslovakia was taken we felt trapped, and then my parents realised it was a mistake to stay, that we should have gone to Canada; but there was no chance to go any more, and day by day things got much worse.

John Fink
German Jewish electrician, Berlin

We German Jews experienced the Nazis from 1933; people in the countries which were overrun by Germany, like Poland and Czechoslovakia, they experienced German Nazism only since 1939. But we had the hard times bit by bit and when they put the screws on tighter and tighter, it was terrible to hear of people committing suicide and others being taken off to concentration camps. Everyone knew how bitter it was to fall into the hands of the *Gestapo*. There was no secret about that. It's not only the Jewish people who suffered, there were many Germans — especially the Social Democrats and Communists — who were taken away and never came back.

1939

WAR

I remember immediately the war started there were a few German planes shot down and a German pilot and his crew were paraded across Warsaw. That was my first sight of a German uniformed pilot and his crew and I thought they looked very nice young boys of nineteen, twenty or so, in German uniform. I couldn't see any problem.

The Munich Agreement, which surrendered Czechoslovakia to the *Reich*, convinced Hitler that England and France would not dare to confront him over further expansion eastwards. But, after the Nazi occupation of the rest of Czechoslovakia in March 1939, Britain and France guaranteed that they would go to the aid of Poland should her independence be threatened by Hitler. During the summer of 1939, Nazi threats against Poland increased with demands for the Free City of Danzig and the Polish Corridor. On 23 August 1939, Hitler signed a non-aggression pact with Stalin which gave him the "green light" to invade Poland. On 1 September 1939, German forces launched their *Blitzkrieg* — lightning war. The long agony of the Polish people was about to begin.

On Sunday, 3 September 1939, after Hitler refused to withdraw his troops from Poland,

Britain and France honoured their guarantees to the Poles, declaring war on Germany.

As the Nazi invasion of Poland continued, random acts of violence, killing, destruction and arson were undertaken by mobile SS units entering alongside the *Wehrmacht*, with the aim of terrorising the population at large and dividing Poles — many of whom were active anti-Semites — and Jews.

John Silberman
German Jewish schoolboy, London

War clouds were gathering, everyone knew it was likely that there was going to be a war, but everybody also believed that it was going to be short-lived, because here was the mighty British Empire, the country that had won the First World War, plus France — what chance had Germany, only twenty years after she was flattened last time? So we, in our mentality, weren't too upset about the gathering clouds because, hopefully, this was going to be a quick end to the evil in Germany and maybe we wouldn't have to go to America, as planned, but go back to Germany and pick up where we had left off. The mood was: only war will sort this thing out.

Michael Etkind
Polish Jewish schoolboy, Lodz

We listened to the German radio, sometimes in Polish, sometimes in German. (Earlier in the year) they were broadcasting a speech by Hitler. My mother was listening. I didn't understand much German then but there was one sentence which she explained to me, "The Jews must disappear from Europe." I realised we had been sentenced to death. It was a very frightening moment.

Marsha Segall
Young Lithuanian Jewish woman, Siauliai
I finished high school in 1939 which was my downfall because I had intentions to study in France. My sister, who finished school in 1937, went to London to study at the London School of Economics. I intended to go on the fated day of 1 September 1939 with a young couple who lived in Paris and came on holiday to see their parents in Lithuania. Neither they nor I left Lithuania because the war was declared and Poland was attacked by the German army.

Lili Stern-Pohlmann
Polish Jewish child, Krakow
In the summer of 1939 we were on holiday in Poronin, near Zakopane. People were very uneasy: they were reading the papers and listening to the radio. I remember my father saying: war is imminent. My parents decided to cut the holiday short and return to Krakow. When we got home my father said, "Right, I'm going to send you to your grandparents in Lvov and I'll join you in a few days." On 31 August 1939 he put my mother, my little brother and myself on the train. Little did we know that was the last train from Krakow to Lvov. Usually it was a fast train, but now it was

stopping at every little station, with crowds of people waiting to board this train. We arrived in Lvov to a scene I will never forget. As we looked out of the window for my grandfather, who always met us, there were soldiers lying on the platform, one next to the other, asleep — the platform was paved with them. During the night of the 31 August/1 September, the Germans bombed the Lvov railway station, and all those poor boys were killed.

Anna Bergman
Czech Jewish university student, Prague

The panic started in 1939. I had a valid passport, valid permission from the Germans to leave the country plus a visa and job in England — all the documents. I was single with no ties, but I didn't want to go, couldn't imagine that anything would happen to us. I remember on 1 September 1939 we were swimming in the river and one of my friends had all the necessary documents for Australia, and here we were kissing and embracing, celebrating the fact that we *couldn't* go any more. It was so *mad*, we were living an illusion, we were so happy that we stayed.

Adam Adams
Polish Jewish schoolboy, Lublin

Life started to change in September 1939 when I noticed big posters about mobilisation. I remember thinking: "Good, I won't have to go to school." How immature I was! I didn't know what war was going to bring us. And when the German army came in like a parade, I was on the road watching it. In my eye, I have this little photograph of myself, singing as they came a song which goes something like, "To love and be loved and be twenty years old . . .", not realising how life is going to change in a few weeks; not months, *weeks*.

John Fink
German Jewish electrician, Berlin
I remember the day the war started. The radio was blaring about dive bombers attacking Warsaw and how the Slavic people don't even deserve to live, that they should all be defeated. The big word was *"Lebensraum"* — more room for Germans to live. I then lost my job and was sent to work for a while in the Air Ministry.

Michael Etkind
Polish Jewish schoolboy, Lodz
The Germans arrived in force after 1 September, they were everywhere; *Panzers* were driving through all the main streets, you've never seen so much traffic and machinery passing through!

Martin Parker
Polish Jewish electrical engineer, Warsaw
I had survived the First World War, and knew the problems. I bought two tons of potatoes, three tons of coal, a hundred kilos of sugar and a hundred kilos of flour, and this helped us a lot. The money which I had from my engineering business I started changing into gold. My wife's friend's father was a manufacturing jeweller and from him I bought second-hand earrings,

rings, chains — this type of thing, easily disposable. I had a kilo and a half, quite a lot then. Later the price of gold went up.

Stanley Faull
Polish Jewish schoolboy, Warsaw

When war broke out everything came to a complete standstill. Between 1939 and 1945 I had no schooling at all. At the time that Czechoslovakia had been taken over, my father and the family and his friends used to discuss it in the evenings and I remember my father saying that he was surprised that the Americans, British and French weren't stopping them. "He just marches through and takes over." "He" being the corporal, the decorator-painter. I remember they used to make fun of Hitler, they treated him as a joke. Even when the war broke out they said that it can't last for more than six months because he's incapable of standing up against Britain and France. I also remember my father saying, "It's not possible for him to extend Germany as he wants to because they will stop him." And I, as a boy, thought: well, my father says so, that must be it.

I remember immediately the war started there were a few German planes shot down and a German pilot and his crew were paraded across Warsaw. That was my first sight of a German uniformed pilot and his crew and I thought they looked very nice young boys of nineteen, twenty or so, in German uniform. I couldn't see any problem. I still believe that the German Air Force and *Wehrmacht* (Army) were decent people, it was the Nazi machine — the *Gestapo* and the SS (*Schutzstaffel*) —

who were on the extermination side, and not just Jews; gypsies and Russians as well.

Adam Adams
Polish Jewish schoolboy, Lublin
The next photograph in my eye happened very, very quickly. A German officer was allocated to our house. He was dressed like a god in a beautiful uniform; he was a highly educated man from Vienna. I remember him playing our piano, always beautifully dressed in a fantastic uniform, and I would look at him and admire him.

John Richards
Austrian Jewish Kindertransport refugee, London
In the morning this person came to pick me up and we went by train from Bury, in Lancashire, where I had first been sent, to London. I remember the date because it was 3 September 1939 — the day war was declared. We were sitting in this person's house eating a meal. I could speak a little bit of English then; they had the radio on and I heard this man's voice saying, ". . . this country is at war with Germany." I looked at the people in the room and said to the man who had fetched me, "Does this mean that I can't go home any more, that I won't see my mother and father again?" He tried to explain in a very kind way what it was all about, then he said, "Maybe if God is willing, maybe you'll see your mother and father again; maybe." And it was the way that he said it . . .

Clive Teddern
German Jewish Kindertransport refugee Edinburgh

I had come to Britain in March 1939 on one of the children's transports as a fifteen-year-old boy. I always remember the broadcast on that Sunday morning. The family I was staying with in Edinburgh were very emotional about it. You knew that war would happen, in a way I was almost *glad* it happened and I wanted to do what I could to assist the war effort in my own simple little way — like filling sandbags and things like that. In a way I was glad it had come to a climax — well, partly glad, because obviously there were other considerations — I realised that contact with my parents would be lost. I did not foresee that the Holocaust would happen. I felt the war would be over soon; everything would be finished and I would be going back to my parents. I had visions of my standing on a ship and sailing up the river Elbe — that kind of thing.

Stephen Dale
Young German Jewish refugee seaman, London

I was due to take an exam to be an officer in the Merchant Navy when war broke out. Now, under some government regulation, I couldn't take it. Nor could I go back to sea as a merchant seaman. "Oh, then I'll join the Royal Navy." "You must be joking! The Navy won't take people like you, but you can join the Army." But this would have to be the Pioneer Corps where you weren't allowed to carry weapons, and being in a second-class unit didn't appeal to me at all. Anyway, by that time it was 1940 and my refugee friends and I knew we'd be interned. "Enemy aliens" had to go before tribunals where we'd be classified as A, B or C: A were interned immediately, B had conditional liberties and C, like myself, could do what you liked provided you told the police if you moved away for more than twenty-four hours.

Ludwig Baruch
German Jewish Communist youth, Liverpool
In September 1939 I was summoned to the police and told I couldn't own or ride a motor bike, bicycle, map, and God knows what, and I had to report all my different movements to the police. Then I was summoned to a tribunal in October, given category A, and interned immediately. My father was interned the same day. It caused a sensation in Liverpool I can tell you, because at the time I was the Chairman of the Youth Committee of the Liverpool Trades Council, as well as a member of the District Committee of the Communist Party, and very friendly with the Liverpool Labour Party. It caused a sensation because I was known as an anti-Fascist German. We were taken to Clacton. We had an escort of three young lads. They were flabbergasted: they were told we were dangerous Nazis and there was my old father and me, and they could see it was absolute bullshit. When we were on Liverpool Street Station on the way to Clacton, they were hungry and thirsty and they said, "Look, we're hungry, we're piling our stuff here with our guns." And off they went for their food and we had to watch their guns and equipment! It was absolutely ridiculous. The

first internment camp was Butlin's in Clacton — an absolute bloody mess, you've never seen anything like it, complete chaos.

At the end of October, I was taken to Seaton camp. I was in Seaton internment camp from late 1939 until 1 July 1940 — my father and I were in the category A. There were German anti-fascists there of all persuasions, some priests and a few rabbis as well as sailors from German ships which had been captured by the Royal Navy after the outbreak of war. There were also some Nazis and German nationalists and leading Nazis too. There were also German and Austrian Communist Party groups. We anti-fascists wanted to be separated from the Nazis but the British couldn't admit that some of the internees were anti-Nazis so this was refused. But we had no real problem even with the leading Nazis; our relations were always correct. There was no aggro at all. I can tell you that by the time the *Graf Spee* was scuttled on 17 December 1939, their morale was very low, already they feared the worst, especially when they heard of the suicide of the captain of the *Graf Spee*.

Leon Greenman
British Jewish businessman, Rotterdam
My wife told me that I had promised her a child.

I said, "We'd better not because I still think we're going to have a war. I don't know why, but I feel it."

"Well," she said, "you promised."

I said, "Okay, we'll have a child."

Just like that. When war was declared, I was still in Holland wondering what we should do. We couldn't leave the old lady. I didn't know where to turn or what to do. I went to the British Consul in Rotterdam and said, "What's going on? What rumours are there?"

"Oh, we can't tell you that, but you can leave under A or B, which means in a few weeks' time, or under C, when the staff of the Consul leaves."

I said, "All right, we'll leave when the staff leave."

I was thinking of my stock of books and the old lady and my pregnant wife.

Michael Etkind
Polish Jewish schoolboy, Lodz

Then various notices appeared; for example, Jews were not allowed to walk on the main street which was renamed Adolf Hitler Strasse. They were not allowed to go into parks, swimming pools, or cinemas and theatres. All the money in the bank was frozen, all property belonging to Jews automatically confiscated. Then Jews had to wear an armband with the Star of David on it to show that they were Jews; somebody started making them and you bought them at the street corners. The death penalty was imposed for the slightest deviation from the order. People were being hanged for nothing, just to terrorise the population. I am very squeamish and found it strange that out of morbid curiosity, people would go to where corpses were hanging in the square.

Adam Adams
Polish Jewish schoolboy, Lublin

At first nothing was mentioned about Jewish people, nothing at all. My next recollection — again something like a photograph — about twenty people sitting in our room discussing things. They would recollect how during the First World War, nothing happened to the women, only the men. Eventually it was decided that all the men would leave and the women could stay because they would be safe. Twenty of us went to the River Bug, hired a boat and a Jewish peasant as a guide and started to cross the river. I remember it was night, we were sitting in the boat and suddenly the lights came on; there were German soldiers on both sides of the river and they caught us.

Taube Biber
Polish Jewish schoolgirl, Mielec

It happened to be the eve of the Jewish New Year and being orthodox people, everybody was preparing for the holiday. Of course the Poles collaborated (with the Germans) and they showed them around, "Here are the synagogues and this is the ritual bath." The Germans got into the ritual bath, they drove the people into the courtyard and there they poured paraffin over them and burned them. That wasn't enough; the three synagogues were in the square, we lived in that road and peeping through a little space between the curtains, we could see what was happening. They were going round the houses, breaking in, picking up all men, making them stand with their arms up around the burning synagogues.

Michael Etkind
Polish Jewish schoolboy, Lodz
Every few days there would be a knock on the door and invariably there would be a German soldier, often with a *volksdeutsche* (a Pole of German origin) with a swastika on his lapel, and they would simply come and rob: the wedding ring from my mother's finger, look into a cupboard and take whatever they wanted. It was simply that a soldier would team up with a local man who would tell him where rich Jews were living and they would go and help themselves.

Helen Stone
Young Polish Jewish woman, Bedzin
They burned our synagogue *with* the people inside. Opposite the synagogue was a church, and about two o'clock in the morning the priest heard that the synagogue was burning and he ran to the church, opened the door in case somebody ran out of the inferno, and quite a few people did; he saved their lives. I was moved about nine or ten times in Bedzin as they were making streets *Judenrein* — cleansed of Jews.

Roman Halter
Polish schoolboy, Chodecz
One day soon after the war started, the SS *Sturmbahnnführer's* (SS Major's) wife for whom I was then working said, "You must come this afternoon, I

want you to deliver a message." She gave me a piece of paper and instructions and I went on this errand and when I was on my way back to the *Sturmbahnnführer*'s house with the rucksack I had been given, I heard shooting. So I cut across through the forest to the part where I heard the shooting — I knew the place like the palm of my hand — and there was a ravine. I went to the edge of the ravine and looked down.

My Jewish friends were being shot and the people who were doing the shooting were the men who had been recruited by the *Sturmbahnnführer*: all the gendarmes were dressed to the hilt and the young recruits were in uniforms. The shoemaker had two children, a son and a daughter. They were twins and they were taken against a mound; the boy didn't want to let go of his sister, so the *Sturmbahnnführer* said, "Crush his skull," and they crushed his skull. I saw all this. His sister screamed and they dragged them both to a spot and they shot them.

I was quite paralysed. These were my contemporaries. That happened so early — still only '39. I realised that if I were caught here, I'd be shot right away, so I crawled from bush to bush and eventually made a loop and went back with that rucksack and gave it to the *Sturmbahnnführer*'s wife. Then I went home. I didn't want to tell my parents, I just kept quiet about it . . . I carried that secret with me, but it gave me nightmares for a long time. After that life became worse and worse.

1940–1941

THE THIRD REICH EXPANDS

All of a sudden, I must have been about five or six rows from the front, I saw my mother and four sisters lined up and before I had a chance to say, "Mother!" they were already dead.

After the conquest of Poland, Hitler turned his attention to the west. In April 1940, he invaded Denmark and Norway, and a month later Luxembourg, Holland, Belgium and France. The next year he conquered Yugoslavia and Greece. By May 1941, Germany dominated the Continent of Europe. Millions of Jews were now caught in the Nazi net.

After the Fall of France in 1941, Britain faced the real prospect of invasion. Fears of a German "Fifth Column" prompted Churchill's government to round up and intern more "enemy aliens", many of whom were Jewish refugees who had come to Britain to escape Nazi persecution.

In 1940/41, during the first six months of their occupation of Western Europe, the Nazis moved quite slowly against the Jews, lulling them into a false sense of security. But in Poland, where over two million Jews were under Nazi rule, they were subjected each day to further cruelties and indignities. Jews lived in constant fear of round-ups for slave labour, arbitrary arrest and imprisonment, seizure of property, beatings and killings. Decrees were issued at this time for incarcerating Jews in ghettos.

A secret protocol of the Nazi-Soviet Non-Aggression Pact, signed on 23 August 1939, allowed for the Russian occupation of eastern Poland. The Red Army invaded on 17 September 1939, and by the end of the month Germany and Russia had partitioned Poland. Many Jews fled from German-occupied Poland to what they hoped was the relative safety of the Soviet annexed territories. But over 200,000 Jews were deported to labour camps within the Soviet Union. Although suffering appalling conditions in the camps, especially those located in Siberia, a large proportion survived the war. Many of the men went on to fight in the Free Polish forces after their release following the Nazi invasion of the Soviet Union on 22 June 1941.

On 22 June 1941 the *Wehrmacht* turned eastwards, conquering large parts of the western Soviet Union. In contrast to the less draconian policies initially adopted in western-occupied countries such as Norway, Denmark and Holland, Poles and Russians were considered, along with Jews and gypsies, *Untermensch* — sub-human; they were to be reduced to a state of abject slavery through erasure of their cultural identity and political autonomy along with seizure or destruction of their property. Their lands would, in turn, provide the *Reich* with *Lebensraum* — living space — for the expanding German population. Among all these perceived enemies, Jews were considered a special category, the foremost racial enemy.

Leon Goldman
British Jewish businessman, Rotterdam
Just before the bombing of Rotterdam, I went to the British Consul and found the house closed with nobody there. So we were trapped. I still don't understand why they didn't let us know they were going. On 10 May, the first bombs were dropping near our home. I looked out through the window and saw about four or five aeroplanes circling around, letting their bombs drop. I heard something fall behind me and turned around. My wife was busy bathing the child. It slipped out of her soapy fingers onto the floor. I didn't say a word. I picked it up, put it back into her hands and looked at her. We couldn't say anything. So that was the beginning of the war.

Steven Frank
Dutch Jewish schoolboy, Amsterdam
I was not quite five years old, in May 1940, when I first saw the German soldiers march on the streets of Amsterdam. They marched in their greatcoats with rifles on their shoulders and packs on their backs, tin helmets on and bayonets in scabbards at the side; we were excited and followed them wherever they went, even getting lost once and finding it difficult to get back home again. But the first time that I became aware that

101

I was different was when our parents told us that we had to be careful what we did and where we went. And it really hit one between the eyes when the notices, "*Voor Joden Verboden*", went up. It meant we couldn't go into the park because of this notice. "Forbidden for Jews."

At the outbreak of war there were 140,000 Jews living in Holland and these were absolutely petrified that they were going to be sent eastwards to work and any ruse you could possibly find to remain in Holland was essential. There was this "Barneveld List" with names of prominent people in Dutch society. It contained musicians, conductors, professors, teachers, painters — the top echelons of Dutch Jewish society — plus a few lower down the social scale, but with connections. Eventually three non-Jewish prominent men in the city who had previously unsuccessfully pleaded clemency for my father, managed to get us on the Barneveld List.

Barneveld was in the mid-southern part of Holland; we lived in the castle, situated in beautiful grounds, there were no guards or barbed wire. If you wanted to walk out, you could. Eventually it became so overcrowded that a second place was opened in a town not far away. People were very grateful to be there, a bit like a flock of sheep — you feel safety when you're all together.

Anna Bergman
Czech Jewish university student
Later on in September 1941, just before Heydrich came to Czechoslovakia as Deputy *Reich* Protector of

Bohemia and Moravia, the Yellow Stars were introduced. I was probably the only Jewish person who didn't mind at all and I carried my head high. I had a very nice outfit with a suede leather jacket and the star fitted the pocket perfectly. I met a friend of mine walking with her head down and I said, "Don't let them get you down." But I must have been the only one.

Jan Hartman
Czech Jewish schoolboy, Prague
I was ashamed to have that Star. You see it was one thing that the Germans managed very successfully to do, somehow to impress people with the idea that they were the master race. Race is a strange term, but when people speak of race today, I shiver when I hear it used in the German sense. There is one reaction which is cerebral, reasonable, rational and normal; but the other is under the skin, which has nothing to do with the rational. I reject the idea of a master race, but having lived with them and with the way they behaved, it actually gets under your skin. You can get a very strange reaction where you detest them because they are bad and yet you admire them a little bit.

Janine Ingram
Young Greek Jewish woman, Thessaloniki
Later on we had to wear the Star. I am an obstinate and proud person and to me wearing the Star of David was a challenge, so rather than wear it and lower my head, I wore it proudly. I didn't feel there was anything wrong

with being Jewish. I didn't particularly *want* to be Jewish because I didn't know the meaning of it because I'm not a religious person, but as I was born Jewish, I may as well be one. So I wasn't affected by that Star, and probably I didn't realise the danger — that the Star was the only way of getting us where they wanted us.

BRITAIN: INTERNMENT OF "ENEMY ALIENS"

Clive Teddern
German Jewish refugee youth, Edinburgh
Well, I never expected it! I mean, I heard the news — the invasion of Holland and Belgium — but I never related it to anything connected to me. I can't remember whether I heard then that the Germans used parachutists disguised as refugees or if I heard about that later, but I very clearly remember that day. It was a Sunday, 12 May 1940, and I was sitting in the kitchen doing my homework. Somebody came to the door to see me, he asked me my name and said, "I'm afraid I have to take you into custody. Would you please take a change of underwear, socks and your alien's certificate," and so on.

And to me that was a great adventure, I was quite happy about it, highly thrilled, it didn't worry me at all. In fact I was looking forward to getting away from the environment in which I was living in that orthodox house where I had been so unhappy, lonely and homesick. Also, it seemed to involve me more in what went on in the war. So I hopped off quite merrily getting my things together. The family were very emotional, all very upset, and I didn't see what they were upset about. But to me it was a great adventure. I was ready. I was one of the youngest internees, just sixteen years old.

I was taken first to an internment camp in Edinburgh and then on to a camp which had been set up on Lingfield race course. It was from there that the German side of the camp were taken to Liverpool Docks and put on the *Duchess of York*. We didn't know where we were going, we thought possibly the Isle of Man although we were surprised to find such a large ship to take us there.

We were not in convoy. It was very traumatic seeing people in German uniforms, although the strange thing is that the German civilian internees were far worse than the German servicemen. Of course, the moment we went through the Irish Sea it became apparent that we were not going to the Isle of Man. A large number of the Germans who were naval personnel had a good idea of where we were heading and there was a terrific outcry: "Britain has been invaded and they are sending us to Canada so we can't be liberated. But we won't get to Canada because halfway across, the war will be over then the ship will be liberated and we'll throw you lot overboard."

Stephen Dale
Young German Jewish refugee seaman, London
In June 1940, at the time of Dunkirk, lots of people fled from France and western Europe and the

Government didn't know who was who, so, allegedly, Churchill said "Collar the lot!" So my friend Rudi and I were collared before we could join the army. We ended up at Huyton near Liverpool. From Huyton many were sent to the Isle of Man and a good many were sent to Canada. One ship — the *Arandora Star* — was torpedoed on its way to Canada with considerable loss of life; another ship went to Australia. I was on that ship — the *Dunera*.

Ludwig Baruch
German Jewish Communist, Arandora Star

After Seaton camp, I was taken onto the *Arandora Star*, berthed in Liverpool. The boat was a shambles; it had been used to evacuate British troops from Bordeaux. I walked about a bit, looked and thought: this is going to be a very dangerous trip. We got underway. The first person I met in the dining room was a member of the Liverpool Young Communist League, Abrahams. I said, "Where the hell are we going?" He said, "Canada." I said, "Well, I hope we're lucky!"

I was sleeping on a blanket on the floor with my life-jacket as a pillow, and as we were torpedoed there was a terrific bang and I was lifted off the floor with the impact. The lights went out and the boat immediately started to list. We were fortunate in that our cabin was very near the entrance to one of the decks. We went to the boat deck and there was panic. I said to my friends, "Look, there's only one chance, we've got to get off." I could see that the boat deck was wired with barbed wire. I led, and jumped overboard with the life-jacket and put it on in the water. I swam away as quickly and as far as I could, got hold of an upturned bench which had some big air tanks underneath, and when I was joined by a soldier and two other people, between us we managed to sit on this thing, with a corner each. It was not uncomfortable; it was a lovely day with a nice breeze and the water wasn't cold at all. We were sighted by a Sunderland flying boat: there was a huge area with debris, people and bodies floating about, and we knew we would be rescued.

After our rescue by a Canadian destroyer, we landed in Greenock and from there to Edinburgh for about ten days, then we were taken to Liverpool again. Now that landing stage at Liverpool was the worst experience of the war so far as the British Army was concerned. There were about 15,000 internees there from all sorts of camps and we were eventually taken to Australia. On the landing stage there was a group of Pioneer Corps soldiers. Some of the internees had luggage and money — what they did to them! They were beaten up and robbed. The soldiers were in a state of hysteria produced by their greed. I've seen soldiers with their battle dresses undone with money stuffed into their pockets, opening the suitcases and robbing and beating up. Everything was strewn on that landing stage. I had absolutely nothing, nor had the rest of the *Arandora Star* survivors. When we were taken onto the *Dunera*, people were robbed there as well. And the worst of it was that on the landing stage were Liverpool plain clothes policemen watching this. The officers from the Pioneer Corps were there too. It was the most *outrageous* incident I saw during the whole war.

Stephen Dale
Young German Jewish man, Dunera

The first days were terrible because the weather was very bad in the Irish Sea, and people were very sick and the conditions were really awful. People were also very depressed because as we boarded the ship we were maltreated, searched, our luggage broken open and things stolen from us by the troops who were told we were prisoners of war. I'd like to believe that they would have treated us better if they were told that we were internees and not Nazis, but they were ill-informed and treated us like enemies. Against this background of maltreatment, given the bad weather and conditions, the atmosphere was pretty, pretty ghastly. I remember standing by an open hatch to escape the stench; you could look up, but you were behind barbed wire.

I hated the situation and I hated being subjected to these illiterate troops. They were the Pioneer Corps — I mean they were the lowest form of life. People who were not fit to be drafted into other units were taken into the Pioneer Corps. When I was drafted into the Pioneer Corps later on I could see that they really were the dregs of humanity. It was quite appalling.

Ludwig Baruch
German Jewish Communist, Dunera

On the way to Africa we had one panic when the ship was hit by something. I thought it was a torpedo and there was panic on the ship, but nothing happened. Later, when we passed Cape Town, we knew we were going to Australia. We had no contact with the crew; the guards were from the Pioneer Corps and some were quite sympathetic. We were fed, the conditions weren't too bad. It was uncomfortable down in the hold; I slept on the floor, some slept on tables, others in hammocks. It was a question of keeping yourself amused: there was lots of conversation, we were all Jewish and anti-fascists in my hold, we were lucky. We had some chessboards and I played chess all the way to Australia. We were taken out once a day to walk around the deck. One terrible experience: on one occasion a chap in front of me jumped overboard. He killed himself the day his visa expired for the Argentine — the only suicide I witnessed during the whole of internment.

Eventually we arrived in Melbourne, 16 September 1940. People in Britain didn't know where we were, my fiancée didn't have a clue. In Melbourne we were taken off individually from our hold. I was completely in rags by then, had nothing at all, and I walked up this landing stage under armed guard, was put on a train and ended up in Tatura camp, Australia where I was interned until 1942.

109

GREATER GERMANY, 1940/41

Fritz Moses
German child, Strehlen, Germany
I have to say that my father began to have some doubts (about the Party) when the Jews were deported, and also when the handicapped people disappeared. In earlier times, you know, every city would have some kind of . . . well, today we would call them "local crazies". In our town we had "Crazy Marie", and there was a person who had "goose paws". He would always stand in front of the stores and hold out his arms to beg. He always got something, and there were three or four of these and they were kind of everywhere. I only know that my mother said to my father at that time, "Konrad, that man with the goose paws, I haven't seen him for a long time." And he said, "They've picked him up too." People knew what had happened — you know, this euthanasia, the deportation of Jews; but people excluded it from their minds.

Magdalena Kusserow Reuter
German Jehovah's Witness young woman, Bad Lippspringe
One day, in 1940, the *Gestapo* came and picked me up. All my family were in prison and I was really happy because I was left alone, always with the *Gestapo* behind me. I was about two months in Bielefed prison; my father, my mother and my sister Hildegard were in that prison. My two older brothers had been killed. The younger children were put in a reform home with

criminal children. In the prison, we were all in different cells and didn't see each other.

After two months they condemned us: my father to five years in prison and five years' concentration camp, my mother three years, and my sister about two years in juvenile prison. I got six months as a juvenile. I was alone in a cell until the end of the six months. When my time was over, the overseer of the prison said, "Look, I have a letter from the *Gestapo*, you must sign that you won't continue as a Jehovah's Witness, then I'll let you go free." I explained to her that I couldn't; she was very sad, she was nearly crying. She said, "Ah, it's a shame; I'm so sorry." They brought me to the *Gestapo*. They asked me to sign. I said, "No, I believe in the Bible and I will continue" — the death of my brothers Wilhelm and Wolfgang gave me strength. I had to stay four months more until I was eighteen. Then they took me to the concentration camp.

Fritz Moses
German child, Strehlen, Germany
My parents would talk privately about the Third *Reich* and the Jews; I was also curious and listened in. One day my grandmother came back from Breslau and told my father, "Konrad, I was standing on the station platform when a very long train arrived with many women and children in it." And she said, "You know, there was a woman who called out of the train window, 'Dear lady, please bring me a glass of water.'" Well, grandmother went and got the water

111

from this water pipe which had paper cups, and then brought it to the woman. And then an SS man, who was patrolling back and forth next to the train, knocked the water out of her hand and said, "Watch it, those are Jews!" Then the train left the station and she said the woman rolled the window down again and shouted out loud in the dead silence of the station, "A curse on all Breslau's children." And then my grandmother said, "My God, what are they going to do to *us* in the future!"

Barbara Stimler
Polish Jewish child, Kutno

It was February 1940 and I was lying in bed with flu. About twelve o'clock in the night there was a terrible banging on the door. Usually, when they came in, we thought they would not touch the women, only the men, so my father and his friend ran off. They came right up to our room. My mother said, "Run!" I was in my nightdress, without shoes in the snow and I was running; I wanted to go over the railway to our friends. But they got hold of my mother in the street and they started beating her; she told me later that they told her to call me, but she didn't want me to go back. But when I heard her screaming with pain from the beating they were giving her, I went back. They took me to the kitchen, they tore my nightie off me and the jewellery I had pinned on me fell to the floor. But I could see that they were not bothering with that, they were bothered about something else. They told me to get on the bed. I'm not going to tell you what they did with me, but they didn't rape me. My mother came in and when she saw them bending over me, she ran to the kitchen for a knife and was going to stab one of them. Then we heard German voices and these people came. I can't tell you any more. I was in such a state, I was ill for six weeks . . .

In May 1940 we were taken to a disused tobacco factory with just straw on the floor there. One day we were lying on the straw and they came and called my father. They told him to undress and to dance. My father was a stoutish man and they gave him a prayer book, and took a gun and held it next to his ear. We thought they were going to shoot him. Then with three SS men on one side and three SS on the other, they used him like a ball, kicking him. The humiliation! Then they threw him on the straw. After a few days they woke us in the middle of the night and marched us to a disused sugar factory; all the Jews from Kutno were there, about ten or eleven thousand. The beginning was not too bad, but then when it rained and became flooded, we had to stand on the tables and chairs. After a few weeks, people were starving, it was terrible. They started throwing bread over the fence; who could catch it got it, who couldn't, didn't.

Taube Biber
Polish Jewish child, Mielec
The festival of Passover is always a family gathering and a celebration of the Exodus from Egypt. I shall never forget my late father reading the *Haggadah*, the story of the Exodus, with tears streaming down his face as if he

knew that this was to be our last *seder* together. I'll never forget this.

Andrew Bakowski
Polish child, Polish countryside

We used to play around in the dust of the yard. One day, three men — two youngish and an older man — were led through the village by soldiers in dark green uniforms. They went through quite casually, not a march, and as we came up to the fence which separated the village from the fields, we stayed and watched them as they went down this dusty road. After about a quarter of a mile the road made contact with the wood, the road turning to the left and the wood sort of vaguely to the right. The party turned off into the wood and the older boys said, "They're going to kill them, shoot them." We started playing, throwing stones and so forth and then we heard the shots: dum, dum, dum, in the woods. The landlady obviously heard them as well and we were drawn into the house. We were allowed to go into the woods when there were some older boys present. Those woods were used by the German army for manoeuvres and we went there to gather spent shell cases from the rifles. We went in, looked and saw the soil had been disturbed where these men had obviously been killed. One of the boys even found a tooth. And my most vivid feeling about this? I couldn't find any shell cases; there weren't any. There were three people killed — Jews obviously — and yet my memory of it is as superficial as that.

DEPORTATIONS TO THE SOVIET UNION

Alicia Adams
Polish Jewish child, Drobhobycz
The people who came from the western side of Poland, to what was now the Russian part, were told to register, and my father thought he was very clever and went to register in Lvov, the neighbouring big town. So when they started taking people to Siberia in 1940, the Russians looked for us in Lvov and not in Drobhobycz — that was very bad luck because we could have survived in Siberia. Many of our friends and relatives who were taken there survived — in very bad circumstances, true — but they survived.

Wolf Albert
Polish Jewish youth, White Sea area, Siberia
We were Poles and Jews together; the anti-Semitism existed even there! After going across vast distances from Poland to the White Sea area by cattle truck, we marched until we got to a large river. We then went on barges, approximately a thousand of us, one young boy no older than fifteen. The only people who had been in that area were those who pegged out where the railway was going to be built. We were miles away from anybody and the whole world, in the middle of an extremely large forest, small hills and swamps. Our food was dried pieces of black bread and that was all we had, nothing else, nowhere to sleep.

In time, they brought in pickaxes, hand saws, shovels and wheelbarrows. We had cut out trees to build a fence

115

and create our own camp. When that camp was created, the first thing they did was to put up a placard which read, "In the place that you work it never rains" — meaning work will never stop if it rains or snows. There was no clothes change, absolutely no facilities, no conversation among the people, no discussion, no crying or bitterness and the Russians there were treated exactly as we were, even the soldiers and guards. One of the commandants who was very foul-mouthed told us, "This is your Warsaw, this is your Poland; this is where you will stop forever, and the way you arrange it is how you will live."

In the autumn it started to rain non-stop for a month. We had no cover whatsoever. We made fires and they put groups of twenty-five of us to a fire and we used to sleep on big planks of wood and you warmed your front and your back got soaking wet, then you turned round to warm the other side. And the next morning, we went out in the rain to cut through the hills with pickaxes and shovels. Then it got to snow. After a time a group started to make living accommodation — holes cut out about five or six feet deep with wood all round and on the top like a roof; and shelves on the inside on which we slept. We didn't have a blanket or cover, absolutely nothing.

I estimate that in six months no more than fifty per cent were there. Up to forty degrees zero we had to go out to work! For a few days it went up to fifty degrees zero. The first to die were the old and frail and after that the young ones who'd had absolutely everything at home: soft life, fresh rolls every morning. Every five miles there were camps and these were connected. No chance of escape, nothing but camp after camp after camp.

Jacob Pesate
Romanian Jewish factory worker, Bucharest
On 27 June 1940, the Soviet Union gave an ultimatum to the Romanians to withdraw from Bessarabia and northern Bukovina; the Romanians accepted and the Red Army moved in. When I heard this on the radio, I said goodbye to my employer, took the few things I had, and boarded a train and arrived in Czernowitz before the Soviet troops arrived. It was very wise of me because in the next few days, there were *pogroms* on the train by the Iron Guard (Romanian fascists), and several hundred people were killed. On 28 June I was among those who received the Red Army with flowers in Czernowitz.

22 JUNE 1941

Wolf Albert
Polish Jewish youth, White Sea area, Siberia
At one time there was a rumour going around that Germany had attacked Russia — the first news since our arrest. When the agreement was made to let the prisoners go to join the Polish army, we were released after two days. It was at that time that I had to be

117

helped because I had night blindness and couldn't see at all.

John Dobai
Hungarian Jewish/Catholic schoolboy, Budapest
The first real impact of the European war was in 1941 when my father was called up into the army as Hungary entered the war against Russia. But after a few months he came home again because of the influence of the anti-Jewish Laws which declared that people with a Jewish background or Jews themselves could not serve in the Hungarian armed forces, only in the Labour Service on the Eastern Front. He went back to the bank but the apprehension became very strong.

Joseph Harmatz
Lithuanian Jewish youth, Vilna
When the war broke out between Russia and Germany I was sixteen and a half years old. On that day we had gone on a long walk and were outside the city when we heard the bombs falling. When we arrived home, we were told that a war had started between Russia and Germany; but nobody expected that the Germans would be in Vilnius within two and a half days; we believed the Russians were a great military force. The Lithuanians supported the Germans; they had been against the Russian occupation so they cooperated with the Germans against the Jews. For us this was a terrible surprise because before the war we were living together like best friends; and what we saw and heard

later was absolutely unbelievable — they killed Jews in almost every town and village in July and August 1941; only some in the ghettos of Vilna, Kaunas and Siauliai survived. Without their cooperation the Germans would not have been able to do it.

Marsha Segall
Young Lithuanian Jewish woman, Siauliai
The first to march in was the German *Wehrmacht* and the first Germans I saw were those with big dogs looking for Russian soldiers. When we saw the Germans we knew — that's it! And we made our way back to our flat. Right away the Nuremberg Laws were enacted in full. It meant that you couldn't go out in certain hours, or shopping in certain shops, and you were not allowed to walk on the pavement; also, you had to put Yellow Stars of a certain size on the front left side and the back so they could see from both sides that you were Jewish. You couldn't *not* put it on because the population cooperated with the Germans — you couldn't pretend you were somebody else because everybody *knew* you and you would be denounced. They used to grab people in the street and from their houses to do all sorts of undignified work. They also burnt books from Jewish libraries and Hebrew schools on the spot, not like in Germany. One Sabbath day there were two big knocks on the door and two big Lithuanian partisans came. They had my father's name on the list. He just left without saying goodbye or anything. That was the last time I saw my father.

119

Alicia Adams
Polish Jewish child, Drobhobycz

The Germans came into our town during the invasion of the Ukraine in 1941. That was the most frightening experience. They came on motor bikes and I remember watching them and running home. They didn't take possession of the town immediately, but let the Ukrainians run wild and start the first *pogrom* of the Jews in Drobhobycz. The whole family hid in the loft, we heard them downstairs, they came and robbed and killed. After three or four days the Germans took control. Before then we'd had good relations with Ukrainians: I'd lived near them in the country and played with their children; I never realised how anti-Semitic they were. But the Ukrainians who created that *pogrom* were not farmers, they were town-people; they also hated the Russians and smashed the figures of Lenin and Stalin in the middle of the town.

Jack Shepsman
Polish Jewish youth, Nowogrodek, Belorussia

One day the Germans came with lorries and they picked up all the Jews and threw them on the lorries. As I saw what was happening, I begged my parents, "Come with me, I am *not* going on that lorry." We had a very long garden with a little hill at the top and I went up there and looked down to the road where I could see everything: they were picking up the shouting, crying people. I saw my family coming out of the house, the soldiers were shouting and hitting them — quickly, quickly, on the lorry! Then all went quiet. I hid for four days under hay in a shed and went out on the evening of the fourth day. I heard later that my family didn't have a chance: they were taken to this place where the forest started and where long graves had been dug, and when they came down from the lorry, soldiers were standing there with machine guns and were shooting people day and night. At this time they shot about 50,000 people, not only from Nowogrodek but the area around.

Juozas Aleksynas
Member of the 12th and 13th Lithuanian police battalions, a paramilitary force under the Germans, Belorussia
(The Jews) were told to gather in places such as public squares and market places. The local police would drive them out of their homes. The Germans would have lists of prominent Jews such as doctors and engineers; they would be selected out and all the others driven out for shooting. The pits were already dug, they were behind the town, often on the hills. The Jews would be taken to the pits by the Lithuanians, the Germans would be surrounding the town.

When the Jews were gathered in this large area, they were taken to the pits in which they lay down and were shot. Some soldiers stood on the bank to shoot, others took the Jews to the pits. We shot them after they had climbed down and lay down, then others would lie on top and so on. At the end some bleach was put on them. When we finished we left the place. We could not refuse to shoot. If somebody couldn't shoot because

121

they felt ill, the Germans always checked the pulse or temperature, but not when they were ready for shooting. If somebody said, "I cannot," the Germans ordered, "Stand! Align with the others," and that's it.

We were given Russian guns and rifles. The clothes of the Jews were burnt. There used to be a disgusting smell — it was very disgusting. You had to see it to understand. They were all shot, mostly in the chest or head . . . it could be a thousand or just one or two hundred. We did not have to force the Jews to those places, they were given the command and they went like sheep, no resistance at all. The children were with them, small ones and bigger; everybody was killed — a mother, a father and child would lie down together. We thought about this ourselves — how parents would feel if their child was shot in their presence — and we shot the parents first because the child would not feel as much. Sometimes women would cry, but in most cases they didn't, neither did they shout. Germans used to take pictures of all these shooting procedures. We felt bad about that and cursed them.

Officers didn't shoot, they just gave orders. Only at the end if they saw someone still living did they shoot him with a pistol. We came to the shootings as machines. You didn't realise what you were doing. Terrible.

Josef Perl
Czech Jewish youth, unknown eastern camp
In the late summer of 1941 I was caught by an SS and was marched into this camp with a gun in my back.

After ten minutes' walk into that place, I saw a column, five abreast, of naked people — women, men, old people, young people. After the column went past me, the SS ordered me to stop and undress and pushed me into the column. We marched into a forest where a huge long ditch was already dug. I don't know what it was filled with but I could see vapours rising. I could hear: tat tat tat tat tat tat, a machine gun going. But when you don't see it, it doesn't somehow connect with anything. But as you come nearer and nearer and you begin to see faces, you know who's being killed. All of a sudden, I must have been about five or six rows from the front, I saw my mother and four sisters lined up and before I had a chance to say, "Mother!" they were already dead. Somehow time stands still. You become like a lump of salt. But what woke me was the sight of my five nieces and nephews being marched, and the murderers had the audacity to ask them to hold hands. When the bullets hit those babies, the bullets lifted them three feet off the ground before they fell into the ditch. I would have been almost the next one but all of a sudden the bombers came over, we were ordered to lay face downwards, but everyone started running higgledy-piggledy, and I started running and ran deep into the forest.

Aleksandra Nizie
Polish child, Trawniki, Poland
It was still light, we went when they (the killers) took themselves off . . . I said to my sister, "Come, let us go see what's going on there." So we went through the

orchard to the end — right? We looked and the earth was moving. I said, "Look, Jula, how the earth is moving!" And blood flowed in streams. You see, when they brought them (the Jews) to the work camp, they were all well-fed, handsome, well-dressed people, not just anybody; and in Trawniki there were a few like them as well. They had it good.

They had covered the trench up straightaway. And they must have spread lime, something like white ash; but it soaked through because the blood flowed out of them. And on the third day they had already begun to burn. They left behind some Russians who I think helped these Ukrainians. And they took one by the head and the other by the legs and threw them on the fire and they burned. They'd made a sort of metal scaffolding, you know. I saw it, I saw it — yes, I *saw* it! Not only I, but many hundreds of people saw this. They burned for about two weeks or maybe more; the stench was terrible.

Alicia Adams
Polish Jewish slave labourer, Drobhobycz
At one time I worked as a cleaner for a *Gestapo* man. He was one of those who shot people in Bronica wood with machine guns — about two thousand at a time. He always used to drink beforehand. Once he said to me, "You are very nice, I will never kill you with the others." Then he showed me a beautiful flowering tree and said, "I will kill you separately and I will put you under that tree." I once painted a self-portrait with that tree. I sold the picture and called it "Childhood

Memories", but I'm certain the buyer didn't know what kind of memories they were.

Jacob Pesate
Romanian Jewish youth, Czernowitz

After the shock of the German invasion, 22 June 1941, I left with the train eastwards towards the USSR on 1 July. My family stayed behind. Czernowitz was then re-occupied by the Romanians who returned with an SS Division. The Germans and Romanians behaved very brutally; people were shot on the streets, leading Jewish personalities were picked up, including the chief rabbi, and about another hundred or so, and shot. Restrictions were imposed on the Jews; it was a very difficult time. At the end of August my father was arrested. In October a decree obliged the Jewish population, then about 50,000, to move into a ghetto in a very small part of the city. My mother with my brother and sister went to live with a distant relative who happened to live within the ghetto.

Soon after, another decree was issued that Jewish people have to be deported and they were taken on trucks to the station. Surprise, surprise, my father was already there! They all went on the same train, eventually to Transnistria, the piece of land between the Dniester and the Bug rivers. This was November 1941, a very harsh winter. On the way sick people died; they were thrown out of the train because of the overcrowding; people had lice and were infected with typhus and other deadly diseases. They were stopped on the Dniester because there was no bridge for the

125

train to cross; from there they went on barges across to the other side and from there they were forced to walk in the bitter winter, children, old people, and women, carrying whatever they could in very inhumane conditions.

When they got across the Dniester, they found many members of the family from southern Bukovina with whom they'd had no contact for a year. Since my brother, a diabetic, couldn't get insulin, he died soon after arrival. My mother got typhus and died on the way as did my uncle and grandmother. My father and sister reached a small village, Berchad, where they joined a Ukrainian Jewish family who took them in; from there he wrote a letter which I received in Buguruslan, in the Soviet Union. Eventually they were forced into a camp there; they were not allowed to work or have contacts with the outside world. They didn't get any rations, and the only way to survive was to exchange the few things they had with the peasants for food. Life was very hard, but officially they were not in extermination camps, they died of hunger and disease. The Germans occasionally wanted workers to do heavy work on the eastern side of the River Bug. However, all those that went over the Bug never came back — they were all killed. Those in the camps were completely isolated.

Ruth Foster
Young German Jewish woman, Lingen
In December 1941, my parents received instructions that they were to be deported to the "east" on the 10 or

12 December. Being an only child, I volunteered to go with them. In the meantime Jews had to leave their homes and were put into *Juden* houses, just for Jews. There was a curfew from 6p.m. until 7a.m., we also had special ration cards with a "J" on them, meaning *Juden* — Jew. And only at certain times could we go shopping and then only in certain shops ... The transport we were on was called the "Bielefeld Transport". We ended up in the Riga Ghetto, in Latvia.

John Fink
German Jewish electrician, Berlin

Jewish people all over Germany had to work. My father had to work on the railroad, my mother had to work in a factory and my sister was working as a tailoress. We knew people were being sent away in the beginning of 1941. People were picked up, especially the older people, and nobody knew what happened to them. We heard that they were sent to the "east". In those days we didn't know much about foreign countries or even where the "east" was. We didn't know that they were being sent to Riga or Lublin, into ghettos. In 1943, Goebbels wanted to give Hitler a birthday present: he wanted to tell him that Berlin was *Judenfrei* — cleansed of Jews. I was sent away from Berlin on 12 March 1943, one of the last big transports.

Dr Friedrich Carl Scheibe
German child, Suhl-Heinrichs/Thueringia

One morning as I was going to school, there were a lot of people standing on the footpath without moving.

127

What I saw made a very deep impression on me which I will never forget. A strange column of people appeared who walked like very old people, placing one step carefully in front of the other. I had the impression that they were wearing about three overcoats, one over the other. Many couldn't walk; they lay in a cart. In front of this group was a young man who had a large sign around his neck with the words, "The last Jews depart from our city." Behind the column of people were Storm Troopers who shouted, "Germany Awake, Judaism croaks!" Hundreds of people looked on; it was deadly quiet, no one joined the SA in their shouts. There wasn't any discussion afterwards; people didn't talk about it.

Fritz Moses
German child, Strehlen, Silesia, Germany
Problems with our name, Moses, stopped later because there weren't any Jews left then; they were all in work camps.

1939–1942

THE GHETTO (i)

At first it was a relief when we went into the ghetto.
You could walk on the streets without being afraid
that some Polish boy would come and point out that
you were a Jew, or that a Hitler Jugend would come
in and order you to do something or that a German
soldier would come and grab you and you wouldn't
come back . . . So initially, a sense of security.

With the extension of Hitler's power over western
and eastern Europe in 1940 and 1941, the Nazis
were confronted with the problem of dealing with
vastly increased numbers of Jews under their
control; this is when the medieval practice of
separating Jews into ghettos was revived. Such
segregation gave the Nazis fuller control as well as
making it easier to exploit Jewish labour for the
war effort.

The first ghettos were set up in Poland and they
were to form a model for the network which later
spread across the map of eastern Europe. In
October 1939, following a directive by the
Security Police Chief, Reinhard Heydrich, the first
ghetto was set up in Piotrkow. This was soon
followed by another established in Randomsko in
December 1939. By mid-1941, nearly all Jews
in occupied Poland had been forced into ghettos,
including those in the cities of Lodz and Warsaw

(1940) and Krakow and Lublin (1941). By November 1941, a model ghetto with showplace status was set up in the eighteenth-century fortress of Terezin (Theresienstadt in German) in the occupied Czech lands. With the German invasion of the Soviet Union, other ghettos were established, including those of Kovno, Riga, Vilna and Minsk, to house the large Jewish communities in the western Soviet Union and the Baltic states.

Ghettos in larger towns and cities were usually sealed and guarded, with the population completely cut off from the outside world, apart from a few exit permits granted for those working for the Germans. In the case of smaller Jewish communities, designated areas were often left unsealed, but with freedom of movement strictly curtailed. With the influx of Jews from surrounding areas and later, other countries, ghettos of all types became ever more crowded with conditions becoming increasingly squalid.

In 1940–41, instead of murdering Jews outright, the Nazis waited for conditions in the closed ghettos to take their toll. Conditions in these crowded slums were appalling. In Warsaw, according to Nazi statistics, for instance, of the city's 1,800 streets, only 73 were assigned to the ghetto and 30 per cent of the city's population lived in just 2.4 per cent of its area, six or seven persons in each room. Warsaw was the largest ghetto containing, at its height, 490,000 Jews together with a few hundred gypsies. In addition to extreme overcrowding, Jews were systematically starved and worked to death. Medicine and fuel were scarce and often non-existent, and access to clean drinking water was limited. Sanitary conditions, never good, declined rapidly as starvation and disease took hold. In Warsaw the situation was alleviated somewhat by trading across the wall. This was at great risk both to Jews and Poles, the death penalty being the fate of those caught. Nearly 100,000, 20 per cent of the Jewish population of Warsaw, perished in the city between September 1939 and July 1942 — 61,000 dying between January 1941 and July 1942. Death rates were also high in other locations.

In Lodz, smuggling was out of the question, given the tightly sealed nature of the ghetto. The relatively high survival rate there until July/August 1944 can be attributed to the "work to live" policy adopted by its *Judenrat* (Jewish Council). In all, some 500,000 Jews were to perish in ghettos from starvation, cold, overwork and disease.

Jewish leaders — mainly men — were selected to form *Judenräte*, which were run by a Nazi-appointed *Judenälteste*, leader. A Jewish police auxiliary force — the *Ordnungsdienst* — was also established to keep order and enforce rules and regulations. Although initially welcomed, these organisations played controversial roles within the ghettos. The *Judenräte*, although usually aiming to make life as bearable as possible, were forced to cooperate with the Nazis. Where to draw the line between cooperation and collaboration created huge dilemmas for the Jewish leaders. With the intensification of deportations to the "east" from March 1942 to February 1943, one of the most distressing services demanded of them was to provide lists of deportees. Some, like Adam Czerniakow of Warsaw Ghetto, on hearing that death, not work, awaited his "relocated" Jews, committed suicide rather than be a party to Nazi crimes. Others, such as Chaim Rumkowski of Lodz Ghetto, cooperated to the point of what appeared to be collaboration, arguing that at least part of the Jewish community would survive.

Despite the horrendous conditions and constant anxiety, not all Jews surrendered their human dignity or humanity in the face of Nazi attempts to dehumanise and degrade them: those Jews with some means set up soup kitchens; clandestine schools were opened, religious life continued in secret and cultural activities occurred in many ghettos. Orphanages were also set up, the most famous being that of Janusz Korczak in the Warsaw Ghetto. Jewish historians created secret archives in which ghetto life was documented for posterity, Emanuel Ringelblum's *Oneg Shabbos* — Enjoyment of the Sabbath — being an outstanding example. In the Kovno Ghetto in Lithuania, members of the terrorised population created and buried a vast archive documenting German crimes against their community. Dozens of men, women and children in ghettos throughout Europe recorded their experiences in letters, diaries, personal journals and drawings. All these activities indicated spiritual resistance on the part of large sections of European Jewry.

Rena Quint
Young Polish Jewish child, Piotrkow Ghetto
The ghetto started in 1939, and I believe it was the first ghetto. I remember people moving into our apartment which was in the ghetto area and I remember that it got very crowded. A lot of the people were very sick and people were hungry and were dying. The main incident that sticks in my mind from the ghetto is when there was an *Aktion*, a round-up. I remember the women and children were screaming and yelling when we were being separated and herded into a large place, which I now know was the synagogue. I was there with my mother and my brothers and if anybody moved there were beatings and shootings. I remember this feeling of pandemonium. And there was a door in that room and there was a man on the other side. He beckoned to me and said, "Run, Run!" I was very young, and naïve, I don't know how a young child can let go of her mother, I don't know if she pushed me or if the hand of God pushed me, but I ran and ran to this man. I don't have proof, but I believe he was my uncle. That whole shipment of people were sent to Treblinka.

When I ran from the synagogue, I was taken by this man to my father. First he hid me in a cellar and when that was no longer feasible, he cut my hair, gave me a new name and dressed me like a boy. Every day I went

135

to work in the glass factory with him. I had to learn how to think and act as a boy. The glass factory had been a Polish factory taken over by the Germans and my work was bringing water for the glass making and moving glass jars. We worked all day — it must have been something like a fourteen-hour day. I was close to my father and to these other men I called "uncle". The people in charge of us were sadists: they were there to push you on and get the work out.

Michael Etkind
Polish Jewish youth, Lodz Ghetto

At the beginning of March 1940, notices appeared that a ghetto would be formed in part of Lodz and my uncle, who was very enterprising, went into the ghetto area and found a large room on the third floor of a big tenement block. Then we were informed that Jews living in other areas of Lodz would have to move into the ghetto area in April. A few days before that date, German soldiers and policemen went into the flats in the more expensive areas of the town and shot about two hundred people in order to stampede us into the ghetto. From then on you could see hundreds of people on transport sledges — snow was still on the ground — or pushing hand-carts in the direction of the ghetto. It was into this one large room that my uncle, his wife and two children, then my mother with her three children, all moved. Can you imagine moving from an apartment of four or five bedrooms into half a room!

The ghetto area was the poorest part of Lodz, adjoining the Jewish cemetery. It was rather like the

East End of London and I would say that maybe half of the Jewish population lived in that area before the war, and the other half had to move there which made it very crowded. In addition people had to move out of the streets where trams were running. Therefore you had a population of a quarter of a million squeezed into an area where there should have been 80,000, and they would have had cramped conditions to start with.

At first it was a relief when we went into the ghetto. You could walk on the streets without being afraid that some Polish boy would come and point out that you were a Jew, or that a *Hitler Jugend* (Hitler Youth) would come in and order you to do something or that a German soldier would come and grab you and you wouldn't come back. Also, Jews are great optimists; when the war started everyone was saying that by the spring of 1940 it would be over. When the ghetto opened . . . well, another two or three months, not to worry. Rumours spread that the Russians had parachuted down five miles away and any time we'd be liberated. All the time you had those hopeful, misleading messages somebody invented. So initially, a sense of security.

Roman Halter
Polish Jewish youth, Lodz Ghetto
When we arrived in the ghetto in 1940, we were the first to be allocated a space — this was roughly ten by six foot, and we were at the start of this timber structure, so other families had to go through us to enter their spaces. My father, who was over sixty, went

into a home and so did my grandfather. This was hard for us because we felt this was the beginning of the end. My sister-in-law who lived with us in this space managed to get starvation rations for us, and so life began inside the Lodz Ghetto. Very soon we lost lots of weight. I used to go and visit my father and grandfather. It was easier talking to my grandfather than to my father — my father harped back to the hanging of his son, my brother, and the loss of his family; also from being uprooted from the community and the loss of the whole community, because he felt that we were *all* Poles, whether Christians or Jews, and we had all shared the life in that little town of Chodecz. From our meagre rations we managed to scrape a few things to pass to him because suddenly these people over sixty had an even smaller ration than us.

Andrew Bakowski
Polish child, Warsaw

The first evidence of something happening so far as the Jews were concerned started slowly. At first we didn't know it was the ghetto area, it wasn't referred to as such. Then things began to change and they started to build walls on the periphery of the ghetto. Then the station began to receive more Jewish transports. At the beginning I'm not sure I knew they were Jews, but soon I reckon we did. It's one of those things you don't talk about with your parents, but you talk about with the kids. "They're Jews." Transports would arrive and large columns of people would make their way across the front of our house heading in a westerly direction, turning north into the ghetto area. They would move in quite an orderly way, quietly. We would see them from our windows, you could hear people talking, you could see guards walking, not many. Some of them wore badges — the Star of David — some of them would wear uniforms — they were bus conductors, or postmen, and there were families, and people with cases. Occasionally they would stop for the trams, and they would then go into the ghetto.

Danny Falkner
Polish Jewish inmate, Warsaw ghetto
The Jewish population of Warsaw of course consisted mainly of artisans. There were businessmen and labourers but in the main they were artisans who had contributed a great deal to the economic life of Poland. They were now all concentrated in the ghetto and the Poles were deprived of their products: leather goods, woodworks, tailoring. So a two-way traffic developed: raw materials were being smuggled into the ghetto and ready-made articles smuggled out. By these activities people managed to make a living.

Jerry Koenig
Polish Jewish child, Warsaw Ghetto
The situation in the Warsaw Ghetto was truly horrendous — food, water and sanitary conditions were non-existent. You couldn't wash, people were hungry and very susceptible to disease because of their weakened condition. It's amazing what happens to people when they're deprived of basic needs. For my

139

brother and me there was no school and the only entertainment was taking a walk. It was unbelievable the number of dead people you saw in the streets. When we came home after a walk it was mandatory that we took off our clothing to search for lice, because they were the ones carrying typhus and typhoid fever. The only way you could survive was by supplementing your diet with things bought through the black market. But you can imagine that if the sellers were risking their lives to obtain these things, then the price is going to be extremely high. So it was no secret in the family that eventually our financial resources would run out and we would face the same situation as others.

Roman Halter
Polish Jewish youth, Lodz Ghetto
The people in the home started dying very quickly of starvation. My grandfather realised this was not a life for him and when I came along one day, although he couldn't stand and was quite ill, he was lucid in his mind and said to me, "You know this is the murder of our Jewish people and the life in the ghetto is not for me. I am fairly old now and you must not be upset. I will say goodbye to you, and please see that I am buried in the proper way and say the *Kaddish* for me." I said, "Don't talk like that, grandfather," and he said, "No, you must listen to me: remember when you were very small I had this pocket watch, I'd like you to have it now, and it will remind you of me." It was the kind that you pressed and the lid opened. And then I told him of the massacre of my friends in the ravine at Chodecz.

And he said, "When you survive" — "*when*", not "*if*" — and he went on, "when you survive, you must tell the world exactly what happened because such barbarities have not occurred before in history and people will not believe it."

Szmulek Gontarz
Polish Jewish youth, Lodz Ghetto
It's like a town: it had to have its own organisation, its own police, its own officials and officers and so on. They organised factories where we worked even though the products went to the Germans. All this took some organisation and there was a Jewish committee (*Judenrat*) who prepared all this. At the beginning they were very sympathetic to the people, but as experience has shown in many other equivalent situations, people change. These people, although they were Jewish, their sympathy had gone. We were being badly treated. We didn't see the Germans any more, they were outside, we just saw our own people mistreating us.

Janina David
Polish Jewish child, Warsaw Ghetto
Schools were forbidden, but parents organised small groups of children, four or five at a time, and of course there was no lack of teachers. We met once or twice a week in somebody's room, usually in a different room every week because there was the death penalty for the children, the teachers, the parents and in fact everybody in the house if we were discovered. We had classes in just the basics, we couldn't learn physics or

141

chemistry properly as we couldn't have laboratories or make experiments; we learned all that from books which were pre-war and out of date, but we learnt with great enthusiasm. People learnt foreign languages: Latin, Greek, German, French, English. People were continuing with higher education; there were university professors who were also giving courses in everything.

Abraham Zwirek
Polish Jewish youth, Plock and Suchedniow Ghettos
Openly you're not supposed to have any religious life, but religious customs among Jewish people became very strong, although conducted in a quiet way. I think there were more religious people than before the war. Even myself. As we couldn't go to the great synagogue, they conducted prayers in various small homes. If no rabbi was available, then there was always someone very well learned, like my grandfather, who could conduct it in a very nice way and people joined in. One or two would stand outside the door to see the Germans were not approaching because we were not allowed to have a gathering to pray.

Anna Bergman
Young Czech Jewish woman, Theresienstadt Ghetto
By the end of November 1941, the first group of men were sent to Terezin to build it up. It was a barracks' town, but the place was cleared of non-Jewish people; then it became a place only for Jews and the German administration. My husband went in November and I followed at the end of December 1941. About fourteen

young men, for no good reason, were hanged on our arrival; I think they wanted to frighten us, to make us aware that this was no joke. We were the first ones, pioneers of a sort, and the Germans promised — and they were very careful how they put this — that if some "transports" of people left Terezin, we would be allowed to stay. They gave this promise to the first arrivals, an age group of between eighteen and thirty-five, the most capable young people, and they kept their promise for three years. We were the few who didn't have to worry about the transports.

Maria Ossowski
Young Polish woman, Warsaw

The tragedy of the children who came out of the ghetto to beg for food was that they could not speak Polish — they were from places deep in eastern Poland and only spoke Yiddish — so it was really difficult to help such people because if you don't explain a few things to them, how can you really give them proper help? One day, I remember very clearly, a kid of this sort appeared on our street. My auntie took him in, gave him a bath because, poor thing, he was full of lice and dirt, so she cleaned and fed him. And I had to run to my friend's house where they had young children and bring the boy some clean clothes, not saying why I suddenly needed them. Before the curfew we simply put him out on the street, there was no other way and he marched off in the only direction he could. We looked out for him again but he never came back. Poland was the only country which had the death sentence for helping a Jew, and this was for you and your family.

Helen Stone
Young Polish Jewish woman, Kamionka Ghetto
We were married on 1 January 1941. When Bedzin was made *Judenrein* — cleansed of Jews — we went into the ghetto of Kamionka, just outside Bedzin. We were sewing uniforms for the Germans in a huge sewing factory, and those who worked there had a card proving we worked some place. My husband worked as well, something to do with wood which had been his business. I got pregnant and if I hadn't had an abortion the child would have been three weeks when I went to Auschwitz and I wouldn't be here talking to you now.

Ruth Foster
Young German Jewish woman, Riga Ghetto
When we left the train we were stiff, we could hardly walk because by then it was minus twenty degrees and lots of people had frostbite. We had to leave our hand luggage on a heap. The wind was howling and there was ice and snow on the road. We had to get in rows of five and march towards the Riga Ghetto. SS men with rifles, truncheons and big dogs were herding us and with loud-hailers they were calling, "Who is not able to walk — old people and mothers and children — you don't have to walk any further, there are some vans waiting for you. Get on these lorries and you'll meet your loved ones again soon." Later, I found that these lorries were portable gas chambers and the people were

gassed on them and taken to the forest and buried there, some of them even alive. But we didn't know this at the time, we only knew that these grey vans never arrived at the camp. A very nasty incident happened on the way. In front of us were a young couple who lived not far from Lingen. The father had a little child on his hand and the mother had a child in her arms. One of the SS came and said to the little child, "Would you like a sweetie?" The child very shyly said, "Yes." So the SS man said, "Open your mouth." The child did so and he shot through the mouth of the child. My father said, "My God, what's going to happen here!"

Ezra Jurmann
German Jewish youth, Riga Ghetto

We arrived in the ghetto and were taken to a group of houses which had obviously been left in a hurry: there was complete turmoil, they were completely deserted and they had not been heated. In a pantry there was a pot of potatoes frozen solid. There were pots, pans and plates thrown all over the place. Complete chaos. Ominous. On the walls a message said, "Mama, farewell." My mother must have seen it, though she did not show any reaction. She immediately set about clearing up, scrubbed the floor, got hold of some wood and started a fire in the kitchen range. Mr and Mrs Levi, another lady, my mother, my brother and myself, shared this place. My mother scrubbed the floor, cleaned up, created order, set up some sort of beds. There were blankets and mattresses lying around, everything in disorder. The young woman who helped us with our luggage and brought us there said, "Latvians lived here." She did not say Jews, but Latvians. I do remember idly wondering, very very briefly, what had happened to those Latvians and where they were now.

Ruth Foster
Young German Jewish woman, Riga Ghetto
We found out later that three days before we arrived, they killed 30,000 Latvian Jews who came into the ghetto from Riga and the surrounding towns. They herded them into a nearby forest where previously the Russian prisoners of war had dug graves for them, they had to undress completely, leave their clothes in neat order, and then they had to go to the edge of the pits where they were mown down with machine-guns. So when we came to the Riga Ghetto, we lived in these houses where those poor people had been driven out and murdered.

Margie Oppenheimer
Young German Jewish woman, Riga Ghetto
It was in December 1941 that I was deported from my home town of Oelde, Germany to the Riga Ghetto in Latvia. We arrived on 15 December. I worked as a nurse at first, very difficult because we had nothing to give the patients — no medication, no dressings, nothing. And the majority of people were frost-bitten. Fingers and toes were lost. I remember this nine-year-old boy, all his toes were black with

146

gangrene, and I just cut them off with scissors. He didn't feel a thing and he made it. Another time this lady had gangrene right up to her knees and she was dying. I called the doctor. I started laughing hysterically, I could not control myself; it was a reaction that I cannot define. That was the night when I said, "I am not going to work as a nurse any more."

Ezra Jurmann
German Jewish youth, Riga Ghetto
We slept that first night, we were exhausted. At least we now had water. Sometimes there was a distribution centre and we got a slice of bread and margarine. On occasions we got some cabbage leaves, the outer leaves. In late spring we sometimes got lots of rhubarb leaves and fish heads. What else? A handful of buckwheat or groats, called *kasha*. The food was totally inadequate, especially bearing in mind the cold and people having to work. You'd go out and get weaker and weaker, your movements slower and slower. You'd get starvation signs such as pulmonary oedema — swelling legs, water in the ankles. Then, if you were lucky, pneumonia came and took you away.

Kitty Hart-Moxon
Young Polish Jewish woman, Lublin Ghetto
The overcrowding in the Lublin ghetto was the worst thing because in 1942 they were bringing thousands of people from other countries — people who

couldn't speak the language, they couldn't communicate with the local population and they had nowhere to live. At least we could speak the language and we could still find accommodation because my father still had some possessions that he could barter with. But people from these different countries couldn't do this — they had no means of earning a living or finding food. I got caught many times going out foraging for food and mostly I was denounced and caught by the Poles. You see Germans didn't, *couldn't* really, identify the Jews; unfortunately the Poles would identify the Jews for the Germans. So when I foraged for food on the "Aryan" side and bartered goods that my father would give me — perhaps he still had some jewellery that I had to sell — it was the Poles who would say, "Ah, here is a Jew! Oh quickly, there is a patrol, we'd better hand her in." And very often I was handed over to a patrol, beaten up and thrown back into the ghetto without having brought anything back; or even taken to the German headquarters somewhere to scrub floors.

I think the ghetto was a time of incredible fear but gradually you became accustomed to fear and I think you took chances and you really became fearless. I witnessed a lot of executions in the ghetto, most executions took place during the round-ups. People were thrown from windows and those who resisted were simply shot or they were clubbed to death with rifle butts — people died before they even managed to get on the lorries.

Halina Kahn

Young Polish Jewish woman, Lodz Ghetto

Because I didn't look Jewish I used to go to the black-market. I took the Star of David from my coat and went into the shops saying, *"Heil Hitler!"* One Sunday morning I bought ten or twelve pounds of potatoes and went on the tram and stood in front with the potatoes. When the conductor came, I went to get some money, and as I took it out my star fell down; there was a young *Hitler Jugend* (Hitler Youth) nearby and he put his boot down so that the conductor couldn't see the star. When the conductor went he gave it back to me. I was completely struck: he had saved my life and he was a *Hitler Jugend*.

Daniella Hausman

Young Polish woman, Warsaw

When the Germans came to the block of flats where I lived and started taking the Jewish families out, we realised what was going on. We knew about the ghetto; it wasn't far from where I lived. We noticed them walking out of the ghetto every day for work, guarded by the Germans. People couldn't walk near the Jewish column but we tried to throw some parcels of food to them. I felt very sorry for them. Looking from my flat I could see the entrance into the ghetto and one day I recognised some Jewish people who used to live in our block, others noticed them as well, and everyone went downstairs and tried to talk to them. They looked very bad, very thin. We all tried to give them some food or clothes.

149

Martin Parker
Polish Jewish inmate, Warsaw Ghetto

We lived in the centre of everything. Hundreds of people were milling about, begging. Some were wrapped in rags. Two sisters were walking about singing songs which I was surprised to hear. One was from the *Tales of Hoffmann* — they were going around in rags and singing that. Musicians were going around the streets, begging for money — qualified musicians, the best type of music. People threw money from windows for them to buy something to eat.

I was very worried for my family all the time, but they never went out of the house. And when there was such famine, my wife and others who could afford it arranged to give meals to the hungry people in the house. Every day between two and three o'clock, the people were given this meal. They had been hanging around waiting from one o'clock — this was their only meal of the day. People did share, there was a sort of committee that went round and collected from everyone who could afford to give something. Fortunately we had things to give, a bit of this, a bit of that, coal to burn and potatoes.

Jerry Koenig
Polish Jewish child, Warsaw Ghetto

One of my family's important assets was a farm — large by Polish standards — near the little town of Kosow. Dad became friendly with a local family, the Zylberman family, also farmers. When we were in the Warsaw Ghetto, Dad and Mrs Zylberman corresponded with each other. Mr Zylberman was saying, "I don't understand why things are so bad because things are normal here." His suggestion was that we should try to escape and go to their house, live with them and maybe help with the farm chores.

There was a street-car that actually traversed the ghetto area. The rules were that when it entered the ghetto area, all the passengers had to get off. While it travelled through the ghetto you could get on the streetcar if you had the fare, but as it was leaving the ghetto, everyone would get off and the streetcar would exit. There was a man who had the right contacts and by bribing him we got on the streetcar. At the right time, the arm-bands identifying us as Jews came off, everybody looked the other way and we were on the other side. We reached the little town of Kosow partly by walking and partly by train. When we arrived, we found that Mr Zylberman had not exaggerated — it was a very pleasant surprise for us because things were absolutely normal there. We didn't know it at the time but a tiny Polish village nearby, by the name of Treblinka, had been selected as a death camp.

Stanley Faull
Polish Jewish youth, Warsaw Ghetto
The easiest option was to report to the railway station for work promised in the east and tell yourself, "Look, we'll get our bread, we'll get work, we'll be together as a family, and if we've got to help the war effort, well, we've got to help, at least we'll survive." Tens of thousands of people went and were never heard of

since. The "work" was not work, it was extermination: they went to Treblinka and other places of extermination. In 1942 certain people ran away from those camps and they came back and told the story. And the elders of the community listened and said, "It's unbelievable, we can't believe this because you can't imagine a cultured race like the Germans would have a policy of gassing people and burning them, it's not *possible*."

I listened — I was then about twelve — even today I can visualise these people; I felt they were just dreamers and telling the story to frighten us because it was so *inhumane* to do a thing like that: take them in cattle trucks, select them, take their clothes off them, gas and burn them! The truth was unbelievable in 1942. And my father said, "Whatever happens, even if they're right, we're going to stay here as long as we can."

Barbara Stimler
Young Polish Jewish woman, Lodz Ghetto
I managed to get a room for myself and my mother and I also found work for her in the kitchen; so as she was working, she got soup — only those who worked got fed. Suddenly she got ill, she started to swell from hunger; her legs were very bad, she could hardly walk and had a terrible pain on one side. They took her to hospital, when she came back she was paralysed on one side. My problems then started: there were some little worms working on one leg — that leg was so thin, it was terrible. One day they closed the street (for round-ups for deportations); I could walk about because I was wearing the nurse's uniform. What did I

do when I went to work? I carried my mother, put her in a hole in the garden and left her there, praying to God that when I came back she would be there. She was, thank God, and I carried her back. I had to leave her in the room when I went to work. I left two chairs, one with a bedpan and one with something for her to eat, because I was working all day long. The hospital people where I worked were kind, they gave me the bedpan and some soup for her when I was going home.

Michael Etkind
Polish Jewish youth, Lodz Ghetto
I ended up working in the post office, as a postman. Any kind of uniform in the ghetto was useful. By the end of 1941, more and more people who were not working were being sent out of the ghetto. They got notices and their food was cut off, and they were ordered to the railway station to be moved out in cattle trucks. Nobody knew exactly what was happening, but nobody wanted to be sent out of the ghetto. As a postman, I was the one who was bringing those notices to those people. We were nicknamed the "*Malchamoves*" — the biblical "angel of death". It wasn't pleasant because when you gave the notices, the people would burst into tears. These were the people who couldn't work: too old or too young or just incapable because they were so weak from starvation. Sometimes you'd see a piece of soap with a letter RIF on it, and the joke which spread through the ghetto was that this RIF was Yiddish for "Real Jewish Fat": Jews were being evacuated and turned into soap. Those jokes started at

153

the end 1941, beginning 1942, so rumours that Jews were being exterminated were about even then.

Roman Halter
Polish Jewish youth, Lodz Ghetto

In the spring of '42 there was a selection where the sick, those who didn't work and the young were to be deported. The ghetto was divided into two zones with each zone being cordoned off by the SS and the Jewish police. You had to stay in line and the SS would walk around saying, "to the right", or "to the left". One woman who lived in our zone, was the wife of the doctor from our town who had sent me to hospital when I had my appendix out. She was a very noble character and had a little girl with her. The SS who did the selection took the child away. She went up to him and said, "*Please*, she is all I have in the world — spare my child." He pushed her away and she said, "In that case take me as well." He pushed her aside again. Then she tore her blouse and exposed her breast and said, "Shoot me!" He took out his pistol and shot her. The child was screaming and her mother was lying dead, bleeding from the chest. Then suddenly it was too much for the SS man and the selection had to be halted.

Another man carried on the selection and my mother and I were taken and put on carts. My mother by then had big swellings on her legs which reached to her feet and she had great difficulty in walking. When we were on this cart, she said, "You have to save yourself." She told me that when we came round the corner she would tell me where to jump, and I was to take my wooden clogs off and run in a zigzag fashion. It was very compelling: she spoke to me as if there were no one else in the cart, although it was full of people. She said something like, "May God be with you." We came round this corner and she said, "Even if they shout and shoot, don't stop."

At the very end of the path there was a wooden toilet and I ran through the arch in a zigzag way and ran to the fence. On the other side was the Jewish Fire Brigade and another zone began. I jumped over and stayed close to the fence as she had told me. When the Jewish police came running, they thought I had jumped into the mire of the toilet and so they opened the lid and fired some shots into it. I lay very close to the fence on the other side. After a while I went to the Fire Brigade people and told them I had escaped and said, "Please don't give me away." They said, "Fine, stay here until dusk." When I went back to the place where we lived, the eiderdown was still on the bed. I crawled into the bed and slept for a very long time.

Martin Parker
Polish Jewish inmate, Warsaw Ghetto
In July 1942, when the big deportations started, they gave the Jewish police an order to bring 6,000 people every day to go "east", and if they didn't bring 6,000 then they had to bring their own relations and parents. These policemen became *merciless*; they had horse-drawn carts, they'd close a house, everyone had to

come down, and they'd go from door to door pulling people out. They were not liked; we knew they were treacherous and we disliked them for cooperating with the Germans. I wouldn't do it for anything in the world. They worked because they thought they could save themselves and their families and get some allocation of food. Eventually, when it became more difficult to make up the numbers, they broke doors and dragged people out, pushed them down the stairs and onto the waiting carts.

Edyta Klein-Smith
Polish Jewish child, Warsaw Ghetto
During those times of heavy selections in 1942, they would try to catch people as they were running to their homes after work. On this day we were running and we could see that we weren't going to make it to our house. Then my stepfather remembered that someone had a hiding place in a nearby building and we ran into this building. This hiding place was very small and it was packed, but our relatives were there and they let us in. The wall was closed so completely on the outside that you couldn't see anything. The Germans were running through the building shooting and pounding on the doors. One of the women had a baby and this baby started to fidget and cry. Nobody said anything. She didn't say anything and she just smothered the baby. I only realised that she had killed it when the raid was over and the wall was opened. She just looked at us and she walked away.

Danny Falkner
Polish Jewish inmate, Warsaw Ghetto

At this time I was hidden in a cellar on a street leading into the *Umschlagplatz* — the concentration place from which deportations were sent to Treblinka. It was a hot summer day and Korczak was leading a group of children — maybe a hundred or two hundred — and he was leading them to the *Umschlagplatz*. Korczak was a doctor by profession but he did not want to go into normal medical service, treating those who could pay. He wanted to give society what he felt society needed. He became head of a Jewish orphanage, then a mixed orphanage of Jewish and non-Jewish children. In the ghetto, he found it very difficult to maintain the orphanage because there were no funds for it, but he used to go around with a sack to collect food for the orphans. He was prominent in science and educational circles, he wrote many articles about child rearing and child care. I was told that he was approached by a German before entering the *Umschlagplatz*, telling him he could save his life, but the children would have to go. He refused the offer, he said, "Where my children are going, I must go as well." And of course he perished in Treblinka.

Christabel Bielenberg
Anglo/Irish woman, Dahlem, Berlin

I was in Berlin having had Christopher, my little baby, and I was with a very good friend of mine and we were having supper. A Dutchman, the head of Unilever at the time, was supposed to come to dinner, and he arrived very late. When he came in he said, "I can't sit down because I want to tell you something first." He said that he'd been in Czechoslovakia, travelling back from the east, and he'd got out at a station's platform to stretch his legs and had been stopped by two SS; but before climbing back into the train he'd noticed a train on the next platform, a cattle train, and he'd seen children's hands sticking out through the slats of the cattle trucks. I remember the silence that came over the five of us; we couldn't eat anything.

Michael Etkind
Polish Jewish youth, Lodz Ghetto

With my postman's cap and badge I could walk anywhere and could observe the selections. I noticed some terrible scenes where the Chief of *Gestapo*, Fuchs, was active. I remember one tenement: all the people came down for selection, the younger people were less afraid and one of the young men came in front, more or less confident that he wasn't going to be selected for deportation. Fuchs took out his revolver and told him to kneel — I was about twenty yards away and could see quite clearly — the man went on his knees and Fuchs sort of hesitated, holding the gun, and then slowly said, "Get up, turn around, and now kneel." And he started counting, "One, two, three . . .", and slowly walked away and left that man. He didn't shoot him, he was just playing with him. Later on after dark, when the selection for the day had finished, we went to see the young man. He was in bed — a young, healthy man, but he was so nervous, shaking, frightened.

Esther Brunstein
Young Polish Jewish woman, Lodz Ghetto
We saw the Germans with their big vans. People around me were screaming, everyone had someone there: a mother, a father. I actually saw, with my own eyes, new-born babies being thrown down out of the window on to the big lorries — from second, third floors, just thrown down. We could see the blood splattering and we could see the Germans laughing and joking and I was beside myself.

Roman Halter
Polish Jewish youth, Lodz Ghetto
At one stage the SS came along and told Rumkowski (leader of the Jewish Council) that he had to supply so many children. And Rumkowski called a meeting that we had to attend. He stood up in Lodz Square and said, "I appeal to you to give up your children. We have this demand; in order for you to survive, your children *must* be given up." He stood there and uttered those words. I found that speech of Rumkowski's *terrible*. At a certain point you have to say, "No, I will not do this, I will not say this."

Michael Etkind
Polish Jewish youth, Lodz Ghetto
Some resented Rumkowski's role in the ghetto, but many did not. Had he survived he would have been

159

murdered after the war; as it was he was killed in Auschwitz. But indirectly, because of him, more people survived in the Lodz ghetto (for longer) than in any other; not those he meant to survive — himself, his family and his friends — but people like myself. He did collaborate, but would you accuse the British soldiers who were building the bridge over the River Kwai of collaboration? Those he put on the deportations list, because they were not working, hated and resented him; but the people who because of him survived, were very grateful to him. Czerniakow in the Warsaw Ghetto was in the same position, and when the curfew for mass deportations took place there, more or less at the same time as the Warsaw Ghetto was being liquidated, he committed suicide, took poison and killed himself. What do you think of a captain of a ship who, when the ship is about to sink, takes poison or jumps overboard? It is *impossible* to judge.

Halina Sand (daughter of Martin Parker)
Polish Jewish child, Warsaw Ghetto
My parents were in despair because we were told that children were being taken. I was very frightened. They tried for a while to hide me by pushing me into one of those handcarts and piling the baggage on top of me. And I remember it was a hot September day in 1942 and my clothes were sticking to me because of the sweat. When they started searching the handcarts my father took me out. They were lining everybody up by then in the cobbled street. And everybody was kneeling in ranks of four. It is very hard to kneel on cobbles. My

mother took me with her into the rank where she was kneeling and wrapped me up in the coat she had been carrying and laid me in front of her as though I were a parcel. The other people in the rank complained. They said, "You won't be able to hide her and they will take all of us." I don't remember how long it was. It just seemed to go on forever. I knew my mother was there, but my father was in another rank. This seemed to go on for eternity. What they were doing was going through the ranks and taking out all the women who didn't look as if they would be good workers. Well, that was the last of them, they were never seen again. By this time most of the children had already been taken. I was almost . . . I must have been the last. I didn't see what was going on because of course I was wrapped up. What I am saying now is what my mother told me afterwards, not what I saw for myself.

The Germans would walk up to a rank and inspect it. And everyone they thought was too feeble to be worth keeping would be yanked out, usually being first struck across the face with these heavy batons that they carried, and dragged away. And my father, who could actually see this going on from some rows behind, said that had he seen my mother being taken away he would have gone for the German who was hitting her. And that would have been the end of us all. But it didn't happen, I don't know why. She was probably flushed and looking well that day. She was carrying a heavy rucksack on her back and the Germans went past her without a second glance. Those immediately in front and those immediately behind were being dragged out of the ranks. Then everyone was ordered to move forward and close the gaps in the ranks. My mother moved forward on her knees and as she did so the coat unrolled and I fell out. I remember that very well because of the blinding light.

This only lasted a second; a moment later I was wrapped up in the coat again. She said there was a German standing by and she still couldn't understand why he didn't see because there was a moment when I was clearly visible. Finally, they ordered everyone to stand up and said we were going back to where we'd come from in the ghetto. Of course I could not be a parcel now that I was standing up. My mother put a coat over my head and other people had coats and piled them on top of that, and they pushed me on. I was a kind of walking parcel. They closed ranks behind me on the way back to the ghetto. Then my father suddenly appeared. We went back to our bare flat. And I remember my father sat down on the stripped bed and wept. That is the only time I have seen him cry; and to cry . . . well, to cry like that with ghastly, dry sobbing — I'll never forget that.

Adam Adams
Polish Jewish youth, Lublin Ghetto
Aktionen (round-ups for deportations) usually happened at night. I remember the hiding place we had behind the wardrobe and how we would sit together through the night. They would come into the room shouting and shooting, there would be flames all around. I cannot describe to you . . . Imagine, winter

162

nights, suddenly you hear noises, voices, you hear shooting, the fear is *indescribable* and the running, everyone scrambling. The human behaviour in such a situation is to preserve your own life, so you don't look at what you're doing, you *run*, maybe you're running over other people, but you don't care. And that is the terrible thing — you lose all human dignity, that was terrible.

Michael Etkind
Polish Jewish youth, Lodz Ghetto

About 1942 the gypsy camp was formed on the edge of the ghetto. I think about five thousand were brought in. It was winter, very cold. They took a block of tenement houses and broke all the windows so they would freeze to death. One of the postmen had it on his route on the way to the cemetery and saw what was happening. They were not given any food, and then the *Kripo*, which was the criminal police, a branch of the German police, went in and were stabbing and killing them. And as they did this they made some of the gypsies play their violins. The postman whose route it was on, came with terrible stories for a couple of weeks during these killings. Then the Jewish drivers of horse-driven carts had to take the corpses to the cemetery where they were buried in mass graves: men, women and children — starved, frozen to death, or killed, a few hundred corpses every day. There was a case where the Germans were on guard between the ghetto and the gypsy camp and one of the Germans threw a baby wrapped in a

163

blanket; the guardsman was kicking it like a football until it hung on the barbed wire.

Ruth Foster
Young German Jewish woman, Riga Ghetto

In a way it was quite ironic because there we were in the ghetto, but we were together with family and friends, with cousins and uncles who had also been deported. My father met a lot of old friends he hadn't seen for a long time. But what could you do? We didn't do much, we didn't have a good time, we didn't dance or anything. We went to work and were pleased to get a bit of bread. We stayed within our own four walls because the *Kommandant* would go round the streets and whenever he saw Jews walking about, he would take them to the old Jewish cemetery in Riga and shoot them, no questions asked.

My father had to share the fate of those poor people. He was working for the SS in Washington Square, Riga, sawing wood. A German soldier passed from our home town and said, "Wilhelm, what are *you* doing here?" My father only answered, "Bring me some bread." The soldier did. In the evening, as my father's party came back to the ghetto, there was a control. There was a young boy with him who worked in the SS kitchens and he had taken some potato peels for his mother to make something with, and another friend of my father's who had been given a sandwich by a soldier. All this was found on them as they marched into the ghetto. They were taken aside and handcuffed and the Jewish police came to our billet and asked my mother and me to go to the *Appellplatz* — which was a market square in the Riga Ghetto — where lots of people were assembled. We had to stand in the front row. Those three in handcuffs were put in front of us, a distance of five or ten yards, then the *Kommandant* came behind them and, with his revolver, shot them dead. They fell dead in front of our eyes. That was the life of my father.

Ryvka "Rene" Salt
Polish Jewish child, Zdunska Wola Ghetto

In August 1942 the real nightmare started when early one morning we were woken up with shouts, "All Jews out! Into the streets!" We had to get dressed quickly. We heard rumours that old people and children were being killed, so we took our grandparents and one young cousin of three years and hid them in the attic, thinking we would be back. We went out into the streets which were already crowded with people and followed one another until we came to a very big field. When we were all there, they ordered us all to sit down. Then, again, through loud-speakers, they ordered parents to give up their children under the age of eighteen years. Anyone who didn't actually see the scene could not imagine the cries of the mothers, "Almighty God, help us!" And you could see the little children running towards the officers, the bigger ones holding their little siblings in their hands. While all this was going on, my mother was trying to hide me on one side and my little sister on the other. Before long they got hold of my little sister and my mother got badly beaten up. My sister, then ten, said to the officer, "Please don't hit her, that's not my

165

mother." And I was told that she was running away with tears running down her face.

When they had taken all the children, we were lined up in fives and taken to the local (Jewish) cemetery where there was a selection: right to live, left to be taken away. That went on until it was dark. We were left sitting on those graves for three days and three nights. They installed electric lights around the cemetery and continued to make selections. People tried to make me look older: someone gave me a scarf to wear and powder to make me look more mature. But just before we left, I was spotted by a German officer; he pointed at me and said, "You, stand up! How old are you?" I was so nervous, I couldn't answer. My father said, "Oh, she's eighteen, I know her." The officer stood there looking at me — I was twelve and looked about eight — he looked me up and down and he could see that I wasn't eighteen years old. Finally, he said, "She can sit down." No one could believe it; it was God's will. When we left that cemetery, there were only three children left; I was one of the three. I can never forget it: the guilty feeling that they got hold of my sister and not of me.

1943–1944

THE GHETTO (ii)

I felt elated that the Jews had fired the first shots, we could see that the Germans were not immune to violence, that violence could be exerted against them as well. Of course we knew it was an impossibility to conquer, or resist them completely. We knew that our fate was sealed. But we wanted to bring down as many Germans as possible.

Despite the terrible retribution and reprisals meted out by the Nazis for Jewish resistance, numerous cases are documented both by individuals as well as groups. Underground resistance movements were formed in many ghettos; these, led in the main by members of pre-war political and youth movements, were often without the knowledge of the *Judenräte*. Underground couriers helped to create networks among isolated ghettos and gathered information on localities as well as organising the smuggling of arms in preparation for mass escapes and armed revolts, these usually occurring when the liquidation of a ghetto was imminent.

The Warsaw Ghetto Uprising is perhaps the best-known of all ghetto revolts. Ever since news of mass murder by gassing had filtered through to the ghetto, members of the Jewish Fighting Organisation (ZOB) had been planning an armed

169

revolt. When the final liquidation of the ghetto began on 19 April 1943, the 750 ill-equipped Jewish men and women members of ZOB rose up in a desperate fight against the 2,000 battle-hardened *Waffen* SS troops and their Ukrainian auxiliaries. For twenty days they fought, using a network of cellars, bunkers, sewers and rooftops. By 16 May, resistance had practically ceased and the Germans started razing the ghetto. Fifty-six thousand Jews had been captured and sent to concentration camps, and about 7,000 were shot during the revolt. News of the uprising spread, giving heart to incarcerated Jews throughout occupied Europe and becoming a lasting symbol of heroic struggle.

Danny Falkner
Polish Jewish inmate, Warsaw Ghetto

The first sign of the Resistance was when the chief of the Jewish police was murdered in the ghetto. This was a sign that seemed to be recognised by the Germans because there was a three-month pause in the forceful elimination of Jews — October, November, December, and no actions. During that time the young people organised themselves into small units, planning resistance. I was partially involved with one of the groups. One evening after curfew, a young man, who we knew worked with the *Gestapo*, came and said, "I can't give you any details but I'm warning you to be careful tonight, something might happen."

I was walking up and down the room wondering what to do with this information. In the same street there was a temporary Jewish hospital and the director was a friend of mine. In spite of the curfew, I decided to go and pass this information on to him. I carefully made my way to the Jewish hospital, knocked on the door and finally this friend appeared at the visor. I explained that something was expected to happen. He didn't believe it because we'd had three months of quiet. I said, "It's upon your conscience to do something to hide the people whom you are sheltering." These were prominent intellectuals and personalities given "jobs" there.

At four o'clock in the morning, I think it was 5 January 1943, from a distance we heard the marching steps of troops. When they came through the ghetto gates, the column divided: one went straight to Mila Street and the other straight to the Jewish hospital. We heard shootings and explosions and after a while the troops marched out again. I learned that the first shots were fired in Mila Street where a unit of Jewish Resistance attacked the troops. They felt the first signs of victory as German soldiers were killed. I made my way to the hospital to see my friend. I heard that when the Germans came into the hospital with machine guns, they shot all the patients in the beds along each side of the long hall. The staff were also shot. The only survivors were those hidden in various hiding places in the hospital. This was the first attempt of the Germans to subdue and eliminate the ghetto. But they saw that the Jews were armed and intended to fight.

I felt elated that the Jews had fired the first shots; we could see that the Germans were not immune to violence, that violence could be exerted against them as well. Of course we knew it was an impossibility to conquer or resist them completely. We knew that our fate was sealed. But we wanted to bring down as many Germans as possible.

Martin Parker
Polish Jewish inmate, Warsaw Ghetto
Eventually, when things became really critical, we realised that we had to get out. Several people had mentioned that my wife looked "Aryan" and we started pushing Mr Idzikowski, my former business partner, to find accommodation for us in one of the dachas around Warsaw. He found a couple who accepted his proposition to take a few Jews and hide them, promising that they would be paid well. The agreement was that my wife and daughter, Halina, went first; we got documents for them which cost a lot. Then my mother-in-law and sister-in-law left on 3 April, 1943, and my brother-in-law and I on 8 April. We were all smuggled out on a lorry leaving the ghetto. We arrived at a house in Otwock and were hidden by Jozef and Ola Jaworska for one and a half years.

Maria Ossowski
Young Polish woman, Pawiak Prison, Warsaw Ghetto
Eventually, like many people of my generation and older, I got arrested by the *Gestapo* and sent to Pawiak, which happened to stand in the middle of the ghetto

itself. I was given the task of keeping the courtyards of the women's prison in good order, sweeping, picking up the rubbish. In April 1943, when the Jewish uprising started, my task became impossible as the Germans fought the Jewish fighters first of all with fire — they went from house to house starting fires. So throughout the uprising, the ghetto was burning from top to the bottom, and the streets next to the Pawiak were as much affected as the others. I had to clear the bits which were falling on that courtyard: papers, bits of wood, all sorts of dusty and blackened pieces. Because of my position I could see what those sitting in the cells couldn't see. I have to tell you that with my own eyes I have seen people jumping from the floors to their certain deaths because the houses were totally destroyed by the burning fires. Nothing is clearer in my mind in all the terrible happenings of the war, than watching a scene like that.

Stanley Faull
Polish Jewish child, Warsaw Ghetto
I was there at the time of the uprising and I have seen young boys and girls running around in the middle of the night across roofs, through sewers, getting together and discussing the situation in my presence. By then there was a shortage of people in the ghetto so there was furniture and things to barter, not for food, but for arms. The Polish underground did help, but of course the only arms they gave were 1914 old rifles, too rusty to use. I remember seeing boys and girls, who were no older than seventeen or eighteen, going to kill Germans

173

and taking their machine guns away. They said: we don't mind giving our lives so long as some can save themselves.

Daniella Hausman
Young Polish woman, Warsaw

I remember the ghetto uprising very well, it was really tragic. From the window of where I lived, we could see what was going on because the ghetto was at the back of our block. I saw terrible things. I saw a silhouette of a woman pushing a child into the fire below.

Martin Parker
Polish Jewish inmate, Warsaw Ghetto

During the uprising, the Germans were going from house to house ordering people to come down or they would blitz the houses, and the people were jumping from the houses, killing themselves. My wife, who had escaped outside by then, saw with her own eyes Jews jumping from windows. She heard Poles standing nearby laughing and saying, "The Jews are being fried." If I hadn't escaped when I did, I too would have perished because the ghetto was hermetically surrounded and those inside killed or sent away. A whole army was brought in to fight the Jews, and they had to withdraw several times until they brought more reinforcements. Jews were then living in sewers. The men and women came out, shot the Germans and then went back to the sewers. Someone had to show that Jews are not cowards.

Stanley Faull
Polish Jewish child, Warsaw Ghetto

When eventually the ghetto was systematically destroyed by fire and you couldn't breathe because of the smoke, everything around us, and on top of us, was burning. So we had to get some air and the temporary brick wall, behind which we were hiding, was knocked down. I went out with my mother for the first time in many weeks. And there were people in German uniforms speaking Russian, so they weren't Germans. We were sent straight to Majdanek camp. We were separated from my father at that time. What happened to him, I don't know. My sister was away with the Resistance and my older brother was with my uncle in England. Somehow just the two of us were left.

Andrew Bakowski
Polish child, Warsaw

The ghetto situation was brought to a climax on the day I had my tonsils out. As we returned from this operation and turned from Marsazlkowska into Jerozolimskie, we saw a queue of fire engines stopping outside our house and facing west. The smoke was beginning to rise up from the ghetto: the ghetto rising had started and we could hear shooting. The area nearest to us was subdued early; eventually the place was burnt out. I don't recall any transports after that. It was just the ghetto burning for quite a while. There was a glow at night and you would hear adults talking about it, but they would fall quiet when you came into the room.

Jack Shepsman
Polish Jewish youth, Nowogrodek Ghetto

By 1943, things were getting desperate in the ghetto. Eventually we got agreement to dig the tunnel; just one hundred people knew about it, we needed these to dig and sew up bags to put the sand in. We started digging; people stood in the tunnel to pass the sand out which was then put into bags and passed on. The sand was yellowish and had to be hidden, so we put it in the lofts of the houses, being very careful that it wasn't too heavy. We had carpenters and they started pinching wood from the Germans and cutting up sheds — the sides and ceiling of the tunnel were lined with this so they wouldn't fall down. We had good directions worked out showing where, and the distance to dig. We dug for six to eight months, working day and night. Our electricians made lights inside the tunnel and people were trained to get used to being down there, and not start fainting when the time came. There was a wooden bed over a square hole which had a cover; when we heard noises, we covered the hole and pushed the bed on top and there was nothing to see. There were steps down and up the other end, and the tunnel was of the right depth so it wouldn't collapse if lorries passed over it.

On 10 February 1943 the decision was made to go out. We planned to get all 250 people out at once — to finish the ghetto once and for all. This was the end of the Jewish population of the area. Everyone was given the name of a person and told to find that person and go out after him or her. Not everyone left; Jack

176

Kagan and some others hid because they couldn't walk. I was in the middle. We all got out; about sixty took the wrong direction and instead of walking into the forest, went into the town and they were caught. The rest, 190, came to the partisans. We heard later what a great shock this was to the Germans — the whole area was talking about how the Jews broke out from under the noses of the Germans.

GHETTO EXISTENCE

The model ghetto/camp of Terezin (Theresienstadt in German) had been set up in November 1941, to meet a unique objective; the main aim, as Eichmann explained, was to "save face". Among inmates were the so-called *"prominente"*, well-known personalities: German Jews over the age of sixty-five, Jewish invalid veterans of the Great War as well as Jews awarded the Iron Cross, First-Class during that war. Given its showplace status, the ghetto was exhibited, under Adolf Eichmann's supervision, to delegates of the German Red Cross on 28 June 1943 and to the International Committee of the Red Cross on 23 June 1944, when two films were made for propaganda reasons. Accepting to inspect only those areas carefully selected and given the *Verschönerungsaktionen* — beautification — by the Nazis, the delegates played into the hands of the Nazis by giving Terezin a measure of respectability at a time when they were working flat out, feeding its inmates into the gas chambers of Auschwitz-Birkenau, by then the main death camp.

The ghettoisation and deportations of Jews in Salonika (Thessaloniki) took place in the spring of 1943. Deportations of Jews from Central, Western and Southern Greece and the islands of Rhodes and Corfu took place in the spring and summer of 1944. In all, more than 85 per cent of the pre-war Jewish community of Greece, some 80,000 Jews, perished in the Holocaust. The last ghettos established were those set up in Hungary after the German occupation of March 1944. By then most of the earlier ghettos were depopulated or liquidated — the fittest inmates selected for slave labour, the majority deported for extermination. Due to its usefulness to the German war effort, the Lodz Ghetto was not liquidated until August 1944. Terezin lasted until the war ended.

Janine Ingram
Young Greek Jewish woman, Thessaloniki Ghetto
One day, about two months after we went into the ghetto, we were arrested — the whole family. It was the first day of May 1943. I shall never forget that day. Two German soldiers and a Jewish functionary came to collect us and took us to the *Gestapo*. The first five hours we were made to stand with our faces against the wall, nobody said anything. We were not allowed to talk amongst ourselves. It was a very hot day. I just looked

sideways at my mother, whom I loved very much, and her face was very tense. I can remember to this day how a big stain of sweat was going all the way down her back and she looked as if she was going to collapse at any minute. Then five hours later a German officer came in and for no reason he pulled my father out and beat him to a pulp. My father was also a diabetic and it is very difficult for a diabetic to lose a lot of blood so we were very worried, but we were not allowed to move or tend him, or even look at him; our faces were against the wall.

We were feeling very tired and I realised that this was the day when I would die. As my birthday was on 29 May I would have been twenty at the end of the month. I really didn't want to die. I felt it was very unfair. I realised how I'd never prayed to God in my life and I apologised to God for not praying and said, "If you really want to show me that you are listening today, show me a sign, get us out of here." I bargained with him, I am ashamed to say.

Marsha Segall
Young Lithuanian Jewish woman, Siauliai Ghetto
In '43, we had got to know that children were taken out of the ghettos of Vilnius and Kaunas. We hoped that we would be able to save some of ours. We tried: churches, monasteries, just people *everywhere*, hoping that they would take children, but it was a brick wall. And on 5 November 1943 we got up to find ourselves completely surrounded by three kinds of guards: Lithuanian, German and mainly Ukrainians. They said nobody

should leave the ghetto. The second command came that all the workers should go as usual to their work places, and of course a lot of parents guessed that it was coming here — the children taken. And they tried to hide them as much as they could in cellars and attics, and those who looked bigger they tried to smuggle into their work places. But to describe what happened later is very difficult, because when the gates opened and the workers left, hundreds of Ukrainians jumped from lorries and started running from one house to another in the street, grabbing the children from the hands of their mothers and chasing them to where the lorries stood.

The children, during the three years in the ghetto, were instinctively and terribly frightened of the German and Lithuanian guards and they tried to run back to their mothers. And the screams and shouts of the mothers! — there are no words to describe this. And babies, little children, *lovely* children. The guards looked everywhere: they opened every cellar and just pulled them out like catching rabbits, and from attics, from gardens, from *everywhere*. Mothers tried to give them wedding rings, everything they had. To describe how the children were herded to these lorries is impossible. And in our house we had a small family; the little boy was a beautiful child with huge grey-blue eyes and I always used to tell him stories in the evenings. I loved him. He was found hiding in the garden behind bushes and he was taken. He jumped from the lorry; then we knew they were beyond rescue because he was shot in the leg. I don't need to tell you the state of the mothers who came back from work in the evening to find their children gone.

Rena Quint
Young Polish Jewish child, Piotrkow Ghetto

When they no longer needed us in the ghetto, we were rounded up again and packed into those cattle wagons; at one point we went down on to a platform and there was an announcement that the women and men would be separated. I didn't know what this meant, but my father must have realised that you had to get undressed when going into a camp's reception and he said, "You can't come with me because if they give us a shower, they'll find out you are not a boy." He met a schoolteacher from our home town and he asked her to take me and look after me, and he gave her some valuables and pictures and told me that we would meet again in Piotrkow. Well, he never kept that promise.

Lili Stern-Pohlmann
Polish Jewish child, Lvov

On 31 May 1943, when I was in hiding with a German civilian administrative worker, Frau Wieth, suddenly we saw that the sky was red — an unnatural redness in the middle of the day and from the direction of the ghetto. We had this uncanny feeling that something horrendous was happening. After a while my mother arrived from the ghetto, completely beside herself, saying, "The ghetto is burning, I escaped at the last minute." She then told us the harrowing story of how her mother, my grandmother, said to her when the

Nazis started the liquidation of the ghetto, "You must leave me and go to Lili." My mother refused, saying that I was in good care. But her mother insisted and one moment, when her back was turned, my grandmother opened the window and jumped out from the third floor. Can you believe that! She did it so that my mother would be free to come to me. But she wasn't dead, and my mother called an ambulance, and asked the doctor to help her end her life, to put her out of her agony. The doctor agreed to do this and took her away. She was such a courageous lady, only a small, little creature.

Jan Hartman
Czech Jewish youth, Theresienstadt Ghetto
Terezin was the first chapter, that's when one started to know what it was all about. My mother had studied painting and that's the way she managed to make contact with the SS government of Terezin and to enter the painting service there. To explain what this was: Terezin was set up to be useful to the war effort of Germany and one part of it was a factory to produce paintings for the German people. It was almost like painting on an assembly line — like in a Charlie Chaplin film (*Modern Times*). One would specialise in the sky, another in the forests, another in the houses, in the people, in the hand, in the pigs and so on — I'm almost joking! But the work was of a poor quality and done by a small group of about six or seven people. She managed to get my father into it and because I was

gifted in painting and drawing, she managed to get me in too.

It wasn't a particularly rough time for me. As a sign of how things were, my development, like my brother's and other young people's, stopped completely. Our hair wouldn't grow, nor would our nails and, being in puberty time, that was completely stopped. We would be hungry to the extent of dying of it, especially if you were old. That is perhaps the one nasty thing I remember, seeing the dead people in front of houses, because every day the dead were taken out into the street and laid down.

Anna Bergman
Young Czech Jewish woman, Theresienstadt Ghetto
Everybody lost their menstruation, they say it's a symptom of being locked up. We all lost it and thought we were pregnant, but in my case, after two months or so, it came back normally. In Auschwitz, it didn't arise for me because I went there pregnant, but I think the women all lost it there. I became pregnant with my first child in Terezin; another five couples were in the same position. You were allowed to arrive pregnant, or to come with a little child; but to become pregnant — that was a crime! At first they wanted to abort the children, but we were too far gone. So they made us sign a paper to agree that the children would be taken away and they used the expression "euthanasia" on this. But it never happened; the children were born and lived, but my

183

little boy died after two months, of pneumonia, he was not killed.

As the men were separated from their women, how were these children conceived? It sounds incredible for normal middle-class people brought up in the usual way, but we were twelve girls in our room and sometimes twelve men slept there. You lose all inhibitions: nobody listens, or looks at anybody — it's unbelievable but it's true. This was the only lovely moment we had: we were all young and healthy; but when I see before me — all those men and girls, twenty-four people doing what we were doing . . .

Zdenka Ehrlich
Young Czech Jewish woman, Theresienstadt
Now the art in Theresienstadt was something absolutely unique. I joined the movement. We got permission to produce plays, to give concerts, all this was allowed. So immediately everyone went to work. The designers occupied the top attics, adapted it for a stage, and plays were performed, plays that were translated. I was in six of them. I remember Shakespeare was translated — *Love's Labour's Lost* was one. Original plays were written and performed, some by Czech authors. Lots of poetry. A theatre workshop was set up by a producer who was a very famous name at the National Theatre. Concerts were given, music composed, artists' instruments were allowed to come in, and it became something absolutely unique.

I must say, ridiculous as it sounds, that the climate was ideal for any artist: there were no material worries, no taxes to pay or wondering what to eat or where to live — just give all your energy, love and enthusiasm to the arts. But it was only part of our work. For instance, I worked in the kitchen. And one of the most important parts of the theatre was the satire and this escaped the Germans. There was one particular man, called Karel Svenk. He was a Communist, very, very left, and he was extremely talented. And he composed a song which became almost a national anthem for us inmates, "Everything is possible, don't despair, keep your head up, one day all this will finish and we'll laugh" — not *all* sadly.

Anna Bergman
Young Czech Jewish woman, Theresienstadt Ghetto
There was a performance of Verdi's *Requiem*, the first public performance with all the trimmings, and the Germans came to listen to what the Jews could do. This was performed with all the hidden meanings stressed. Well, they finished and waited and waited, and the conductor turned round, and everyone waited: to applaud or not? And then the Germans started to applaud. You can't imagine the *irony*, the absolute stupidity: the Germans came to the performance, they applauded and they left. And the Jews applauded, everyone was in tears. It was *magnificent*. I saw the concert performance of *The Bartered Bride* by the Czech National Opera, and to hear it *there!* There is one exchange where the pair worry: will they, won't

185

they get married? "How will it end?" said she, and he said, "It will end well." The whole of Terezin was beside itself at this.

Zdenka Ehrlich
Young Czech Jewish woman, Theresienstadt Ghetto
Then the German headquarters started to present Theresienstadt as a model ghetto and one day Eichmann came with some members of the Red Cross. It was highly organised of course. Before the visit everybody was engaged in town cleaning. The streets were virtually washed on the knees with brushes and soap and were spotless. People who lived in shop windows — shop windows were also living quarters — they were evacuated. Things were arranged in the windows as though these *were* shop windows. Children were rehearsed on what to say when the *Lager Kommandant* (camp commandant) arrived: they would crowd around him and he would give them each a box of sardines.

We, the young ones, were put into a group of young athletes. We were allowed to swim across the river, and back of course, to show the freedom! Normally we were not allowed to swim in the river. Music was played in the square, people were walking around like in a spa, everything was arranged. Sure enough, an open car came, with Eichmann standing there in the middle as they drove through. And that of course was used for German propaganda. After that transports went every single day. The hysteria was growing in momentum and more and more people came in and out. On the way out we knew only the words "Going east".

Edith Baneth
Young Czech Jewish woman, Theresienstadt Ghetto

Then came a *terrible* day. It was winter 1943, bitter cold, snowing. For one reason or another the Germans suddenly wanted to count the whole ghetto. We were taken out and walked for about two hours to an enormous meadow. We were put in rows, standing, standing, standing all day. We were not allowed to go to the toilet, had to do it where we were. It was bitter cold, snowing, ice, no food, *nothing*. It was already dark and nobody came counting or anything. And we had the feeling that something terrible was going to happen. A lot of people collapsed, a lot of old people fainted. My mother and I were huddling together to keep each other warm. My grandfather was with the old people away from us, we couldn't help him. Over twenty-four hours standing in that place! Then suddenly they ordered — go back. After that a lot of people got very ill and a lot of old people died. And every morning you saw the dead thrown out on the streets, and every morning you had to pick them up and take them away.

My grandfather got very ill, and he had diarrhoea and never recovered from it. I visited him in the place for the old people when he was nearly dying, and I won't forget that terrible room with the smell of urine. My uncle managed to get him into what was called the hospital, but he died on 20 March 1943. My aunt came with me to the burial. I loved my grandfather very much and seeing his hands and feet hanging out of the cart . . . they were all just skin and bones. And we could only follow up to the point where they left the ghetto. In one way my mother and I were almost relieved; he was sixty when he died, we then thought it was better for him than to go on suffering — how very *practical* was our thinking!

Halina Kahn
Young Polish Jewish woman, Lodz Ghetto

I was working on the *Bahnhof* (railway) where the deportations went from; we had to prepare the buckets to put into the wagons. The selections took place day and night and we had no idea where our people were going — the Germans said they were going to better-organised factories, but they were all going to Auschwitz and Majdanek. We had no idea what these were like. When the trains came back empty, we had to clean the wagons up for the next group. They were cattle trucks with a little window on top.

Day and night the transports left. After a few months we found little pieces of paper stuck in the corner of the wagon. The people had written, "It's hot, it burns." When the cattle trucks returned they were in a terrible state, they had only one or two buckets for seventy or eighty people and they were relieving themselves in the wagons; we had to clean them very quickly with disinfectant to make them ready for others. When we had time we would put drinking water in, because they weren't given any water either. And they were screaming, "Water, give us some water!" We did whatever we could. Sometimes we could hear our people singing *Hatikvah* — the last song — as they waited in the closed trucks. When my mother was deported and in the truck with the whole family, she said to me through the little window — this is a Jewish saying — "My child, when you survive, I hope you're going through your life without needing a doctor or solicitor." Sorry to say, not always true!

Gertrud "Trude" Levi
Young Hungarian Jewish woman, Szombathely Ghetto
After 19 March 1944 when the Germans marched in, things moved fast: we first had to hand in our bicycles, then our jewels and our savings books and eventually most of our money was taken from us. On 7 May we were told to take one piece of luggage and move into the ghetto. This consisted of two streets sealed off by barbed wire. We were lucky, there were only six in our room. In other rooms there were up to fifteen people: women, men, children, all strangers thrown together. The atmosphere was so tense that my friend and I collected the kids aged two to six and took them to the courtyard of the synagogue so they wouldn't be cooped up among so many tense grown-ups . . . We were in the ghetto until the end of June, then we were marched out to our first concentration camp situated on the outskirts of the town in a filthy, oily, disused motor factory.

John Chillag

Hungarian Jewish youth, Gyor Ghetto, Hungary

When the next bit of legislation came into force at the end of April 1944, the *Arrow Cross*, were not only the most vociferous, but physically assisted in pushing and forcing the Jewish population into ghettos.

I was in a strange situation, having been born and brought up in Austria. I was bilingual and the ghetto Council used me as a runner between them and the German authorities. This meant I could retain my bicycle. So I could cycle out from the ghetto mainly to the German authorities with various errands, but also could use the opportunity to visit relatives in other parts. I went a number of times to the town prison to take food and various things and speak with my uncle. This was "official duty", no risk there. I remember one occasion — that was 6 June 1944, the day the invasion [D-Day landings] took place — I can't remember what the errand was, but I went to a German officer. He had the German radio full on and it was broadcasting the first news of the invasion. I cannot remember his actual comment, but it was something like, "It won't be long now for you." As I walked back down two flights of stairs, there was a shot upstairs. I found out that he had shot himself there and then . . . I also delivered messages to the SS. They treated me, as they would say, "correctly". I was treated as a piece of dirt or scum, but not maltreated. I had an official function for them.

But all this was an illusion, it only lasted for a couple of weeks. After that all the ghetto inmates, including me, were driven out into the ghetto square where we were all quite brutally strip-searched, including internally. We were then marched off to the other end of town. There they established a regional ghetto where Jews from the surrounding district were also sent. The conditions in that ghetto were far, far worse than our crammed, but still bearable, situation in the first one.

From this second ghetto into which we had been moved, half the people were rounded up and marched one Sunday morning in June to the local railway marshalling yards, and with a little bit of encouragement from rifle butts and staves we were driven into the cattle wagons. I was then seventeen. One thing which is quite curious — I don't know how the human mind works, but I remember looking out of the slit in the wagon, and I remember it was one of the most beautiful scenes — mountains and all — that we went through. The next day we arrived at a railway siding, and we arrived in what turned out to be Auschwitz — a place nobody had heard of before, certainly none of us.

Roman Halter
Polish Jewish youth, Lodz Ghetto

By 1944 we were becoming quite important as a metal factory. We were then producing more sensitive, precision work and many felt this gave them a greater chance of survival. Then, in early summer of 1944, we were told that a very high level inspection was coming and everything had to be very clean and in working order. We had at that time a couple who arrived from Germany. He was a highly trained engineer, a very able

191

and creative soul. We all queued up to collect our soup with our aluminium containers, and we would go back and wolf it down, but he and his wife — who also worked in the metal factory — would sit down and lay the table with napkins, first have the liquid of the soup and then put the potatoes on the bread board, sprinkle salt and pepper, cut the potatoes and make conversation as they ate. I was fascinated by this; it seemed ludicrous and I asked them once why they did it. They said, "If you lose your self-dignity then you are lost and you really become what they want you to become — *Untermenschen* (sub-human)."

This engineer from Germany knew all about metals and invented a machine for making bullets quickly without damaging them. So when the inspection came, all the leaders of the metal works were lined up, together with this engineer. Albert Speer (Minister of Armaments and War Production) arrived with others from his department and some SS. He went from man to man along this line of section leaders without shaking hands. Then it was pointed out to him that this engineer was the man who had invented this bullet machine. This emaciated engineer stood there with the highest German decoration on his breast which he had been awarded during the First World War. And Speer talked to him; of course the engineer spoke beautiful German, he also felt himself German as his family had lived there for hundreds of years. They spoke almost as equals.

The inspection team passed on, then the SS Colonel saw this man wearing the decoration. He stopped and said, "Where did you buy this?" He said, "I fought for it," and he gave the names of the places where he had fought. The SS said something to another SS behind him who pulled the decoration; the engineer fell down. Then the SS put his foot on his chest and pulled it. Speer stood there and watched, impassive, as if he were watching geese flying over his head. He said absolutely nothing. His face did not show surprise, sorrow or empathy; he just stood. And when this man had his Iron Cross ripped off him, our leader said, "May we have permission to pick him up because he is going to explain the machine?"

The next day he died and two days later his wife died. It somehow seemed that his heart was ripped out with that decoration.

Halina Kahn
Young Polish Jewish woman, Lodz Ghetto
When the last people left the ghetto in 1944, my husband and I were in the last seven hundred that remained. A few months before the Russians came, the guards took the men out at night from the factory to the Jewish grounds to dig graves there. The men had to keep quiet about it. They were working through the night and my husband came back in the morning very quiet, very distressed. I asked him, "What kind of work do you do when it's so dark?" He said, "It's not important, I am here." Later I heard they had to dig seven graves, for the seven hundred of us that remained, each grave for a hundred of us.

Jan Hartman
Czech Jewish youth, Theresienstadt Ghetto

We heard that there were transports going to Poland and the place was Auschwitz. The image I had of this place was that it would be a place rather like Terezin for the production of things. My father and mother stayed in Terezin. When we were leaving, we were in a narrow area like a sluice-gate all boarded up, but there was a hole somewhere where we could get back to say goodbye for the last time to our parents. My father, who was a hunter, told me, "You remember how a hare can survive when the chain of hunters comes. If the hare jumps and runs zigzag, they will get him; but if the hare stays in his little hole, it will survive. You remember that." That was the rule that helped my brother and me survive: never volunteer for anything.

Anna Bergman
Young Czech Jewish woman, Theresienstadt Ghetto

I became pregnant for the second time, this time consciously. Now listen to this marvellous philosophy! When my first child died we decided to have another — this was after the invasion of June 1944 — we thought that if we returned to Prague after the war there would be nothing there for us and we would think twice about having a child to care for; but if I returned pregnant, or had a baby, that child would be *there*. My husband was deported on 28 September 1944 and he never knew I was pregnant because I wasn't sure then. When the men left, the Germans told us that anyone could follow their husbands of their own free will and meet them in another place, Auschwitz, which would be like Theresienstadt. I was one of the first to go. I needn't have gone because I was in sheltered work at the time. I could have stayed there until the end of the war and I knew that; but in October 1944, I was one of the first ones to volunteer to go to Auschwitz, a camp I knew nothing about.

1940–1944

THE CAMPS (i)

*I was with a friend whose parents were in the same
transport but had been sent to the other side during
the selection by Mengele. When we got into our barrack, she asked the women already there, "Where are
my parents? When will I see them again?" And they
started screaming with laughter, "You stupid idiot,
they are in the chimney by now!" We thought they
were mad, and they thought we were mad.*

By 1 September 1939 the concentration camp
system had been vastly enlarged to accommodate
almost 25,000 inmates. The camp system then
consisted of seven main camps: Dachau, Buchenwald,
Sachsenhausen (originally called Oranienburg),
Flossenburg, Mauthausen, Neuengamme and
Ravensbrück, a camp for women and children.
These had numerous sub-camps. All units
operated uniformly under a central command with
strict training of camp guards who were organised
into the *Totenkopfverbände* — a SS unit. With the
subsequent occupation of most of Europe, these
camps were expanded into a network of thousands
of camps, organised into 23 major categories that
criss-crossed the Continent, holding about two
million prisoners.

The main categories were: *Konzentrazionslager*
(KZ or KL), concentration camps; *Arbeitslager*,

199

labour camps; *Durchgangslager*, transit camps; and *Vernichtungslager*, extermination camps, which existed for the sole purpose of implementing the "Final Solution" of annihilation, the vast majority of its victims being Jews.

Victims were transported to their final destinations in various ways. Some of the victims from parts of the *Grossdeutsches Reich* and western countries were transported in regular passenger trains. Jews from Eastern Europe were transported in closed, overcrowded, freight or cattle cars, mostly without food or water, ventilation or sanitary conditions. Many deaths occurred en route and, whatever the method of transport, on arrival the system was to harry the exhausted, bewildered and terrified people from the wagons into a traumatic reception procedure at double speed. This was accompanied by the harsh shouting of orders, the swish of whips or sticks and the yelping of dogs, which combined to humiliate, disorientate and confuse.

In all concentration camps living conditions were well below those considered essential for bare survival. Inmates suffered from hunger, malnutrition, extreme cold in winter, heat in summer, overwork and fatigue. Appalling sanitary conditions were the norm and medical help was scarce, and often non-existent. Brutality, horror and human degradation added to the misery. Prisoners had no individual rights: they were no longer known by their names, but tagged like cattle with numbers tattooed on their arm or on their striped uniforms. The life of a concentration camp prisoner was one of constant uncertainty, fear and sheer hell. Further torment occurred in those camps in which Nazi doctors conducted so-called "medical experiments", usually without anaesthetics or regard to the pain their helpless victims endured.

Not all concentration camp inmates shared this fate. Many of the incarcerated, Jews included, sometimes managed to obtain more "privileged" positions which enabled them to obtain extra food and clothing. These are not to be confused with the *Kapos* — prisoners appointed by the SS to control and guard the other prisoners or head a *Kommando* (labour battalion). These were mainly professional criminals and included some who had been certified criminally insane. Although there were exceptions, in the main *Kapos* — women as well as men — behaved in a brutal manner and were often feared more than the SS.

The labour potential of the camps was recognised and exploited by the private sector of the German economy. By 1942, major corporations opened factories in or near the camps gaining access to cheap, plentiful, renewable sources of skilled and unskilled labour, hired out by the SS. Under this system, close to 9,000 labour camps of various types and sizes were established in the *Reich* and throughout the occupied territories. The same harsh conditions

201

operated in all camps with specifics varying from camp to camp. Once the work was completed the camp was liquidated; its Jewish inmates, if still fit enough, were transferred to where their skills were needed next. When their usefulness to the *Reich* had finished, the same fate awaited them: shipment to Auschwitz or some other extermination site to be gassed and cremated.

Auschwitz-Birkenau, a conglomerate of forty sub-camps, was considered both a concentration camp and an extermination camp, sharing this dual status with Majdanek. Of all the Nazi camps, none is more infamous. As well as Jews, it housed a variety of groups: prisoners of war, political prisoners, Polish and other European intellectuals, convicted German and Austrian criminals and gypsies. Jews were transported there from all parts of Europe and most of them were sent immediately to the gas chamber and crematorium, only the fittest being selected by an SS doctor — from 1943, this was often Dr Mengele — who decided who should live and who should die. Temporary survival meant squeezing as much work out of them as possible before they succumbed to weakness and, ultimately, their journey down the *Himmelstrasse* — the "heavenly road" — to the gas chamber. It has been estimated that as many as 1.1 million victims were gassed in Auschwitz from February 1942, 90 per cent of whom were Jews.

The industrial part of Auschwitz added a further dimension to the camp. During the war, IG Farben exploited the forced labour of thousands of Jews as well as other groups, including British POWs, while operating the Buna factory at Monowitz, which is also known as Auschwitz 111. Zyklon B, the main poison gas used in the gas chambers of the extermination camps, was manufactured by an IG Farben subsidiary, Deglesh.

Unlike Auschwitz and Majdanek, Belzec, Chelmno, Sobibor and Treblinka were classed as strictly extermination camps, set up solely for the murder of Jews. Each camp had a few workshops to service the camp's SS contingent and their Ukrainian helpers. All these camps, as well as Auschwitz and Majdanek, were located in occupied Poland.

The Nazis had been developing and perfecting their use of poison gas since their "euthanasia", T4 programme against Germans deemed to be mentally or physically disabled had started in late 1939. With the Final Solution under way the goal was to eliminate as many Jews as quickly and as economically as possible. Each *Vernichtungslager* used a different method of gassing. Although there are no survivors from the gas chambers to tell of the full horror of the Final Solution, descriptions have been given by surviving *Sonderkommandos* — prisoners working on body disposal — of the heaps of tangled corpses which indicate desperate struggles for clean air and life as the gas wafted upwards from the floor. Other witnesses to the mass killings have spoken of the apparent painful deaths that occurred.

Gassing of inmates on a much smaller scale also occurred in the concentration camps of Mauthausen, Sachsenhausen, Ravensbrück, Neuengamme, Stutthof, Natzweiler and Dachau. A chamber was built in Theresienstadt in early 1945 to gas the few remaining survivors although this was never used.

Whatever the scale or method of extermination, inmates were subjected to a standard system of deception during all stages of the murder process so that calm and order could be maintained. Measures were taken to disguise the gas chambers and, when stripped naked for the final act, victims were usually told this was for a "shower" or that they were to be disinfected in preparation for transport to other camps.

The Nazi campaign to exterminate the Jews was pursued systematically, methodically and vigorously; its uniqueness lies in the industrial scale on which it was organised and implemented.

John Lawrence
Austrian Jewish schoolboy, Vienna

My mother's family lived in Oswiecim for well over three hundred years. They had a very large estate and when pictures were first shown on television I saw my family name — Jakob Gross & Sons — crossed out in black paint, at the railway sidings. Almost the whole of that estate was used for the concentration camp as well as Birkenau and all the others that were attached. Oswiecim was a lovely town, a beautiful little place with a river running through it. Every year around Christmas time we used to go there. My uncle was a very generous man and he always fitted us out with a sleigh and Shetland ponies. The last year we were there was December 1937. He said, "Look at the house, it's so big, why don't you come. Hitler is going to march into Austria any day now, come and live here." Thank God we didn't. My uncle was the Mayor of Auschwitz and although a secular Jew, the leader of the Jewish community there. He went to the gas chamber — almost the last man to go in; he refused to give hiding places away, so they took him.

Barbara Stimler
Young Polish Jewish woman, Auschwitz-Birkenau
Before we got to the wagons they gave us bread. In the middle of the wagon there was a barrel with water. We were like sardines. In one corner a young couple were sitting with a baby, warming some milk or water with a candle to give the baby something to drink. The stench in that train! I cannot tell you. It's *impossible* to visualise. We were like animals. I don't know how long we were travelling, from Lodz to Auschwitz is not very far, but I suppose we were going about a day and a night because when we got to Auschwitz it was still dark. They told us to get off the train and leave our luggage, that would come afterwards. They were separating men and women. The screams! Can you imagine when a husband is

205

separated from a wife or a son separated from a mother? It was just *terrible*. I had left my mother behind in the ghetto. I was feeling sick and had diarrhoea. I was in a terrible state. They were counting and counting us. And when it got a little bit lighter, I realised there were wooden barracks with electric wires around them. Then from one of the barracks a girl came out; she had a very short dress, no hair, no shoes. I thought that it was a mental institution. I didn't realise that in about two hours I would look exactly the same.

Maria Ossowski
Young Polish woman, Auschwitz-Birkenau
During the journey, one thing happened which amuses me to this day. Of course we were not given any facilities to attend to our bodily needs. Some of us were carrying parcels, so we had brown paper and we made space in the corner and used the brown paper. Of course it became very smelly. They opened the door at one time. As I was nearest to the door, I took good aim and threw it from the wagon. To my amazement, a German soldier with a bayonet ran after it, held his bayonet up and caught it. I don't have to tell you what happened to his arm and his clothes! That was one of those happenings which really brings a grin to your face whenever you think about it.

Leon Greenman
British Jewish inmate, Auschwitz-Birkenau
The train journey from Westerbork to Auschwitz was about thirty-six hours with no food or drink. We just sat

and gave each other the baby. There wasn't much sleep, you were thinking and dozing off. I said to my wife, "If I don't come back, you may marry again, find a good man who is good for the child." And she said, "If I don't come back, or if I'm ill or something like that, you take a wife who is good for the child."

Helen Stone
Young Polish Jewish woman, Auschwitz-Birkenau
On the way to Auschwitz my father noticed that my mother hadn't got a belt on her dress and he wanted her to look nice. "If you look nice, you look young," he said. And I remember that he gave money to another woman for a belt. He gave it to my mother to put on and she really looked lovely — but *fifty*! That was old then.

Roman Halter
Polish Jewish youth, Auschwitz-Birkenau
There were slits in the boards of the wagon. When we looked through the sun came up through the early morning mist — a lovely sun — and we realised we were in a camp. Suddenly, you could smell the fear inside the compartment and people didn't speak very much, and some of them prayed and others just hugged their nearest and dearest.

Leon Greenman
British Jewish inmate, Auschwitz-Birkenau
We were bullied out of the train and stood about waiting. It must have been about half past two in the

morning. It was dark, a blue light was shining on the platform. We saw a few SS men walking up and down. They separated the men from the women. So I stood right in front of the men and I could see my wife there with the child in her arms. She threw me a kiss and she showed the baby. All of a sudden one of the women ran away from where she was towards her husband, hysterically. Maybe she sensed something. Halfway she was met by an SS officer and he let a club down on her head. She dropped to the ground and he kicked her in the belly. Then one of the prisoners in a striped uniform commanded us to follow him. Well, we turned to the left and walked a little way for two or three minutes. A truck arrived, stopped near us and on the truck were all the women, children, babies and in the centre my wife and child standing up. They stood up to the light as if it was meant to be like that — so that I could recognise them. A picture I'll never forget. All these were supposed to have gone to the bathroom to have a bath, to eat and to live. Instead they had to undress and go into the gas chambers, and two hours later those people were ashes, including my wife and child.

Stephan Kucharek
Polish engine driver, Treblinka
It was only when the supervisor told me that I must take the train to Treblinka that I knew that they brought Jews there. What could I say? Nothing. One had to go. I left half of the train at Malkini and took the other half to Treblinka. Some were freight coaches,

others public like those that came from France. I knew this because this was written on the coaches. I did see the coaches when they were empty and I can't describe what it was like! A mess of shit and piss. One took risks, you know. There was this one occasion, 15 September 1942. It happened at the station in Treblinka. I checked the train and this Jewess gestured to me, she was probably hungry. I had this ham sandwich, but I knew that Jews wouldn't eat anything with ham in it, but reckoned that a hungry person will eat anything. So I got out of the engine, walked over the coals — she was in the first coach behind the engine — well, I simply threw the sandwich and she caught it. But the sons of whores — the Ukrainians — took it away.

Zdenka Ehrlich
Young Czech woman, Auschwitz-Birkenau
The scene around me was full of commotion, people were screaming, crying; there were children, there were dogs, there were the guards beating everybody across the head and screaming, "Out, out, out!" When we all jumped out of the wagons we were put into a long, long column and told to march forward. It was not a station, no platforms, just these barracks, the barbed wire, nowhere else to go — it really was the end of the line. On the right were these creatures in rags, and naked women, I thought: what are they doing here? I will never be like them. Then I saw some men on the other side in striped gear. And in between, all you tried to do was avoid the guards, the sticks and the dogs. So you kept inside the column and marched. You were carried

like a flood, it must have been for a mile. Then, three men in uniform; the uniforms were spotless, the boots were gleaming like mirrors. I'll never forget the impression of the man in the middle, Dr Mengele, I just glanced at him; he was very good looking. Not a menacing face at all, rather . . . not benevolent, but not menacing. I remember his boots were so shiny, he was absolutely immaculate. He had white gloves on, not exactly like a traffic policeman, but a sign of distinction and importance. He lifted his hand as he looked at everybody who marched past him and just made a very slow gesture, a very light gesture and said, "right, left, left, left, right left, right . . ."

They put us in a huge room to count — five, five, five. Straight afterwards a woman with a whip chased us into the next room, there were mountains, but *mountains* of rags. Clothing that you had never seen, not even in theatrical wardrobes — Fellini would be pleased to have the imagination to put together the things that we saw. Behind each mountain of these rags was a guard, a woman guard, always with a whip. We had to run in front of it, she grabbed something and threw it at you. The next pile were shoes, men's, women's, everything together. A pair was grabbed and flung at you. So what I finished up with was the most extraordinary outfit you can imagine: I got an olive green ball gown of light material with pearls on it and an irregular hemline — it was like something from a Chekhov or Dostoyevsky play — and a short coat which had probably belonged to a ten-year-old girl, and shoes which saved my life. They were a pair of men's ballroom black patent shoes, huge. In this outfit I left the building and in this outfit I survived the war.

Helen Pelc
Young Polish Jewish woman, Auschwitz-Birkenau
We were told to take our clothes off, they stripped us. We had to leave everything. Here in my ear is this big hole — they couldn't take my earring out quickly enough. After this, the showers; then we had to stand naked with arms up in the air, and they shaved you everywhere. Then you went out the other side and they chucked you a bundle: I had wooden clogs and a long dress that I couldn't walk about in. I was calling my mother. I hardly recognised her, nor her me because we had no hair; and I had a head of lovely red hair! They would search you everywhere: our mouths, our ears, the women's private parts and poked about. Good gracious — how *could* this little lipstick of my mother's have survived! How could she have done it? Where was it hidden? It was so small, this little lipstick, about one inch and a quarter. But later that little lipstick was very useful.

Roman Halter
Polish Jewish youth, Auschwitz-Birkenau
There was this big trough of disinfectant which looked like iodine and we had to submerge ourselves in that. If we didn't submerge fully, a SS would stand on you with their boots until even our heads were submerged. With the rough shaving we'd had, anyone who was cut suffered tremendously because it stung so badly. Then

211

we were moved to showers with water. After getting uniforms, we were given numbers and then taken to our blocks. The women were not put in the women's block, but in this big block next to us. The *Kapos* and their deputies came to rape the women at night and there were terrible screams and groans coming from that block, and the husbands in our block wept because they could understand the shouts. It was a free-for-all, a sort of reward for the criminals, the German psychopaths who were sent to Auschwitz-Birkenau and who were in charge of the blocks.

Jan Hartman
Czech Jewish youth, Auschwitz-Birkenau

We got into a barrack, it was night; and there in that barrack we must have been well over a thousand or more. The people were standing in such a way that we couldn't sit down, for hours we were standing. And I remember not very far from me somebody who must have had a religious disposition, a deep voice, kind of preaching that this was a trial, that we have to get through it; this is proof that we are worth something and to stand up, and so on. In those heavy circumstances, he tried to lift the people and tell them they would survive. Who knows who he was, but I remember that after hours and hours of standing, the whole barrack, thousands of people, were able to sit down on each other's knees. Then, for the first time I started to be aware that I was in the Birkenau part of Auschwitz-Birkenau, a huge place, kilometres, kilometres.

Anna Bergman
Young Czech woman, Auschwitz-Birkenau

I was with a friend whose parents were in the same transport but had been sent to the other side during the selection by Mengele. When we got into our barrack, she asked the women already there, "Where are my parents? When will I see them again?" And they all started screaming with laughter, "You stupid idiot, they are in the chimney by now!" We thought they were mad, and they thought we were mad.

Jan Hartman
Czech Jewish youth, Auschwitz-Birkenau

The next part was getting my number tattooed. Two young slaves — I would describe them that way — came along; one of them had a book, a typical German book, nineteenth-century type, nothing in it but numbers. And the other one took a pen and bottle of ink and with this, very quickly and adroitly, tattooed us. In Terezin nobody asked your name but the boys and other people knew who I was. But in Auschwitz you became a number, you didn't know anybody. The only person I knew was my brother, we stuck together.

What struck me about the camp was the smell. By then we knew it was an extermination camp: we saw chimneys and the fire was very high. "You go through the chimney" — that was the standard saying. I never heard about the gas chambers, so I didn't know how people were killed. But we saw the chimneys and we associated the flames with the transports coming in . . .

213

there was the smell of human flesh being burnt, a certain smell, it was the air. Also, the air was not clean: you were breathing the dead. Another thing was the water pools; some days it had been raining and you would see how the water was coated with a matt film of ashes, greenish-grey. By that time I knew what it was.

Michael Honey

Czech Jewish youth, Auschwitz-Birkenau

The *Sonderkommando* (special Jewish crews forced to work in the gas chambers and crematoria) foreman told me, "We have to empty the gas chamber by loading the bodies onto trolleys, rail trolleys like you use on building sites. You have to heave them onto these trolleys because they are not flat trolleys, they are tipper trucks. So we have to heave them high into these tipper trucks then by rail take them to the crematorium where they are burnt. There are rows of ovens, each oven is big enough to take three. So we take a fat man or a fat woman, a smaller person and a child. This is how we save fuel. The fat of the fat person helps to burn the others." He said the hardest thing is to dispose of those who come from the camp and die of natural causes because they are so emaciated, there is no fat on them. They take so much fuel that the Germans stop the burning and leave the bones on the plate so that the next lot will burn the bones until there are only ashes left.

John Fink
German Jewish youth, Buna-Monowitz, Auschwitz-Birkenau

There was this satellite camp of Auschwitz — Auschwitz 111 — which was actually a labour camp. I worked in Buna where the IG Farben industry was located. There they were making soap and other things from coal, but the main product was artificial gasoline, or petrol. The firm had to pay the SS for each slave labourer and naturally they only wanted people who could work. They worked them to death because how long could you labour with just the little bit of food we were given! I was assigned to a small electricians' *Kommando*. We were a small group, only twenty men. In fact there were only two real electricians; the others were what you would call "*Lager* (camp) electricians" — they were smart enough to say they were electricians in order to save their lives. I was a tradesman, used to a hard life, but there were professional people there — university educated people like doctors and lawyers who had lived very well in normal circumstances, but in those conditions, they couldn't stand up to it. If you couldn't work that was the reason to be beaten and taken away.

Premsyl Dobias
Sudeten Czech inmate, Mauthausen

We were taken to the *Appellplatz* and were told which *Kommandos* (labour battalions) we would be working in. I was horrified that I was taken to the granite quarry — that was the worst kind of work in that particular

215

camp. There was only one thing worse and that was the so-called *Strafkompanie* (punishment company). The *Strafkompanie* had a red circle under their number and that meant they were special prisoners, most of them were annihilated after several days. In the morning we had to run and form up under the number of our barrack. We were counted, and when it was established that all the numbers agreed, that there was nobody missing, we had to form *Kommandos* under certain *Kapos* and we were taken to the granite quarry.

We were the first outside the camp, through the big gate, and we were passing groups of SS because they were stationed on each side of the road to the quarry. While we were passing, we were hit by rifles. When we came down the road we suddenly saw the granite quarry underneath us. We had to run so fast that most of us lost our clogs and had to run barefoot on awfully sharp granite stones which were so painful that we screamed with pain. Our feet were bleeding and many of us got infections from the dirt and very soon died. When we came to the top of the hundred and eighty steps, down at intervals were the SS and as we passed they were hitting us. We were coming down eight abreast, nobody wanted to be on the sides of course. While we were running down, being chased, many prisoners fell on the irregular steps. When they fell, they knocked over some of the prisoners in front like cards or dominoes. Prisoners were falling down the stairs, hitting themselves while the SS were standing there laughing.

Alfred Huberman
Polish Jewish youth, Skarzysko-Kamienna

We arrived and were sent to Work C which was an ammunition factory. This was July 1942 and I stayed until October 1944 which I imagine is a record — the survival rate was three or four months. Most of the time I worked on boring holes in shells. TNT, a yellow stuff which looks like semolina when it's dry, was melted in big boilers, then put in buckets and then poured into shells. Women would stand with copper needles and mix it up to get rid of any air bubbles. Then the shells were taken into little cubicles where holes were bored to fit the detonator. I stood in one of those cubicles and when the hot TNT solidified, I bored the holes out. The dust would come out on your face, and ate into your lungs, and you became yellow with it. We worked on twelve-hour shifts. Work C was the worst place, the survival rate was very poor and thousands died there.

In that camp we had Ukrainian guards and they were ghastly, worse than the Germans. They stood on the watchtowers and sometimes shot at people just like target practice. There was one, and if you displeased him and you were working on the railway line, he'd put your neck on the line and stand quite casually on it until you suffocated. They had the freedom to do what they liked, they were always anti-Russian and anti-Jewish.

217

Abram "Adam" Bulwa
Polish Jewish youth, Dora
There were over 30,000 people working in Dora on the V2 (*Vergeltungswaffe 2* — the "reprisal weapon 2") missile. The food was terrible: two ounces of bread a day and on Sunday a special treat of tea without milk, and that was it. We had to work twelve hours a day — 7a.m. until 7p.m. — and we had to walk about two miles from work to the camp, led by SS and their guard dogs. Every few days as we were led out we saw fifty men hanged on each side with a band playing German music. They said it was due to sabotage, but this was just normal practice. We used to pass the crematorium going to and from work and thousands of bodies were lined up outside to be burnt. This was regular, normal. If you didn't get used to the conditions, you were a goner. Dora was the most terrible place on earth, I'll never forget it. I have nightmares about that camp today.

Dr Helmut Kübler
Luftwaffe General Staff, Nordhausen
I had to go to the camp at Nordhausen where the V2 was built. As we got there, a work gang was marching for relief in the bunker and I had the impression that they were doing good nutrition-wise; they looked completely nourished, red-cheeked. Of course they were prisoners and had to do what the guards demanded of them, what is otherwise expected of prisoners, especially during those times when those who weren't prisoners didn't have anything to eat! I

had the impression that they were doing well. Recently I read another article; I think that today's propaganda is ridiculous, written by someone who hasn't the foggiest.

Premsyl Dobias
Sudeten Czech inmate, Mauthausen

Not many of us are alive who remember the cruel murdering of Jewish prisoners in 1942 in that granite quarry. I witnessed it. While we were working underneath the granite quarry, we noticed high up above on a very sheer cliff there was some gathering of prisoners. We were asked to clear a part underneath. We knew subsequently that the people murdered were Jewish because when we saw them dead at the bottom we noticed the mark of the Star of David on their jackets.

Suddenly we noticed that a prisoner was thrown down the sheer rock, he hit the side, we could see blood and he fell right down to the bottom where there was a little lake or pond. While we were watching, horrified, we noticed that on the top there was a circle of SS behind the prisoners. The prisoners were pushed close to the rim and as we looked, the one behind was forced to push the person in front down until their turn came. This was down a sheer rock about one hundred feet I would say, and they drowned in the lake. There is now a memorial at the lake commemorating the action. The Nazis at the time laughed that the ones thrown to their deaths were "parachutists".

Taube Biber
Young Polish Jewish woman, Plaszow

One day Amon Goeth, the *Kommandant*, wasn't satisfied with the work we did in the different workshops, it wasn't enough. He was a bloodthirsty beast and he called an *Appell* (roll call). We were standing in fives, and suddenly we saw these enormous tables with all the soldiers standing around. And as Goeth was passing, he selected twenty-five young girls and twenty-five lashes were given on their backs. When it was over and we went back to the barrack and we saw these girls all black and blue and with their blood running, we just yelled. We weren't human any more — the yelling, the screaming, the crying!

The Germans got to know about the children hidden in our barrack. They handled it in a very nice way: a nursery would be arranged for when the women were working. We were standing on *Appell* one day — always in the most tragic moments, the music was blaring — on this occasion it was "Everything passes"; and we were waiting, waiting, standing for hours. Suddenly we saw a lorry with all the children on it; next to me stood a mother with twins of eleven, and those poor girls were crying, "Mother, mother! They're taking us away." And they did, the children disappeared.

Josef Perl
Czech Jewish youth, Plazow

The *Kommandant*, Amon Goeth, was a sadist. He used to have a little balcony and his greatest pleasure was to shoot people from the balcony. If he didn't kill twenty

220

or thirty people before breakfast, he didn't enjoy breakfast. He never talked to the prisoners, he just shot them. He had a beautiful white horse looked after by a Jew who used to train horses, he also had two big dogs and they were trained to tear a person in half in ten seconds, he never went anywhere without them. One day I was on a job making cement. I would mix it with sand, put it in a bucket and give it to the person filling gaps under the huts. I was filling the bucket and all of a sudden I saw two white hooves in front of me. I looked up and Goeth took this stick and hit me across the face with it: "Nobody looks at me!" When he went the *Kapo* came over to me and said, "He spoke to you, you should be dead now." I thought, "I must get away from here."

Premsyl Dobias
Sudeten Czech inmate, Mauthausen

We were working on another *Kommando* when two SS with machine guns came over. They appeared to be very friendly. Pointing to a nearby farm, they said, "We are going to form a new *Kommando* for that farm over there, to feed pigs." We need prisoners who first of all must speak German, and they must be from an agricultural community." Well, everybody wanted to feed pigs. I suddenly saw that my chance for survival had come — I could stay indoors and could even eat with the pigs. So my hand went up and some Spanish prisoners, who also spoke German, volunteered as well. The volunteers formed a line and the SS went from one to another asking questions. When they came to me I said that I was born on a farm and was used to feeding pigs. Obviously it wasn't true, but I lied because I wanted to save my life.

There were about twenty-six volunteers and they only wanted twenty. So they went back through the lines and pushed some back. When he came to me, he pushed me out of the line. I immediately put my hand up and said, "I am strong and I come from a farm." The SS came and kicked me in my genitals, but as I saw the foot coming, I turned round and he kicked me on the side and pushed me back. I was out. They counted twenty and said, "Turn right and march up to the farm, we start immediately." We others had to go back and start working again.

Tears were running from my eyes because I thought my chance of survival had gone and I was bleeding from that painful kick. Suddenly we stopped, petrified. We heard the sounds of two machine-guns. As soon as the prisoners crossed the invisible line of the camp, they were mown down by machine-guns from the turrets. They were dead, lying there. I could have been one of them. The SS started to laugh and they turned back and ran towards us. "Who else knows how to feed pigs?" I shall never forget that as long as I live: shot while trying to escape.

Antonie Krokova
Czech gypsy child, Lety

It was late afternoon and we were free in the camp and my sisters were with us. Most of my sisters were older, eighteen, nineteen years old. They stuck together, these poor girls, because mum wasn't alive any more. And the two cops were standing there with another two on the side, and one came up and started chatting to them. We watched as he chatted to them, right? He was looking at my sister and suddenly he grabbed her and she pushed him away. Then this other guy started, and my sisters were defending one another. Then the third came and pulled my sisters apart. He was a strong guy, you cannot beat a strong guy — it wasn't allowed anyway. So he slapped her a couple of times, and threw her on the ground. They were trying to keep us away, we were crying and they forced us back. And we ran to tell what was happening, calling the names of our sisters. Our dad ran that way and he caught one of them. The other man saw that and shot him dead. My brother ran there too, he was fourteen then and he got shot too. So they shot all four of them dead: my sisters, my dad and my brother. They dragged them away and that was it. We had to keep quiet. We weren't allowed to cry either because they threatened that they would shoot us too.

Magdalena Kusserow Reuter

German Jehovah's Witness child, Ravensbrück

When I arrived I met a Jehovah's Witness friend from Bad Lippespring, and we were happy to see each other. Then I was taken to the block for Jehovah's Witnesses — Block 17. About two days later they called me to the *Kommandant* who had a big Bible on his desk. He opened the Bible at Romans, "Read this." And it was written about how everybody should obey and so on.

223

He asked me, "Why don't you obey?" I said "*Herr Kommandant*, we have to read the *whole* chapter to explain this. Just one verse I cannot explain." He then gave me a talk for half an hour in his Bavarian dialect which I didn't even understand. Then he dismissed me, "Go back to your sisters, you stay here in the concentration camp."

Steven Frank
Dutch Jewish child, Westerbork, Holland

Suddenly in September 1943, the German Army came into Barneveld camp and we had about half an hour to pack our belongings. We were being sent to Westerbork. Transport there was in a normal carriage. This was a completely different place, suddenly we had this enormous number of people there from all walks of life, mostly Dutch but some Germans too. The camp was situated in eastern Holland, in heathland in a woodland clearing, surrounded by a barbed wire fence about six feet high and a moat with dirty turquoise-blue water in it. Outside the fence were sentry boxes on stilts with German guards and searchlights; the railway line went into the middle of the camp. Suddenly things changed completely; we were out of our privileged environment into the reality of what the Germans were doing to Dutch Jewry.

Pretty soon I learnt to be streetwise. I remember once I was zipping around the edge of this building and I came face to face with two guards with an Alsatian dog. They let the dog off the leash and he came bounding up to me and started biting me. I put my arms up and was bitten on my arms and legs. I can still hear them laughing — they thought it was a bit of sport, then suddenly they got bored with it and called the dog off. After that if I got to blind corner, I'd stop and look around it before proceeding. You learned to look after yourself.

Stanley Faull
Polish Jewish youth, Majdanek

When we entered Majdanek, the area we were taken in looked very, very vast. But I was young and it looked to me like a holiday camp because you saw a number of buildings with a very big square in the middle. As we went in, I remember seeing very young children taken with their mothers on one side. I was then old enough to be selected for work in 1943, and having by then got the certification that I was an "engineer", I was an important person so far as the German authorities were concerned. This was my first camp away from my parents and I found my feet as it were. But I was very fortunate because after a few days, I was detailed to go to the kitchen. That saved my life because it meant that I could work and eat. My job was to take the soup out in the big containers, bring the empties back in again and clean up in the kitchen. It was a ten-hour job every day, but it was warm, the food was there and I was fit enough to enjoy it. If you became ill, the "hospital" was really a staging area for the gas chamber as there were no doctors or nurses and very little medicine. So one had to keep fit in order to survive: food was number

225

one, clothing number two and then to keep away from trouble.

There were three executions during my time in Majdanek. By that time I understood that these people had tried to escape from working parties outside the camp and that the penalty was death, and we all had to see what would happen to us if we tried to run away. So they were taken up and publicly executed. This was really a psychological thing, "Don't run away." Also, the place was situated in a marshland and there was nowhere to run to and the Poles could get a reward for picking people up and taking them to the police. Also, at that time it seemed normal to me that if you did something wrong, you're going to get hung. Now had I been older and known what normality really was, I would think it inhumane to do it without judge or jury, but when you're very young and you don't know what is normal, then you accept this is the right thing. This is one of the reasons I survived: because I couldn't differentiate between normality and abnormality. My job was to try to survive, to force myself above what I was seeing.

Kitty Hart-Moxon
Young Polish Jewish woman, Auschwitz-Birkenau
I realised first of all that the camp had its own language and I was at an advantage because I could understand it: it was part German, part Yiddish, part Polish. You had to have the language to find your way around. And it had its own expressions: the most important was to "organise". This was a universal word for barter —

to buy, to sell, to get food. And if you lived by this principle, you learnt how to get around certain situations — to try to get into a better work party, for instance. There were work parties where you couldn't survive and you had to get away from those. The better work parties were those that were within the camp compound. Those outside were a disaster because you were exposed to the elements, you were beaten, you had to walk to work in all conditions, in the rain and snow in winter, in the heat in summer. But if you could work under cover somewhere, then you were immediately at an advantage: work in the kitchen was a tremendous advantage, sorting out clothes another; if you could work in the hospital compound, you were at an advantage. There were also people you had to get away from, people you should not associate with. The key to survival was instant adjustment, and having the sixth sense of where danger came from; and finding a way of being totally invisible, hiding behind the crowds so that your face would never be known to anyone in charge — the people that were most feared. Those were the sorts of things you had to learn and I'm afraid if you didn't learn these within the first few days, you were doomed.

Maria Ossowski
Young Polish woman, Auschwitz-Birkenau
The misfortune of the Greek girls was that they didn't know any other language than Greek; they couldn't speak Yiddish or German, and that made their life a

double misery because you had to understand what all the shouting was about, and the shouting was all in German. I remember they were still quite lovely because they were fresh arrivals in May 1943 and they were singing beautiful songs. They didn't last long, not only the lack of food and hard work, but the climate took its toll and they perished extremely, *extremely* quickly. I remember how, once, one of those Greek girls out on a *Kommando* was so ill she had fallen somewhere in the ditch and nobody spotted her. The whole camp was standing for three hours or more because if one was missing on the *Appell* (roll call), the posse went out to search for the missing person. In the end they found her, they dragged her into the camp and set the dogs on her. And this is how she died. That was the day I spat into the face of my God. But I recovered later because you had to have something better to believe in than what was around you.

Josef Perl
Czech Jewish youth, Auschwitz-Birkenau
When we arrived at Auschwitz, we were seasoned, experienced concentration camp people, already in our striped uniforms. I was a *big* child, I looked about nineteen or twenty, and I decided in order to stay alive, I would volunteer for everything. If they wanted volunteers I was there: whether to fetch food, carry bodies, whatever, I was there. The thing was that you couldn't show yourself for long; if you were too exposed you didn't last. Just imagine: you are

228

walking along and you're sticking in the mud, then you lose your shoes! If you lose your shoes, you lose your *life*. I can't begin to explain the *fear*, the heartbeating, and the gauntlet we had to run.

Freddie Knoller
Austrian Jewish youth, Auschwitz-Birkenau

I was always, and still am today, the eternal optimist. I was able to talk to myself and say: I will get out of this mess; I *will* get out of this ordeal and I'll be able to tell the world what has happened here; I must survive, and I will survive. I believe this optimism saved me, because I saw other people who gave up, who did not wash themselves, did not take care of themselves properly. In winter I undressed in the open, washed my body every morning. I think because of this attitude and my eternal optimism, I was able to survive. Once you give up, you are a goner, you are finished.

Michael Etkind
Polish Jewish youth, Auschwitz-Birkenau

The name *Muselmann* was well known. It referred to those who had given up the will to live. Hunger and despair, the giving up of hope, something about the eyes, something about the way these people walked, dragging their feet with their heads lowered down. Once you looked into their eyes, you could see quite clearly that they hadn't got long to live.

Freddie Knoller
Austrian Jewish youth, Auschwitz-Birkenau
The organising of food was the most important thing, I learned a lot from the Polish Jews who were the best organisers in the camp. There was a sort of black market where we exchanged things. I sold a slice of bread for a bowl of soup. With that bowl of soup I went somewhere else and said, "Come on, give me two slices of bread for this." And somehow or other we organised ourselves in this way. Some people who were working in the kitchen came and sold potatoes on the black market on which we had to spend quite a bit of bread. There was a tremendous amount of activity so far as food was concerned.

Ignacz Rüb
Hungarian Jewish electrician, Buna-Monowitz, Auschwitz-Birkenau
Every four people had a loaf of bread and this had to be divided. We had no knives, only spoons with one side sharpened on stones for cutting. It was always very difficult to divide the bread equally — always quarrels, fighting and screaming. Suddenly I had this idea: a simple, wooden stick arrangement with strings to weigh the bread equally. Everybody used it and things became very calm and quiet. A few weeks later, two SS men came in and asked me if I had made it. I said, yes. I thought they would give me more food because it was such a very wonderful thing. But I had such a beating with a rubber cable, even to this day it still hurts. But the idea was transferred from one camp to another, all

the camps used it; it was so simple, anyone could make it.

Alfred Huberman
Polish Jewish youth, Skarzysko-Kamienna
Really, it became the law of the jungle, you couldn't afford to be nice to others. I remember coming across three Greek Jewish brothers and they used to pinch each others' bread ration. There were no standards: no right and wrong, you just looked after yourself if you could.

Kurt Klappholz
Polish Jewish youth, Blechhammer
The cooks would dole out the soup from barrels and as you got to the bottom of the barrel, the soup got thicker; people would play these strategic games to position themselves in the line in order to get the soup at the bottom of the barrel. You then came back with your soup: was it thick or was it thin? How many pieces of meat did you find? Now some orthodox Jews would take out the pieces of meat and give them, or trade them, with somebody else; from the *kosher* (ritually clean) point of view it made no sense because the fact that meat had entered the soup meant it was no longer *kosher*.

Clare Parker
Hungarian Jewish child, Mauthausen
In Mauthausen on our way back from work we were allowed to stop and the Germans would sit down and

the dogs too, and we were eating grass — clover and shamrock . . . Another thing, I would take the crunched up paper from the mattress we had, and smooth it out and draw on it. And I would draw a plate of food and someone would say, "Oh, can you draw nice sliced bread?" They were going crazy for food. It was always in your mind. Or an apple, I would draw that if they wanted. We were constantly thinking about food.

Anna Bergman
Young Czech woman, Auschwitz-Birkenau

To go to the latrines! There were twenty in one row and twenty in another, all under one roof, so you can imagine what it looked like and what it smelled of. And we would be there doing what we had to do, and the SS poked us with long poles on our behinds as we sat, we didn't have time to do what we had to do — it was awful. And the selection parades in front of Dr Mengele and company! Totally naked, you never knew where to put your hands. I once heard him say, "This time very good material," as if cattle were sent to the slaughter house and this time of good quality. We weren't treated like humans. We weren't human.

Kitty Hart-Moxon
Young Polish Jewish woman, Auschwitz-Birkenau

Men were at a tremendous advantage because many were in their twenties and thirties and they had professions, and the Germans needed their skills in the camp — there were locksmiths, carpenters, builders, bricklayers, tailors — the Germans prized these very much. There were also professional people: doctors, pharmacists. Now the women were mostly teenage girls; older women were not allowed into the camp; first of all they were of child-bearing age so they may have been pregnant and of course no pregnant woman was allowed to live. Then, many women came in with their children and since no children were allowed to live, all women and children were taken straight to the gas chambers. And then the women in their twenties and thirties didn't have any particular profession, they were of no use to the Germans so they went straight to the gas chambers. Therefore most of the women that came into the camp were teenage girls without skills, perhaps they were nurses, but you didn't need any special skills to be a nurse in Auschwitz. Therefore, the teenage girls were used for manual labour and of course the death toll was very high. Having said that, the girls were stronger mentally, they were not prone to depression as I believe the men were. They looked after one another, they formed little families. I was a strong believer that you couldn't survive on your own; you guarded, you fought for your friends the same way you fought for your own life. Men tended to survive alone and this was a very difficult thing to do.

Anna Bergman
Young Czech woman, Auschwitz-Birkenau
They didn't know I was pregnant in Auschwitz which was marvellous because that would have been the end. My little boy who died in Terezin, saved my life *and* my

233

unborn daughter's life because, had I arrived with him in my arms, we would both have gone to the gas chambers.

Helen Stone
Young Polish Jewish woman, Auschwitz-Birkenau

Our menstruation had stopped in Auschwitz; but now I am going to tell you how I got my period. I was working in the sewing *Kommando*. One day I was walking on the *Lagerstrasse* — on the main road. On the electric poles men were working, also prisoners. In front of me, not far, a *Blockälteste* (block supervisor) was walking; they were all dressed beautifully, with dresses straight from the people who had just come; she really looked very nice. And these men on the poles, they started whistling after her. And I remember I just laughed a little bit.

But then I thought, "Why don't they look at me?" I passed — not a whistle, not a word. Nothing. And why was I so annoyed about it? But it was like a pleasant sort of annoyance. It was somehow *human*. It was normal. And I came back to my block. I had the bunk on the third layer, on top. And by the top bunk was a little window there beneath the roof and I could see my face in it. I looked horrible. I had about an inch of hair then, it was standing up like a hedgehog. I put my scarf on and took a little bit of hair in front out. And I pulled out a string from the sacking that was on top of the straw and I made a belt on the black dress that was about five sizes too big and it looked much better.

When I came down some of the girls said, "Hey, you look nice!"

Something was waking up in me; that was the evening I got my period. That was jealousy, the jealous fact that they had whistled after that woman who looked beautiful, and they didn't even *look* at me. Like I was just a stone. Emotion did it: jealousy and the will to look prettier, like a woman.

Martin Hoffman
Czech Jewish youth, Buna-Monowitz, Auschwitz-Birkenau
I was out on a *Kommando*. The *Kapo* seemed quite nice to me and he said to me when we got there, "You don't have to do the hard work, you can stay in the hut." One day he came in and locked the door and started undressing me. I fought back and wouldn't agree and then I started screaming. There was a tremendous banging on the door and he promptly let me put my clothes on and opened the door and standing there was a Polish engineer who was working in the factory. I was rather depressed, but I was afraid to say anything to anybody about it. The next day I was so unhappy that I decided I wasn't going to *Appell* and I hid myself in the barrack. There was a tremendous alarm and searches and eventually they found me and I was brought to the camp leader. I was asked various questions and beaten absolutely senseless. I was blue and black and completely unconscious. I had marks all over me.

Leon Greenman
British Jewish inmate, Buna-Monowitz, Auschwitz-Birkenau

There was one *Kapo* called Schiller who used to bully a lot. He had one of the young fellows who was about sixteen and used to work with us. Then he stopped working and we found he was better dressed and had a happier face, and he would shy away from us when we got too near. He was being used by Schiller. I never noticed it until one night I was lying there after lights out and I heard Schiller say in German, "Not so, but so, yes, so is good." Then the lights went on — probably by one of the other *Kapos* — and Schiller was standing straight up on the top bed and the young fellow was standing opposite him. That's the only time. I thought, "Well, well . . ."

Kitty Hart-Moxon
Young Polish Jewish woman, Auschwitz-Birkenau

Canada represented a country of wealth and I think this is why they named this particular *Kommando* the *Kanada Kommando*, because of the abundance of everything there. It was formed to sort out all the possessions of the people who were brought in from all over Europe. The suitcases from the ramp would be collected and emptied into big piles. We, the girls, were subdivided into different groups. I was on night shift the whole eight months I was there and my prime occupation was to sort men's jackets. So I had to go to this huge pile and sort out men's jackets, then place these on a trestle table and feel all the seams for hidden objects. Very often we had to open the seams and if we felt any objects we had to take them out. Very often at the end of the shift we would collect a bucket full of jewellery, or bank notes, or whatever was hidden in the jackets.

I remember once I was sorting out women's corsets and in no time at all I filled a bucket full of jewellery. After this the jackets or corsets would have to be folded into bundles — there was a quota you had to do in a certain period. It was arranged that we could take ordinary third-rate clothing which they wouldn't want for transportation to Germany, back into the camp, and at the same time we would smuggle valuables that we knew could be used for bartering or saving other people's lives. Very often I'd go into the camp wearing five or six layers of clothes with various objects pinned on my back and would smuggle these back into the camp.

Anita Lasker-Wallfisch
German Jewish cellist, women's orchestra, Auschwitz-Birkenau

What I remember about arriving in Auschwitz, June 1943, was a lot of noise, a lot of dogs barking, screaming, shouting and waiting all night for something — we didn't know what. Then when morning came we were shoved in another barrack and all the ceremony was started: you know, the hair was shaved, the number tattooed and your clothes were taken off you. All this was done by prisoners, not SS people. Auschwitz was run by the inmates, the SS were on the fringe, but the

237

actual work was done by the inmates. The person who processed me asked a lot of questions: What is going on outside? How is the war going? Where do you come from? What do you do?

I told her where I came from and for some reason I said that I played the cello. "Oh," she said, "that's fantastic! Stand here to the side." Everybody else was going through and I was still standing there ... I waited and waited and I didn't know what I was waiting for. I knew the gas chamber looked like a shower room and I *was* in a shower room — I thought: that's probably *it*. But it wasn't, because into this room marched a lady who introduced herself as Alma Rosé who was the conductor of the camp orchestra. She was the daughter of Arnold Rosé, a very well-known musician, and the niece of Gustav Mahler. She was highly delighted that a cello-playing individual had arrived because they didn't have any cellists at the time. So she said, "Fantastic that you are here, where did you study?"

I mean it was a totally ridiculous situation: I didn't have a stitch of clothing on, just a toothbrush in my hand — to be discussing where I studied the cello and how delighted she was that I was there! Now I hadn't touched the cello for two years and I asked for five minutes' practice time and then played her something. And I became a member of the famous orchestra. I was very fortunate to be in this orchestra — I mean everything is relative in life — but it was paradise compared to life if you weren't in the orchestra.

Alma Rosé was a remarkable lady, a very strong personality, a very dignified person. The few of us who survived are well aware that we can thank Alma for it. This orchestra had to be very good — she was used to high standards from her father and she was dead set that we must play very well. She was very strict, a disciplinarian and God forbid if you play a wrong note! We were often furious with her, but better to be furious than to realise what was going on around us. She put blinkers on us and she had put blinkers on herself. "You must play these stupid pieces so well that we could play them to my father," she would say. When something was really acceptable she said, "This is good enough for my father to hear." So we had this concentration on music rather than looking out of the window to where the gas chambers were.

Our job was to play marches in the morning and in the evening at the camp gate as the people went out — there were lots of factories around there: Buna and IG Farben — and thousands marched out to work, and they marched to music. So we did that in the mornings and in the evenings, and in the day we went back into the block and all sorts of music was obtained and we had a whole team of people copying out the music after it had been orchestrated — that's how a whole group of people were saved through being copyists. And then we learnt these pieces and played for the amusement of the Germans: they would come in and want to hear some music, especially after selections when they were quite worn out from their efforts of selecting people to go to the gas chamber.

Edith Baneth
Young Czech woman, Auschwitz-Birkenau

We were put in front of the main gate of Auschwitz with the famous *"Arbeit Macht Frei"* (work brings freedom) and in front of that the orchestra was playing the very well-known music of Strauss — all the SS were there watching us. We were standing there for quite a long time listening to the music, and suddenly humanity came back to us listening to the music which we knew from normal days of life. And we all started to cry, not because we thought we were going to the gas chambers, but the emotion of listening to normal music. I shall never forget that feeling: it wasn't the fear of going to death — that was something expected — it was rather the last moment of . . . oh, there used to be a life before all this! This music brought it back to us.

Harry Lowit
Czech Jewish child, Auschwitz-Birkenau

Kramer was the SS *Kommandant* of the Birkenau *Familienlager* (Czech family camp) and I became his messenger. I was quite a nice-looking child and I suppose that is why I was chosen for this messenger business. I got a special uniform which was a close-fitting black jacket with the black band which had *"Läufer"* (messenger) on it, and riding breeches and boots that were always highly polished. I was told to be pleasing to the eye when I worked for the Germans. I didn't have special accommodation but I was treated better because once I became a messenger to Kramer, he would send me to different parts of the camps with

240

messages. I was getting better food and I could take food from the kitchen and give it to my friends.

When I was moved to Auschwitz camp, I was actually given the job of raising and lowering that bar underneath the arch with *"Arbeit Macht Frei"* — literally, "work brings freedom", on it. I would stand there in summer and winter in my breeches and close-fitting jacket with the black band with silver *"Läufer"* writing on it, and that was my job. And while I was there I ran messages for Höss, although I didn't have much to do with him, not like Kramer. I saw Dr Mengele when running messages to him as he was making selections with his cigarette: flick right to live, flick left to die. I would also go to the crematorium and that would make me one of the very few people who actually went in and came out alive. That was quite a traumatic time because that's when I started to see a lot of bestiality.

Alfred Huberman
Polish Jewish youth, Rehmsdorf
People in the barracks used to talk sometimes about their families. Whether it was make-believe or trying to divert their minds, there was a lot of boasting about how well off they were before the war. They would try to outdo one another. To me it didn't mean anything. I was always one of the youngest. Somebody would tell of how big a house he had or what business he had, and somebody else would try to do better. I remember in Skarzysko, there was a medical doctor and his thing was to spout Polish poetry and some of it was quite

filthy. It was some means of diverting themselves from that situation.

Josef Perl
Czech Jewish youth, Buchenwald
Half of our block was for Hungarian and Czechs and the other half for Poles. Poles always thought they were more sophisticated than the Hungarians and Czechs. We were all in the same bloody hole, but we were the lower class and they the upper class.

Leon Greenman
British Jewish inmate, Buna-Monowitz, Auschwitz-Birkenau
When nobody was looking, I pushed my shovel into a bag of cement and it would pour open. I felt it was sabotage against them. Others did it too and the next morning you came to the work place and there were bags and bags and bags all broken on purpose. Bricks were also broken for the same reason.

Alfred Huberman
Polish Jewish youth, Szarzysko-Kamienna
When I was working in Work C, the ammunition factory, I noticed there were two buttons by the machine that you stood by to bore the two holes in the shells, and I noticed once by accident, that if you switched it on and off quickly, the machine had to be repaired by an engineer. That became a habit with me until somebody warned me to be careful and not to overdo it. Also, when we bored those two holes in the

shells, we had a measuring device so that the detonator would fit exactly, so if those holes were defective the shells wouldn't explode; and if the women didn't mix the liquid long enough, or well enough, then the air bubbles would also affect them.

Freddie Knoller
Austrian Jewish youth, Auschwitz-Birkenau

The three boys came pale-faced out of the bunker with their hands tied at the back. They were marched to the gallows and we all had to stand at attention and watch them walking up the steps on to the gallows. The amazing thing is that one of them was courageous enough to shout down to us before the trap door opened. *"Kamaraden, wir sind die Letzen!"* — "Comrades, we are the last ones." Then the next one to him shouted down, *"Es lebe die Freiheit!"* — "Long live Liberty!" This was really a defiance that we had never experienced from prisoners. The SS man who operated the trapdoor got all red in the face and the *Kommandant* shouted, *"Los!"* — move — and the trapdoor opened and the three boys were hanged. This defiance gave us courage. Some of us were shouting — strictly against the rules — *"Shalom!"* And immediately the SS raised their guns towards us. Then we were taken, marched past the three bodies hanging there. We were proud of those three heroes for defying the murderers that were hanging them.

RESISTANCE

They were not led like sheep to the slaughter; they were taken like human beings to be murdered, and they could do absolutely nothing.

A frequent and provocative question put to Holocaust survivors is: why didn't they do more to resist Nazi oppression? Why did they endure such degrading and brutal treatment without protest or resistance?

Survivors have often explained how such questions show ignorance of the reality of the situation they faced. Once the occupation of the western Soviet Union had occurred, the position of Jews in occupied Europe was particularly hopeless, especially for those in the east: Jews were usually isolated and despised minorities among occupied populations, with little or no hope of moral support or of obtaining arms. Added to this, one has to recall the overwhelming power of the Nazi police state and the cunning methods of deception deployed. Given these constraints, the abilities of unarmed Jews to resist were severely limited.

Yet, despite such obstacles, many cases of defiance, resistance and revolt have been recorded. Although starvation, exposure and disease sapped the strength and will of many ghetto inmates to act, Jews did resist through a range of actions. These included their refusal to surrender their humanity and personal integrity, to daring escapes and going into hiding, ghetto uprisings and revolts. Even in the camps, sabotage and incidents of defiance occurred. There were, therefore, many forms of Jewish resistance that ranged from passive, silent defiance to the more violent, armed action. Given the extraordinary weak circumstances of Jews under the totalitarian rule of the Nazis, one can only wonder at the range and level of resistance that did take place.

One type of resistance was manifested by those who escaped and went into hiding. This involved hundreds of non-Jewish men and women in every German-occupied country, who took huge risks to hide or rescue Jews. Often betrayal to the *Gestapo* meant discovery and murder; nevertheless the actions of these courageous men and women saved thousands of Jewish lives. Motivations ranged from moral or religious imperatives, to monetary gain. Others acted for patriotic reasons, regarding the Final Solution as part and parcel of Nazi occupation which they were fighting. In western Europe such activities were especially prevalent in Belgium, Holland and particularly Denmark. Whatever the reasons, thousands of Jewish children, adults and even whole families survived thanks to those who were willing to put their lives, and the lives of their own families, at risk.

Chances of survival in hiding often depended on the size of the Jewish community and their relative assimilation into the general society — Denmark was a good example of this. In contrast, the masses of Polish Jews, particularly those from the east, stood apart from their non-Jewish neighbours, in terms of their religion, culture, customs and language. Conditions were similar in Lithuania, Latvia and Estonia as well as the western Soviet Union where Jews often feared their neighbours as much, or even more, than the Germans.

Nicole David
Polish Jewish child, St Servais-Namur, Belgium
On 4 August 1942 my parents hid me in an orphanage in St Servais, a suburb of Namur, and they went into an attic in a nearby village. The orphanage was the beginning of becoming withdrawn and wanting to be on my own. Although my parents had explained how the deportations had started, I didn't understand why this terrible separation had come; I was terribly unhappy there. When my parents came and said — due to my recurring tonsillitis — that they were taking me back to Profondville, the village where we had previously stayed together, I was very happy.

One day my father and I went out to buy a paper while my mother prepared lunch. As we got to the paper shop we saw two German *Gestapo* men who looked at us and said hello. We answered and my father and I looked at each other and we thought: something is up. We continued our walk and in fact we went on the riverbank. It was a beautiful day, 7 October 1942. We went into a café and my father ordered an aperitif and I was allowed a sip out of that. When we finished we went back home. Our house was right next to the church of Profondville. As we got back to the square we saw three German lorries in front of our house. Someone from the Resistance warned us not to go further. There was a person waiting for us outside a little hairdresser's shop, who took us to a safe house in a side passage of the square. There was an Italian family there and they agreed to take us in and they kept us all day. As we were leaving the main square I started crying and my father said I had to keep quiet because the Germans would hear. I knew then that I would never see my mother again.

At the end of that day, the Resistance came and took my father back to the attic where he'd previously been in hiding with my mother, and took me to the family Champagne in St Servais-Namur. There were ten children in the family and five were still at home, the youngest being fifteen. We used to call the house a chateau because it had thirty-two rooms. I stayed there for over a year and a half and was looked after like one of the family. Again it was a complete change from my family and a change, of course, from the orphanage. It was a family of aristocrats, strong Catholics, very strict discipline. We went to church every day. Paulette, in whose room I slept, gave me lessons and taught me to read and write. At night she would say, "Don't forget to say your Jewish prayers." My mother, who had made the arrangements earlier, had told them that she wanted me to remain Jewish.

Jerry Koenig
Polish Jewish child, Kosow

We didn't know it at the time of our escape to Kosow, but a very tiny village about five miles from Kosow called Treblinka had been selected as a death camp. While we were living with the Zylbermans and helping them with their farm chores and maintaining a semblance of a normal kind of life, the letters and postcards we had been receiving from our grandparents, aunts, uncles and cousins in the Warsaw Ghetto all of a sudden stopped coming. Then we started receiving people who had jumped off transport trains who were telling us a tale of horror, that the transports from Warsaw were going to this camp of Treblinka. Another sign was that some bodies were burned in the fields and if the wind blew in the right direction the odour from this horrendous place was just unbelievable. So all of a sudden things fell into place, and people began to realise why Kosow was being treated differently from the Warsaw Ghetto: we were a captive audience, they were going to get us when it was convenient for them and in the interim we were a convenient source for the labour pool. And this is the point when dad decided that the only way for the family to survive was to go into hiding.

Lili Stern-Pohlmann

Polish Jewish child, Lvov

[Lili Stern-Pohlmann's story illustrates how incredible, even bizarre, some hiding experiences could be. Lili's mother did dressmaking for Mrs Irmgard Wieth, an eccentric, naïve but kindly German civilian woman, who worked for the Nazi administration in Lvov. When the ghetto was closed off, Lili's mother appealed to Irmgard Wieth to take Lili, and she agreed. Later, during the liquidation of the ghetto when her mother escaped, Irmgard Wieth agreed to shelter her too. By then she was also sheltering a Jewish couple — the Podoszyns. Thus the four fugitives were living in extremely dangerous conditions because Irmgard Wieth's apartment block had been requisitioned for high SS and Gestapo officials, in an area specifically designated for them — they were right in the middle of the lion's den.]

The four of us, my mother, myself, and Mr and Mrs Podoszyn, slept on the kitchen floor which was very near the entrance of Frau Wieth's flat. Our hearing and our eyes were very acute in those days; we were very conscious of what was going on around us. One day, as we were lying half asleep about 6.30 in the morning, we were suddenly aware that there was somebody near the entrance. So very quickly the bedding was packed up and the four of us scrambled into the little scullery. Then we heard a key turning in the lock; we thought it was a burglar, he was trying, trying, trying. The door was opened slightly but there was a chain on it.

Suddenly we heard screaming in German, "Open up! Open up, otherwise I'll shoot. Open up!" Frau Wieth was opening the door. A man pushed her aside and started running around the flat shooting and shouting, "Where is that bastard lover of yours? Where is that swine?" And then it hit us: he had heard about a *Wehrmacht* major who used to visit Frau Wieth once a week, spend the night and leave in the wee hours of the morning. At that time the major no longer visited her. Then it was all quiet and after an hour or so, we heard the main entrance door shutting. She came into the kitchen, "Where are you?" and when we came out she told us that he was Dieschner, her SS officer lover whose apartment she lived in. It never occurred to us that he still had the keys. He was posted to Holland to supervise a concentration camp; none of us expected his return. Now, she told us, "He's here for two weeks on leave; what are we going to do?"

Both my mother and Mrs Podoszyn belied their background: they did not look or behave in a Jewish manner so they decided that mother was going to be the dressmaker, and Mrs Podoszyn the maid and cook. Mr Podoszyn and I would hide in the scullery and the two of them would be in the kitchen openly — the "maid/cook" and the "dressmaker". The story would be that they had keys and let themselves in and out; at night my mother would pretend to leave and then slip back in again, but hide in a niche in the kitchen which was covered with a curtain, in case he came in; and Mrs

253

Podoszyn, who prepared their evening meal, would be allowed to stay and sleep in the kitchen. Then at night when all was quiet, we'd all creep out and sleep on the kitchen floor. When I think of it now, it seems impossible, but what else could we have done?

When Frau Wieth went to work, Dieschner used to come into the kitchen and talk to the two women. He loved talking and telling them how Germany was winning the war and how they were bombing England, and the two women had to pretend they didn't understand or speak German. These two ladies had perfect German, but kept repeating, "*Nicht verstehen, nicht verstehen*" ("don't understand") all the time. When I heard their conversations I had to stuff my mouth to stop myself laughing — only the Two Ronnies could do it! It was so narrow in the scullery where Mr Podoszyn and I were, that I had to sit on his lap.

On one occasion the Nordic god was chasing Mrs Podoszyn and she was crying, "No, no, *no*! I tell lady, oh, no, *no*!" Mr Podoszyn kept putting his arm over my mouth, almost stifling me, and there was my mother shivering and praying outside the door, afraid that I would burst out laughing. Occasionally when he went out, they would open the door, so that we could breathe freely and go to the toilet. And that's how we were for two weeks; at six in the morning, we would gather up the bedding, Mr Podoszyn and I went back in the scullery, my mother would "come in" ostentatiously at seven o'clock, and it would all start again. So I ask you: is that not an Oscar performance?

Janine Ingram
Young Greek Jewish woman, Thessaloniki

A time came when a German officer came to be billed in Maria's flat where we were hiding. She was sitting on the veranda and she saw an armoured car approach and people getting out and looking around, so instead of pushing us into the bathroom, she pushed us into her kitchen in which she had a coal bunker with a little door. She pushed the five of us into that bunker; it didn't have the height of a human being so we were crouching and she poured sacks of coal on top of us. She said, "No noise, nothing."

The German knocked on the door and said, "How many live here?"

She said, "I am a widow and I live with my son."

So he said, "I want to inspect the rooms to see how much room you have and how many rooms we can have from you." So he went in. "Just one bathroom?" he said.

She said, "Yes, just one bathroom. I am a poor woman, I haven't got two bathrooms."

"Well, show me the kitchen."

What stuck in my mind was that on the door of that bunker there was a small opening where the wood had shrunk a bit and through that, all I could see was these boots walking backwards and forwards in the kitchen. I was holding my breath and praying that everybody else in that bunker would hold their breath and not sneeze from the coal or anything like that. I don't think he was there for more than a minute, but it seemed like a couple of hours, and then he said to Maria, "Sanitation here is not up to our standards, I don't want any of your rooms, you can keep them." And he went out in great disgust. We had seized up and Maria had to pull us out one at a time. We were black. She was very good, she had a bit of tea from the British Consulate where she had worked before the war, and she said, "We'll have a cup of tea, all of us together, we'll celebrate."

Nicole David
Polish Jewish child, St Servais-Namur, Belgium
The Allies started bombing an ammunition dump nearby and my father thought it was too close for me. So he found some farmers in the same village where he was hiding and had arranged for them to look after me. Needless to say I was absolutely thrilled to be in the same village with my father. I was only there for a short time. Shortly after I got there, I was playing outside and suddenly saw some German cars coming in the direction of the farm. I quickly went indoors and got into the bed and pulled the blankets over me and pretended I was coughing. The Germans came in, quickly looked at me, and went out. In fact they weren't looking for Jewish people at that stage, but able-bodied young men to send to Germany. My father then arranged for me to go to another village with a different family. Life on the farm was totally different from life with the Champagne family. Food in the two villages where I was hidden was better as there was always a little extra besides the ration. None of the families that hid me took any money.

Jerry Koenig

Polish Jewish child, Kosow

Once Dad had decided we must go into hiding, with the help of two young men, a farming family was found in the vicinity of Kosow willing to take a chance. The reward of the Goral family was to be our farm. The plan was to dig a shelter inside of a barn. It was a large family living inside that small farmhouse: Mr and Mrs Goral, their son and his wife, and three teenage daughters. The shelter was to be big enough to house eleven people including the four of us. All the digging had to be done at night and carried to the fields by hand, but once it was done, it was unbelievable — you had no idea there was anything unusual about that barn. The walls of the shelter were lined with straw, there were branches on the floor to keep water from coming up, and there was a trap door which, when lifted up, was still inside the barn. We actually went into the shelter in the winter of 1942/43 and stayed there twenty months until liberation came.

A mother and daughter were in hiding with us. What nobody knew when they joined us in the shelter was that the young woman was pregnant. We were twenty months in that bunker and it takes only nine months to deliver a baby. Everyone knew the serious implications, but didn't want to think about it; but the lady was getting bigger and bigger and obviously one day she was going to deliver her baby. At the same time Mr Goral's daughter-in-law was carrying her baby and finally the day came when the delivery of the

257

Gorals' baby took place. It was a very difficult birth; a midwife had to be called and she had a little boy who died at birth.

A couple of days later a baby girl was born in the bunker. There was nothing wrong with the little girl, it was an easy birth, the only problem was that she did what all new-borns do — she cried. And of course the lives of eleven souls rode on the ability of keeping this whole thing secret and quiet; everybody realised that it would be impossible to keep the baby in the shelter. The idea was raised that maybe a swap could be made with the woman upstairs, but as there was a midwife involved and this was a girl, not a boy, the idea did not fly.

And so the conclusion was that the baby had to die. And Mrs Goral concocted a potion of poppies — opium — which the mother had to spoon-feed to her baby. And the babe just simply dozed off and died, never regained consciousness. This whole thing had a tremendously traumatic effect on the people in the shelter. My brother and I took it particularly hard — to witness this kind of thing was really a terrible, *terrible* experience.

Martin Parker
Polish Jewish man, Otwock
We were hiding upstairs, with my wife and daughter living openly downstairs. During the day we could not move: I had to induce my family to keep quiet and sit and do nothing — if a spoon fell, well . . . We could not go to the WC. My wife came upstairs every few hours.

We arranged a secret shelter upstairs — in a corner there was a space we could go inside if danger came and sit quietly.

On All Souls' Day, 1943, there was a big Polish demonstration, they were singing patriotic songs with Polish flags flying. I was watching at the window and saw Germans with guns coming into the house. I gave the signal and we all went into the shelter. Halina, my little daughter, was ill in bed upstairs. The house seemed empty, they broke in. They came up to our door and broke it with an axe and came in. You can imagine! My heart was racing.

One soldier went further into the rooms and found my daughter in bed.

"Why are you here?"

"I am ill."

"Who are you?"

"I had a family before the war, my mother disappeared, and my father was an officer in the Polish army and he disappeared as well."

"With whom are you staying."

"My auntie, she went to church today."

He looked under the bed, there was a suitcase. He took the two pairs of men's socks and a piece of soap, put it in his pocket, went to the officer and said, "Everything is in order there."

They were standing before our door for ages; suddenly my mother-in-law wanted to sneeze. I gave a signal to my sister-in-law to hold her nose, and she did. If she had sneezed, I wouldn't be here today. When they had gone we had to stay hidden because neighbours

259

came in to see who was in this house which had been broken into, but they only saw my daughter. Then we heard my wife's song, she always sang when she came back — it was a sign that things were in order.

After this scare I asked Mr Jaworski to build an underground shelter in the cellar, so later we moved down and we lived there for about four or five weeks until the Germans had left Warsaw.

Alicia Adams
Polish Jewish child, Drobhobycz

A *volksdeutsche*, who thought that it would be in his favour if he had hidden some Jews when the Russians came in, took us in. He was charging so much a head for every Jew and he hid us in his cellar where he had another fifteen already hidden. He called us his "rabbits" and in the evening he would call his "rabbits" out and give us some food. As the Russians had stopped on the Polish border, he became frightened so he put us in the shed where he kept the straw; then the Germans came to take the straw away and he put us back in the cellar. One night we heard him talking with his wife. She said, "How are you going to kill them?" And he said, "Well, I kill animals all the time — a sheep, a cow — it can't be so different to kill a man." But somehow he was afraid to do it and we were lucky, we stayed hidden about three months and, at last, the Russians came in.

Adam Adams
Polish Jewish youth, Lublin

Maria Cekalska lived in a little house on the outskirts of Lublin with her three children: a boy of fifteen, one of seven and a girl about ten. She was Catholic, an ordinary woman with a very good heart. It was her good heart and belief in God which made her hide us. A police notice had been put up after the liquidation of the Majdan-Tatarski ghetto that anyone hiding a Jew would be shot, so she was terribly afraid. Then, a cousin of hers, a *volksdeutsche*, came to live in the house, so we dug a hole in the cellar, just over a metre long and about a metre wide and we moved into that hole.

It was like a grave but with an opening with a cover in case the Germans came and looked. On the ground we had this straw, with a bucket for our needs which the boy would come and empty at night. We lived there for about seven to eight months in complete darkness, eaten up by lice. The first few days we were crying bitterly because of the loss of our parents. Then we became hungry and that is when I started living again. We were really starved because this woman was very poor and had three children and the *volksdeutsche* cousin to feed. Sometimes she would make potato pancakes and the little boy would throw some down to us. So eight months of terrible hunger and terrible fear because the *volksdeutsche*, who didn't know of our existence, was above.

You imagine: eight months — unwashed, unclean, in total darkness! That's when I lost the sense of time. It was only because we were so young that we survived.

261

We were so hungry that once, when we got a baked potato and we divided it, we both thought the other had got he bigger part, and we fought over it; we scratched ourselves and were bleeding over this potato. We lived like this for about eight months, then the Russian army moved towards Lublin. When the German army was withdrawing, we went out of this hole looking like cadavers.

"Margot"
German Jewish child, escape to Switzerland

So we survived from 1939 until the beginning of October 1943, hiding in Berlin. Then came the date when we had planned to go to Switzerland. We took the night train and that train going to the border was full of *Gestapo*. The next day was the Day of the Dead, when people go to the graveyards to place their wreaths, so we were dressed in black; mother had a black hat with a veil and black armband and I was dressed as a farmer's girl.

During the journey my mother saw a man outside in the corridor looking in at her. Her instinct told her: *Gestapo*. She always felt that when in danger you go straight to the lion, so she got up and went outside and stood next to him. They started to talk and he said to her, "What are you doing on this train? Where are you going?" So she gave him a whole rigmarole about her work and the bombing in Berlin, and how her boss told her, "You need a few days' rest, go to the grave of your parents and afterwards go to Constance and have a few days' rest."

She told that man so much that he was feeling sick of her. So when she realised that she had talked him to the ground, she wished him a good journey and said, "I think my friend in the compartment is waiting for me." This man she had been talking to earlier had already opened the door saying, "Hey, how much longer are you going to be out there?" It didn't take long before the door opened and the same *Gestapo* man came to ask for identity papers. When mother laboriously opened her bag, he said, "Don't show me your papers, I've heard enough about you, I know your whole *life*. This is your daughter? She doesn't have to show me her papers either."

At the border, the guide took us to a field; we were lying down in the earth and he said, "Now, in front of you, see that building? That is the German border, then there is no-man's-land, then the Swiss house, and then you are in Switzerland. Suddenly, as we were lying there, a bright light went on — there was a spotlight on the roof of the German border post that was going round in a circle and lighting up the whole field. We pressed our noses into the ground and lay still and we counted how long it was; one, and then off, and then on; there was a rotation, an exact time. The man said "Goodbye" and there we were. I could hear my mother's heart.

And then we crawled, and we heard *everything*, we heard the leaves drop in the forest — have you ever heard dropping leaves? — you have senses that you cannot imagine. We crawled across the field and we managed somehow to get as far as Switzerland. Mother fell into a river, I tripped over a wire; we thought there was a bell ringing in the village. Mother said, "I have a torch." I said, "Don't you dare put that on!" We started to argue.

Suddenly I heard a "z z z z z-ing", it was a man with a gun on a bicycle going along the main road with an Alsatian dog, but as we were near the river, the dog didn't smell us. We eventually got off the field and there was a street lamp. We hadn't seen a street lamp with the light on for ages — I mean everything in Berlin was blackout — so we knew we were in Switzerland; and when we embraced under that lamp, that was the best kiss we ever received.

Preben Munch Nielsen
Danish student, member of Danish Resistance, Copenhagen

In 1943, when it was known that the order had come to get rid of the Danish Jews, lots of people in Copenhagen were informed and they went from house to house to warn the Jews. Danes are very practical people, they tried to raise funds, and the *Torah* (the scroll containing the five books of Moses) was taken and put into a Danish church for protection. The only place which proved impossible to help was the Jewish old-age home. This is why most of the people who were arrested and taken to Terezin were past sixty. But most of the Jewish people got shelter. A good hiding place was in one of the hospitals; a large number stayed there for a night, and some of the most elderly were put into bed and stayed there for the rest of the war under false names. One nurse asked a doctor, "Why are they here?" "Oh, call it German measles!" Even in serious moments we laughed. And then from the hospital, sometimes there was a funeral. Starting with the "corpse", lots of cars followed, and from time to time one car went off another way — that's how Jewish refugees were brought out of the hospital.

Jørgen Von Führen Kieler
Danish student, member of Danish Resistance, Copenhagen

It would not have been possible to organise the rescue of the Jews within hours had it not been for the enormous support from the Danish people; it would have been a paradise for informers because all security measures had to be forgotten about. What was important was to get in contact with the Jews and have them shipped over to Sweden. My group of ten students used our apartment as headquarters. We had been divided to some extent; my sisters were pacifists, they didn't want to carry arms; my brother and I had already engaged ourselves in sabotage. Now suddenly we had to forget all about our differences because there was only one thing that was important: to save Jews.

We met on 1 October 1943 in our apartment and it was decided that my sister and one of our friends should try to raise the necessary funds. He was the son of a big estate owner on Sjelland and knew all the big estates on Sjelland. So they went around in a taxi to all the mansions and estates on Sjelland and when

265

they came home on Sunday evening they brought home one million Danish crowns. Another member of the group, a girl, knew a fisherman who had moved his boat to Copenhagen and she went down to see him and asked him if would approach his colleagues and try to help because we wanted boats to transport the Jews across the Sound. His answer was yes, but we would have to guarantee new boats in case we were caught by the police or the Germans and lose the boats. Here we were with our one million crowns and in two days we had a fleet of ten to twelve fishing boats and, in the autumn of 1943, it took us two weeks to transport between eight hundred and one thousand Jews across the Sound without losing a single one.

Preben Munch Nielsen
Danish student, member of Danish Resistance, Copenhagen

The plan was that the Jews were accommodated in houses in small villages near the coast; also in the inn where our boss, the innkeeper Tomsen, was. He was very smart. One day he called the *Gestapo* and said he suspected he'd got a Jew in his inn. So the *Gestapo* came and arrested this "Jew" only to find he was one of the few Danes who had an "Aryan" certificate; and from that time the *Gestapo* believed our boss. At one time in the inn there was the *Gestapo* on one side of the bar and, on the other side, our resistance people; and upstairs Jewish refugees were accommodated!

As young people we would take them down to the inn; we knew exactly where the Nazis wouldn't go because they wouldn't dare. Everybody had the possibility of being involved. The police did everything they could. They were given orders to arrest the Jews, they did and then they brought them to us. There were 20,000 Danes in the Resistance and 7,000 Jews reached Sweden. The rescue of the Jews was a very important part of our resistance movement.

Daniella Hausman
Young Polish Jewish woman, Warsaw

I went one day to visit my cousin, not far from where we lived, and he introduced me to a little girl about four or five, called Marisha (Mary). He said she was a niece of his wife. After a while he came to us asking if we could find a place for that little girl. I said I would try — which I did — and found a friend who lived on her own on the outskirts of Warsaw and she took the little girl. When the Warsaw Uprising started, I didn't know what had happened to her. I later heard how Mary was a little Jewess, a daughter of my cousin's friends, who asked him if he could look after her when they went into the ghetto. It was dangerous because if the Germans found out, Poles who hid Jews were executed.

Christabel Bielenberg
Anglo-Irish woman, Dahlem, Berlin

Ilse Liedke was a good friend of ours and she used to collect food cards for Jews who hadn't got any. We

267

would cut off food coupons to give to her whenever we could. This time she came round and said she had someone waiting at the door and this time it was rather more than food coupons she wanted, that this woman was Jewish. She had dyed her hair blonde and had been staying, with her husband, with a priest in Dahlem; but his parishioners had become suspicious and he couldn't keep them any longer — would I take them in?

We had a very good neighbour, Carl Langbehn — who was hanged later as part of the July Plot against Hitler — and I told her that I had to consult with him as Peter was away. I went next door and Carl said, "Chris, you can't do this, you're endangering Peter, and your children are going to know there's somebody around, you can't do it." I remember crawling back through the hole in the hedge, it was completely dark with the blackout so I never saw the face of the husband who was waiting there, but he said, "Have you decided, *Gnädige Frau?*" I just couldn't say no, and said I could do it for a few days.

They moved immediately into our cellar and I didn't tell Carl Langbehn they were there. I remember the danger: Nicky had the job of seeing to the heating system down there and the bikes were always stored where the man was sleeping. It was only a day or so when Nicky called, "Mum, why do we have to put our bikes in the garden, it's raining!" He was very upset when I told him they had to stay there. Then I had, "Mum, why have I stopped doing the heating? Did I do it wrong?" Then about the third day, I saw Nicky with his nose up against the little glass window at the top of the cellar door.

One day when I got up they had gone. I remember going down into the cellar; I had put some twigs of forsythia there for them and these had died. The bed was neatly made, and I realised that they knew they couldn't really stay. Afterwards I heard from Ilse Liedke that they had been caught buying a ticket at the railway station. That was my most painful moment because I felt that whatever was happening — although I wasn't certain it was murder — that I was involved in the fate of this pair, I was dragged into this awful scene.

THE RIGHTEOUS OF THE NATIONS

Many rescuers have been honoured with the title *Hasidei Umot Ha-Olam* — the Righteous of the Nations — by the State of Israel. Perhaps the most well-known is Raoul Wallenberg, a Swedish diplomat working for the American War Refugee Board in Budapest. Wallenberg, together with diplomats from other neutral countries, rescued nearly 100,000 Jews in Hungary during the deportations of 1944/45.

John Dobai
Hungarian Jewish-Catholic child, Budapest
Rumours about collection of Jews, and increasing pressure on Jews in the countryside, must have reached Budapest in early 1944. But the full implications of

everything came home on 19 March when the German army occupied Hungary. And with the arrival of the Germans, and of course Eichmann, the transport of Jews started, first in the countryside.

It must have been about mid-November that my father reappeared from his slave-labour work. It was around this time that, through the network of friends, father heard about Raoul Wallenberg. The Jews of Budapest were being shipped out from the so-called Southern Station, which was perhaps half an hour's walk from where we were. And that is where Raoul Wallenberg was handing out the Swedish passports. So my father took off his yellow star and went down, either to the Southern Station, or to the Swedish Embassy. But anyway, he secured Swedish passports for us with the direction that we should go and live in one of the houses that Raoul Wallenberg and the Swedish Legation had bought. So, yet another move across the river into the Fifth District; we moved into, I think, number eleven in the street which has since been renamed Raoul Wallenberg Street and which has a little plaque in his memory. It was an area which traditionally had a high concentration of Jews, but wasn't part of the ghetto.

Our lives were saved by Raoul Wallenberg, absolutely. The *Arrow Cross* (Hungarian fascist collaborators) were moving up the street, systematically emptying the houses; another week and we would have been taken as well, absolutely, no doubt. I have no hesitation in being profoundly grateful for the fact that he saved our lives; and recognising that here was a man who was surely totally altruistic — he was not looking for medals or promotion, he was young and handsome, he had money, he had connections, he had everything a person of that age could want, and yet he risked all that for people who were totally unknown to him and he did not judge — and not only Jews, but Communists and in some cases criminals. He said: If I can do anything, I will not allow people to be killed.

JEWISH REFUGEE SERVICEMEN

As soon as the authorities permitted, many of the young Jewish men and women who had made it to the west as refugees, performed their own acts of resistance by entering the Allied services to fight the Nazi regime.

Stephen Dale
Young German Jewish internee, Pioneer Corps/SOE, Britain
The British Government sent out a man called Major Layton to persuade people to join the army. This was to facilitate the return from Australia of those of us from the *Dunera* group who had already volunteered. On 2 January 1942, I took the oath of allegiance and was a member of the Pioneer Corps. Many people in my position felt they couldn't sit back and do nothing about the Nazi threat to the whole world. What were the options open to me in order to do something

useful and active? Service in the army was the only thing open to me and at that time it was the Pioneer Corps. Our treatment on the way to Australia was not so much the pioneers as the officers who gave them instructions. But from the moment of joining, I had hopes of getting out. I did, but it took almost a year. In February 1943 I went into the Special Operations Executive — the SOE, and started training. I was dropped, inaccurately, east of Tramonte, Italy in 1944, arrested by Germans and Cossacks and interned for the rest of the war.

Clive Teddern
Young German Jewish internee, Pioneer Corps/Royal Armoured Corps
I wanted to join the army, I felt that was the best thing I could do. For one thing I think my outlook was more positive and at the time there was this wave of patriotism. When I see it now on films it seems — how shall I put it? — rather trite, rather emotional. But that sort of emotional attitude existed at the time, everyone was doing their bit. In a way it was a form of adventure and a lot of my friends went into the Pioneer Corps and I wanted to be with them. I never felt any dilemma, no. I wasn't fighting against Germany. I was fighting against Nazism. And to me those two things were completely different. I never had the feeling that I was fighting against my own country. My conviction was that I was fighting *for* Germany rather than against it. Amongst all the (German) people I knew — friends, relatives and so on — our position was quite clearly

established. We knew exactly what side we were on, there was never any conflict in our own minds whatsoever.

JEWISH PARTISANS

Across Nazi-occupied Europe, partisan units formed with the purpose of attacking the Germans, later often in support of regular Allied forces. The earliest manifestations of Jewish partisan activity took place in the east in response to *Einsatzkommando* (death squad) actions when survivors of massacres and escapees took to the nearby forests, banding together forming partisan units. These eventually became the main source of Jewish rescue efforts. Partisan units, using hit-and-run guerrilla tactics, were of various sizes and operated throughout eastern Europe: in Lithuania, Belorussia, in the Ukraine and in south-eastern Poland. One of the most famous was the family Bielski camp, which was established in the Naliboki Forest, between Lithuania and Belorussia. Led by Tuvia Bielski, with the support of his three brothers, his band of partisans, numbering fewer than forty in 1942, grew to 1,200 — men, women and children — by the summer of 1944. Bielski partisans, as well as fighting the Nazis, are recognised as being the largest group of armed rescuers of Jews by Jews. It is estimated that 20,000–30,000 Jews fought in

273

thirty Jewish partisan detachments, while others fought in non-Jewish partisan groups. In Yugoslavia, Communist partisans, led by Josef Broz — "Tito" — became the major group and numbered nearly 400,000 men and women.

Daniel "Danko" Ivin
Yugoslav Jewish child, with partisans, Croatia

The official date for my entering partisan units was 10 May 1942. Officially, they are saying that I am the youngest at the age of ten years. I had arms — a pistol — and I was a courier. I was wounded in 1943. Yes, I had a uniform. First, all sorts of bits and pieces; later the Department of Tailoring made me a uniform from a mix of English and American uniforms, with good mountain-climbing boots.

For the first three months I was mainly in Dreznica, then in local villages, then in woods. Then, in 1943, I worked again for the central committee. I was sent, like other people, here and there: we need a courier, we need somebody who knows how to write on type-machine. That was important, to type the letters. The partisans in Yugoslavia started in 1941, and it started in small groups, maybe uprisings in villages — in a big way in Serbia and Montenegro — but it ended up four years later as a really big anti-fascist army. Now as a child I witnessed this. I saw this as fast-growing and fast-changing, and I was not fully conscious that it was something extraordinary, it came to me in a normal way — oh, today we are in the village, tomorrow we are off to the town — that was the way. Because I was a child, it was normal: we are successful, we live, we are growing every day. It was so.

Autumn of '42 we were in the woods. It was the hospital in the woods with the command of Fifth Zone and some other units, without water or salt. You had rotten trees falling down and when it rained they were full of water and if you squeezed this wood then a few drops, very bitter and brownish, came out; that is all we had for about ten to fifteen days, and it was terrible for the wounded. We were also without food, we were cooking grass that you find in the woods, no salt — so very hungry and without water then. One day, my mother was sitting, and I remember my brother looking at her, and I saw sorrow. Suddenly my mother from somewhere took some sugar lumps and put on each a drop of alcohol — she was in the medical unit — I remember for all my life, how such a small amount of food and liquid can be enough for hunger and thirst. To each one of us she gave one of these cubes of sugar. It was fantastic. It was celebration.

Joseph Harmatz
Lithuanian Jewish youth, with Lithuanian Brigade partisans, Rudnitski Forests
It was called the Lithuanian Brigade, although Lithuanians were only few there; but politically they wanted it to be known that there was a Lithuanian partisan brigade fighting the Germans. There were about six hundred in the brigade, split into battalions. Of course in the beginning, when we first escaped from Vilna Ghetto in 1943, we had to organise ourselves. It

275

was difficult, we had no barrack, nothing over our heads and it was already autumn which is very cold and wet in that area. We had no food or arms, and we would go with just pieces of wood to the peasants at night so they would think we were armed.

Taking food away from peasants is not easy because they didn't have enough and they would hide it. And then you had to take it back to the camp, to load it on wagons and horses, and the roads weren't asphalt, and it was difficult and took many, many hours. And some of the peasants would be angry and would alert the Germans and they would wait for us. That was the most difficult thing: providing people with food. To go and blow a train, which sounds very dramatic, was much easier than bringing food, because you would find your place, do whatever you had to do and come back. It would take you two nights sometimes if it was far away, and someone might be wounded, even killed, and you had to bring the bodies back. But every military action was *easier* than bringing food. And with the Red Army's advance more partisans would come in, then you had to decide who's your friend and who's your enemy. We had no prisons. The judgement is either he stays alive or he goes where he goes; and when you are only eighteen and an intelligence officer running the investigations then you've got a problem. But when you come out of it and feel that you're not too much damaged because everything is still in the right place, it gives you some satisfactions. But life was tough, very, *very* tough.

The forest was very dense and we found little islands of sand, and we built bunkers inside and covered them with grass, with trees on the top. The only way we could be seen was because of the smoke coming from the chimneys; we had to have heat because of the cold. And it was very wet and damp. But the Germans were afraid to enter the forest. We had women there who had different roles depending on the type of woman: the elderly women would do the cooking and prepare food and so on; but the youngsters were very important with communications; you know a girl could move around easier than a boy and a blonde girl was a bargain, every one was like a *goddess* for us. And they were very brave, absolutely wonderful; they went in and out and were caught many times, but they had the spirit to come out of it. We respected them tremendously. Yes, there was anti-Semitism in some places; I never experienced it, but I experienced it with other Jewish partisans in other units who came to complain to me.

We didn't really expect to come out of it. There wasn't a night when all those who went out came back. Like in war, having wounded people was a horrible thing. Please remember we had no medicine or doctors, and if sometimes we had a doctor then he didn't have any proper instruments or anything. How can you operate without those things! And people came out of the war without arms or legs and were operated on again and again. The guy, for example, who gave me entrance to the underground, he lost his arm. We were out together blowing up a train and the detonator blew up before he pushed it in, so he lost three fingers and we took him about thirty miles back, bleeding all the time. We had a young doctor and with a simple saw he cut his bottom arm off. After the war he went into hospitals again and again and when he died at the age of eighty-plus, he was *still* in pain. We had nothing, no anaesthetics, nothing, *nothing*. No medicine. So it was tough from every point of view: food, people being killed, suffering, wondering what was happening to your family; altogether it can put you into a situation where you are in despair.

Jack Shepsman
Polish Jewish youth, Bielski partisans, Naliboki forest
The Bielski officers in the camp took all 190 Nowogrodek escapees on. They took people from other areas too; there were 1,500 people in that particular Bielski group, men, women and children, all Jewish. I didn't like it there a bit, we didn't have any arms; I had gone there to fight, to *do* something and they put me in the kitchen — I didn't survive just for that! I had to take revenge for what the Germans had done. One day a group of very nice, fine boys came to the camp. I went over to them and told them I didn't want to be with the Bielskis, that I had no future there to take revenge and, whatever they wanted, I was prepared to do. They spoke among themselves and accepted me. They called themselves the Orognekege, they were half Russian Jewish and half Russian non-Jewish. I was happy with them; at least I was doing something.

Jack Kagan
Belorussian Jewish youth, with partisan group, Naliboki forest

A group of Bielski partisans went out to interrupt a German patrol. On the way back they were extremely tired and lay down to sleep in a farmer's house. A farmer sent his son to the Germans to tell them that Jewish partisans were in his house. The Germans came and shot them all. The farmer was left alone for a while and nobody knew what had happened to those ten boys. About two weeks later they found where they had stayed — it was a safe house. One of the Bielskis with a group went to the farmer and told him they had found out what had happened. The farmer tried to resist, but they killed him and they killed the whole family. The order was that nobody should take anything from this house, in other words it must not look like a robbery of any sorts, it should be seen purely as a punishment.

Jack Shepsman
Polish Jewish youth, Orognekege partisans, Naliboki forest

I went with them for training on how to bomb German supply trains along the railways. They told me to go to the rails and put my ear on the rails. You could hear for miles and miles, especially at night. You would hear, Tsch, tsch, tsch, and then the more normal noise as it came nearer. There were German guards walking backwards and forwards, so we waited until the train was near before rushing the explosives in. Then the train was bombed, there was a lot of shooting and we killed a lot of Germans; they filled up the wagons with ammunition and other supplies and we took to the forest. I had a wagon and horse and that horse knew where the base was and could always find its way home. I learnt a lot in a short time and was very happy with that group. We were not short of food, I knew how the farmers used to bury their food to hide it from the Germans, so I'd go and dig the stuff out, so we had plenty to eat and clothes and shoes. We sang Russian songs around the fire, they were a happy, musical bunch. I was the only Polish Jew there. We all wanted revenge; the biggest punishment was not to be allowed to go out on a job.

1944–1945

THE CAMPS (ii)

My trouble in Auschwitz is that part of me died there, without any doubt at all. You were under-ridden by this ghastly twenty-four hour stench from the ovens and the chimneys — twenty-four hours a day this sickly smell! And do you know, I can still taste it to this day . . . It was ghastly, absolutely ghastly.

By January 1944, the Nazis had been pushed back almost to the Polish border and in the summer of that year, the Red Army renewed its offensive in support of the Normandy landings in the west. By this time, the extermination camps of Chelmno, Belzec, Sobibor and Treblinka had completed their killing, leaving Auschwitz-Birkenau as the major death centre.

Faced with the spectre of defeat on the Eastern Front, the campaign to root out Jews left under German control was stepped up. After the German invasion of Hungary in March 1944, 400,000 Jews were deported to Auschwitz; Jews still living in Slovakia were seized and the last remaining ghettos and labour camps in the east were liquidated. Deportations from Theresienstadt were also accelerated. Transports of Jews continued to be deported from western European states. In little over six months from the spring of

1944 more than 600,000 people, 95 per cent of them Jews, poured into Auschwitz-Birkenau.

Dennis Avey
British prisoner of war, Buna-Monowitz, Auschwitz-Birkenau

Now dreadful things were happening in Auschwitz-Birkenau during 1944. They were gassing and burning thousands of people who couldn't work any more because of their failing strength; I knew practically everything that was going on there. I knew that from all over the Continent people would be brought to Auschwitz-Birkenau: men, women, children, old people; then they were sorted out and some were gassed right away. There were heaps and *heaps* of clothing, glasses, footwear — huge warehouses full of possessions taken from these people. They just put them into the gas chambers using this Zyklon B gas and then they were burned. And this happened day in and day out.

Christabel Bielenberg
Anglo/Irish woman, Dahlem, Berlin

The widow of von Schulenburg remembers him coming back and saying, "You know they are killing those Jews who are being sent to the east." And she said, "What, every one of them?" And he said, "I believe it could be hundreds of thousands." Von Schulenburg was a very sturdy person in the opposition, hanged in the July Plot of 1944.

Else Baker
Young German child, part-gypsy, Auschwitz-Birkenau
When I arrived in 1944, I know I wouldn't have survived had I been left in the big barrack with all the gypsies. Wanda was my salvation. She lived alone in her little room. I remember making a daisy chain for her because towards the crematorium side of the camp there was rough grass growing with clover and little daisies. I very often went into the tall grass towards the end. I had been told not to go near the electrified wire as this would kill me, but I did go near it into a forbidden area. This was close to the people that came from the left; long columns of people, all smartly dressed, walking towards the crematorium. If I had shouted, they would have heard me. Later, I discovered they were Jews. The women were in fur coats, they all looked like film stars with their extravagant clothing — I should think they wore their best clothes, their glad rags.

Gertrud "Trude" Levi
Young Hungarian Jewish woman, Auschwitz-Birkenau
The deportation of the Hungarians started in the summer of 1944. The normal load for the trucks was 60–90 people, we were 120. When we were locked in we decided to deal with the situation in a civilised manner and from our luggage we built up seats and then we sat down very very close, back to back, with very tightly pulled-up knees.

We had two buckets for our human needs; we had to overcome our inhibitions to use them — men, women,

285

strangers, children — but we used them and they weren't quite sufficient for 120! Anyway, with every jolt of the train the muck ran out so we were sitting in it and we couldn't do a thing about it. This was June 1944, a very hot summer and there was very little air in the truck. The two openings had barbed wire over them and the air became really unbearable. We were thirsty, we had a bottle of water to drink, most probably we drank it the first day, thinking that we could refill our bottles, but this didn't happen and we were getting thirstier and thirstier.

In our normal life we talk about being thirsty, but thirsty there meant one's lips were parched, broken, hurting; you were hungry, you had a piece of bread in your hand but couldn't eat it because you couldn't swallow any more. It meant people went into hysterics, people went mad, people had heart attacks, and people died. And we had the dead, the mad, the hysterical and the screaming among us and we could not do a thing about it.

Hugo Gryn
Ruthenian-Slovak Jewish youth, Auschwitz-Birkenau
When the train finally stopped, it was still dark, and they didn't open the trains until daylight. I got out, and that was the point where my whole life was saved. There were these peculiar-looking people in striped uniforms. I made the assumption that they were inhabitants of the local lunatic asylum. They were moving up and down, their job was to clear the trains; but one of them, as he passed me, he's

muttering in Yiddish, "You're eighteen and you've got a trade, you're eighteen and you've got a trade." And my father says to me, "If they ask you anything, you're nineteen and you are a *Tischler und Zimmermann* — a joiner and carpenter. Gabriel, my brother, was eleven — extraordinarily lovely, a very, very bright boy; we came to the head of the line, they ask how old I am, I say nineteen.

"*Betreibst Du ein Handwerk?*" "Have you a trade?"

"*Ja, Tischler und Zimmermann.*" "Yes, a joiner and carpenter."

They don't even ask my brother and he is sent one way with my grandfather and grandmother, and my father and I another, my mother in roughly the same direction. My mother is not going to let my brother go without her, and the last I saw of her was her being pulled back roughly and sent in our direction, although the men and women were separated there.

Later, in the barracks, I asked what happened about family reunions — you know: when are we going to meet the women and the others? How does it work? This man, who had been there some time, said, "You'll never see them again."

I said, "Why not?"

He says, "Well, by now they're dead."

"What do you mean, 'they're dead'? Look, I'm so scared, don't make bad jokes." Will you believe it, I didn't believe what was happening there for at least twenty-four hours.

287

Maria Ossowski
Young Polish woman, Auschwitz-Birkenau

In May 1944, when the Jewish population of Hungary arrived, they were burning 3,000 bodies a day. You have to remember that Birkenau itself was built on the lower lands near the River Sola and it was low, wet and horrible. So the air there was never fantastic, but given the addition of the smoke belching out of those five chimneys, day after day, night after night, breathing in the camp was very unpleasant and it was very difficult to do the hard work. I am ashamed to say that when I knew I was going away into another *Kommando*, six kilometres from Birkenau, what I was thinking was: thank God, no more smoke; because I left in the middle of the destruction of the Hungarian Jews.

Kitty Hart-Moxon
Young Polish Jewish woman, Auschwitz-Birkenau

In *Kanada Kommando* we had a direct view of the people that were being brought into this compound. Between May and September 1944 they were preparing to bring in about three-quarter million of Hungarian Jews, and this was why a new group was formed to sort the things because they were expecting a lot of possessions. I was on night shift so I could observe what was going on during the day.

What I observed was that the women and children had been separated from the men and were sitting in the small wood just across from our barrack; the children would pick flowers, the women would sit and picnic and give the children the food and drink they still had. Then a group would be led into the low building which was Crematorium 4, and you heard a sort of muffled sound. Then from one of the windows from my barrack I could see a person walking up a ladder wearing a gas mask and he would empty a tin into an opening, a sort of skylight, at the top, and he would run down the ladder very quickly.

You couldn't hear a lot, other than the muffled sound; sometimes you could actually hear screams. After a pause you could see smoke coming out of the chimney of Crematorium 4, and a while later activity could be seen at the rear of the crematorium; ash was being dumped at the back into a pond. Now, what I couldn't understand was that the people sitting in the wood were totally calm, they had no idea that the people who had gone in front of them were already dead. They simply had no idea.

The capacity of the crematoria at that stage could not cope with the arrival of three-quarters of a million people, so many of the executions took place at the back of the wood in pits. We saw men gathering brushwood where they had to make big fires. We couldn't take it in for a long, long time. But of course we were there for eight months and we saw it day in day out. Also the huge amount of clothes gave an idea of how many people were actually being killed.

Else Baker

Young German child, part-gypsy, Auschwitz-Birkenau

One evening, we were all ordered not to go out of the barrack. There was no light in the barrack, it was dark. I didn't know anyone there, and from outside came these screams, *terrible* screams and cries of "murderer" could be heard. One of the adults in the barrack defied the order and opened the door. And there was an unholy pandemonium because through the open door the adults could see open fires burning towards the crematorium side of the camp, open fires. And word went round — as a child I was listening — "They're burning people alive, they're burning people alive!" Pandemonium! Panic! God, if you can imagine Dante's images, these wouldn't do it justice: total darkness, people milling around, door slightly ajar, redness in the middle distance, the screams.

I had the courage to ask an adult nearby, "What is going on?" And she turned towards me and yelled, "Your people are burning our people alive." "*Your* people," because she could see that I wasn't a hundred per cent gypsy.

And I said to her, "You can't burn people, one burns coal not *people*."

Antonie Krokova

Czech gypsy child, Auschwitz-Birkenau

I was standing in front of the gas chamber. The first hundred were going in and we were in the second hundred. And then the professors and doctors from Prague came and a professor recognised me because he knew my father very well. The professor asked me in Czech, "What is your number?"

When I heard this I was startled, so I said in German 8140.

And he said, "Can't you speak Czech?"

I nodded that I could.

"So, what is your name? What is your father's name?"

"Well, Vrba." And I started crying.

He said, "This is Vrbova," and he took me out. He said in German, "This one will not be burnt, this is a family that has to be freed."

But mum had been burnt by then. Some of my siblings had died too.

Antonin Daniel
Czech gypsy youth, Auschwitz-Birkenau

We were taken to the showers. Then they said, "You'll collect gold."

We said, "They don't want to give it."

They said, "They must, they must."

They had a kind of water there to grease the fingers when the rings wouldn't come off; and we had small pliers to snip the earrings. We knew what was going to happen to these people after we had taken the gold but we were not supposed to say. I had to tell them that they would get the same kind of clothes as I had and that they were going to work and would go to the block. We took everything from them, stripped them naked, that was what made them suspicious.

291

I told them, "Undress and if you have rings, gold or money, then put it here." Some handed it over and some didn't want to. Then they went into the gas chamber, a place like a shower, until there were lots of them and then it was locked. They didn't know anything about it. The gas was switched on and that was the end.

There was a sort of peep-hole there. We were able to watch. I saw, I *saw*; but if that *Kapo* had caught us, he would have beaten us to death. They fell like flies. It took fifteen minutes and some, well many of them were still alive, they were still breathing. We opened it up to make the gas go away and then we dragged them out. Those who were still breathing, they beat to death.

We mostly went for the women who were light; when they were fat we couldn't manage to drag them — then we got a beating from the *Kapo, "Schnell! Schnell! Schnell!"* — it was no good, we had to carry them as well. There were about two to three hundred in the chamber, it was not always the same. They were Jews: women, children and men too — whole families, yes, yes. They did not put Roma (gypsies) there. When Roma died, yeah, they would throw them into the furnace.

After the gassing we dragged the corpses from there. They gave us kinds of belts, we had to tie them to a leg and pull it to that crematorium. Only Jews were selected (for work in the crematorium), they were very strong kids, see, young. They got more to eat; at the most they were there three or four months; then finished, sent to the gas chambers and others took their place. I had already learned my lesson. I had grown accustomed to it. It did not do anything to me. Nothing at all. It did not touch my feelings in the least — I had grown immune to it.

Kurt Klappholz
Polish Jewish youth, Blechhammer

When Blechhammer became a camp of Auschwitz in 1944, we had a crematorium and I participated in the incineration of corpses from the hospital. I remember vividly what one did. There was someone who kept the ovens hot so that the bodies could be burnt. There was another chap who helped me. What we would do is put one or two bodies onto a metal stretcher which had wheels at one end and this would be placed inside the oven; and at the other end there were handles with which the other person would push the stretcher into the oven. Then one had a huge fork to be placed between the legs of the corpses so as to lift them off the stretcher when inside the oven, so that it could be drawn out. As soon as the bodies were inside the oven, the heat was such that they started to move, then the oven door would be closed and the bodies would be burned.

I must have felt some twinges of — to put it mildly — strong distaste; in particular the movement of the corpses was a grisly sight; but after a while it was something you did without paying too much attention to it. I recall that I preferred to be at the back pushing that stretcher, as wielding the fork was an unpleasant experience. The chap who did it with me was a big,

293

lumbering man. One day he was struck down by some illness and within a few days he was dead. I then incinerated him.

Albin "Alex" Ossowski
Polish inmate, Auschwitz-Birkenau
The most tragic contact we had in the camp was with the *Sonderkommando* (special Jewish units forced to work in the gas chambers and crematoria). What they described, what they had to do, was so horrible. One man said that in the group he had to burn were the bodies of his wife and children. He was crying all night and you couldn't help him or do anything. The *Sonderkommando* lived under sentence of death because after three, four months, the Germans suspected they were going insane and they killed them.

Dennis Avey
British prisoner of war, Buna-Monowitz, Auschwitz-Birkenau
And they said the people of Germany didn't know what was going on! The people of Auschwitz itself complained bitterly about the smell from the crematorium. And all these people coming in daily! There must have been hundreds and thousands of Germans who saw them and yet they said, "Oh no, we didn't know anything that was happening." That's ludicrous. It's a fact: old people and children particularly were killed. The best of the menfolk were allowed to live to work. The rest were burnt daily, daily, daily.

John Fink

German Jewish youth, Buna-Monowitz, Auschwitz-Birkenau

In 1944 suddenly planes came overhead first on reconnaissance flights which didn't mean much to us. But soon after that suddenly they bombed the place, we heard later they were American planes. I was in the generating plant, we went down to the basement and the foundations were shaking and when we came up after this air raid there was nothing left of Buna plant. A bomb fell into the prisoner of war camp too. They were English prisoners and I believe about thirty people were lost. I think they were bombed by accident as they were very careful with their bombing. They didn't bomb the crematoria or anything in the Auschwitz camp, they were only interested in getting this artificial gasoline plant. We thought this was the end for us because they wouldn't need us for work any more, but lo and behold, next morning we had to march out again and start working to clean the place up. The water and electricity was restored and once more the prisoners started working in Buna.

Antonie Krokova

Czech gypsy child, Auschwitz-Birkenau

There was a mother who had four little children. The two-year old needed to pee, but you couldn't make any noise there, it had to be complete silence. We had red food bowls without handles, and she took a bowl so that the child could take a pee and a pooh into the bowl. Then she put it outside and covered it with a

295

blanket. She thought she would take it away when we went for counting — when the counting was over she would go to the latrines and pour it down the toilet. But someone saw and reported it. After the counting, the German came while it was still under the blanket, and he said, "What is that there?" She was speechless, she turned completely pale, paralysed with fear. So he uncovered it and said to her, "*Haben sie Loffel?*" — "Have you got a spoon?" She nodded. "So, take the spoon." Believe it or not — I swear to God this is true — she had to *eat* it. She lived for two, three more days and then she was dead.

Harry Lowit
Czech Jewish child, Auschwitz-Birkenau

The difference between grown-ups and those children who were able to survive was enormous, because the children were much more adaptable. For my part I knew that I was living behind an electrified fence and I accepted that as normal. I believe that what has saved me from a lot of psychological hardship was that I actually accepted the surroundings I was living in and adapted to them. If you don't accept it then you only go one way and that's down. It really became a very cruel world: I attended many public hangings which came up every month, about five or six at the same time. I saw people dying of hunger and being beaten to death, and you were stepping over dead bodies all the time — that became an everyday occurrence. So you get acclimatised and at the very impressionable age of thirteen it seems that you become almost sadistic.

From my point of view this job as *Läufer* — messenger, was a way to survive; but in some ways I felt guilty that I was getting this privileged treatment, but on the other hand I tried to make up for it by helping others. There was nothing to be gained for me to get killed. But obviously, even now I feel guilty that I perhaps cooperated with the Germans, but I did it for self-survival and to help others. And from the story I heard from my uncle who went to Prague immediately after the war in 1945 — he met one or two people who told him, "If it had not been for your nephew, Harry, who gave us extra food, we would not have survived." That made me feel good.

Anita Lasker-Wallfisch
Young German Jewish cellist, women's orchestra, Auschwitz-Birkenau
Eventually in 1944, the day came when someone came to our block — the music block was the only block where Jews and non-Jews were mixed. Then came the dreaded moment, "Aryans to one side, Jews to the other." We thought, "Now we'll be sent to the gas chamber." But that was when they sent us to Bergen-Belsen.

SELECTED FOR LABOUR

With the war going against Germany, an acute labour shortage led to the transfer, in the summer and autumn of 1944, of a large number of inmates

297

from Auschwitz to labour camps, including Jews — the relatively fit young Hungarian women forming a large proportion of the deportees. It was this need for labour until the last days of war that accounts for the numbers of Auschwitz survivors, compared with the pitiful few from the other death camps.

Helen Pelc
Young Polish Jewish woman, Auschwitz-Birkenau
When we were in the barrack where Mengele was doing the selection, we knew about the gassing and thought it would be *it*. My mother got this tiny lipstick out and made my face nice and red and hers too. We had a little more flesh on our bodies and she pushed me into the skeletons — people who were just skin and bones; she pushed me there knowing that they took the better looking ones on one side and the really bad skeletons on the other. My mother was marvellous, her wits and everything: she knew that the people who were fitter looking might still serve a purpose for them. After this we went by train, and then a march, to Kurzbach work camp.

Barbara Stimler
Young Polish Jewish woman, Auschwitz-Birkenau
One day Mengele comes to the block and we all stand on one side, a thousand of us. He stands with two SS men near the door. It is September 1944 and the sun is shining. We have to undress, we hold our clothes on our arms. He takes us by the hand, turns us front and back.

One woman is sent to the other side of the block, and one is sent outside. Now, which is which? We are sent outside, looking behind to see where the fat ones are going and where the thin. We can't do anything: if we have to go, we have to go. They take us to the shower. Now, what is going to come out: will it be water or will it be gas? We are holding our hands, praying to God. *Water* comes out. We all sigh with relief. They give us clothes: a dress, stockings, clogs and a coat and they take us to Pirschcow, a farm in Germany, to dig anti-tank ditches.

Roman Halter
Polish Jewish youth, Auschwitz-Birkenau

Mengele and his officers came to the block and a rope was put down longitudinally. We were all put on one side of it. The order was that everyone had to go up to the rope, stretch out our arms and then on a certain order turn them over palm up. Everybody thought the strongest and best would be selected for work, so they came to the forefront. Mengele would then walk along the rope, looking at the palms saying, "You are a metal worker with such soft hands? What did you really do in Lodz Ghetto, you are lying." And they would be marked and dealt with. So we behind quickly spat on our hands and rubbed them in the floor in order to get dirt into our palms and we sighed with relief when we were marked OK. Those who were marked thought they were for certain death, but nothing happened — it was simply a sadistic thing which was Mengele's way of dealing with people.

Jan Hartman
Czech Jewish youth, Czechowice

One day in 1944 we were selected for Czechowice, we thought we had saved our lives because we were out of Auschwitz which we knew was certain death. We were about six hundred. Czechowice was an oil refinery: oil was all over the place as it had been bombed, completely destroyed and the oil had leaked out of those huge oil tanks. By the time we got there it was winter and there were endless *Appells*, hours and hours and *hours*, people falling down. On one occasion I saw a man fall because he couldn't stand any more, and an SS man came and was dancing on him, pushing him into the mud. The question of solidarity sometimes comes up, but that was very limited — everyone was interested in his own survival. It doesn't mean that you wouldn't help someone else, but you wouldn't care particularly to help him. I mention this because it was winter and cold, and a needle and a piece of thread was great wealth; at one point I needed to sew and a man lent me a needle and a piece of thread. That was *exceptional*. I don't know whether I would have done it for somebody else, I don't know.

Hugo Gryn
Ruthenian-Slovak Jewish youth, Auschwitz-Birkenau, Lieberose, Sachsenhausen, Mauthausen and Gunskirchen

One form of resistance in the camps was to remain decent. The object of our imprisonment was, I think, to strip us of our humanity — to vindicate the Nazi stereotype of *Untermensch* (subhuman). There were many people who remained decent. There were equally many people who were reduced to a level of callousness, even cruelty. I can think of examples of both kinds and experienced both kinds.

George Hartman
Czech Jewish youth, Czechowice

In Czechowice there was a man, a Czech, and he and I got to be very good friends and we would be talking about food and why we wanted to survive. And my brother and I would be making recipes. I said, "Well, when I survive, we'll cut a skinny slice of bread with a huge piece of butter, and we'll have breakfast and cook eggs and ham . . ."

And he would scream, "For Christ's sake, stop talking about *food*, I can't stand it any longer."

But I said, "But we have to talk about something, a *dream*, something we will have when we get back from this horrible camp."

And we did it day after day until he said, "I can't take any more, I don't want to live."

And he just dropped dead. And I tell you, it's the will to live that kept you alive, it was really that fragile. Psychological and spiritual strength, I think, did give some support to the body, and if you didn't have it, you died.

Stanley Faull
Polish Jewish youth, Skarzysko-Kamienna

I was in the engineering camp where Poles who were paid were working as engineers minding the machines.

301

About five hundred of us were picked to work in this particular camp, I was one of the youngest. I had the job as "soap boy", a very big job. Soap was a tremendous currency, you couldn't get it, and anybody stealing soap was shot. So I was trusted with this job. The Pole I worked for would weigh out a number of blocks of soap, I would then put these in buckets and take them to the boiler rooms where hot water boiled and put the soap in the hot water to melt. Then, under his supervision, I would deliver this to the various machines and top them up with this soapy water which was used in place of oil, because there was no oil. I had the most fortunate experience as the Polish engineer I worked for looked after me indirectly. Had he done it directly, he would have been punished.

I was lucky to be in that part of the camp and not in the rocket works. The skin and eyes of those who worked there were so yellow because of the chemicals they used. They became like robots, they weren't human, and after a few months they died and a new lot would take their place.

Alfred Huberman
Polish Jewish youth, Skarzysko-Kamienna
The Hungarians arrived at Skarzysko looking immaculate in comparison with us. By then it was 1944. They were so naïve and we, the more experienced, used to rob them. They didn't believe what was going on, they were still worried about their appearance, they were civilised and they fell like flies

— they couldn't take it. In those conditions you become animal-like, you have to grab and you don't care who you take it from.

Roman Halter
Polish Jewish youth, Stutthof

Stutthof was a dreadful concentration camp. It was close to the Baltic and the beginning of November 1944 was freezing cold. The only way to survive when we stood outside on *Appells* in this terrible wind and cold, was to form a sort of "human oven". We moved into a big block, like a haystack, and rotated one way and then the other way, and those inside had to come outside after a few minutes. Anyone who was excluded from it suffered from cold and pneumonia and died. So really, solidarity existed between us. The SS told the *Kapos* to disperse us. But we soon formed another human oven, then another, then another, because it was the only way to survive.

Margie Oppenheimer
German Jewish woman, Stutthof

When we arrived in Stutthof, we had selection and that was the hardest. We had to undress stark naked and march around outside in a yard surrounded by guards. That was the worst, the most humiliating thing and I will never forget it or get over it. They would make remarks: if there was an older lady with the skin flapping from losing so much weight, they would make remarks. Or if you had to bend down, they would say, "Look at her haemorrhoids!" or "Look at her veins!"

Helen Pelc
Young Polish Jewish woman, Kurzbach

When we first went out to work, we were given a blanket which we made into a sort of envelope coat. Then we were given a shovel and marched out to the field where we had to dig trenches. There were ten SS men and some SS women; one had binoculars and knew every movement we made. The trenches were very deep, between five and six foot, maybe one and a half yards wide. This was the winter of 1944; the ground was hard and it was *very* hard work.

One night my mother got out from under the wires and went to ask a farmer for food. He didn't want to help and she came back with nothing. The next morning, before marching us off to work, Erika, this SS woman, said, "Somebody was disturbing the villagers last night, who was it?" Nothing was said for a while. "Well, I have got patience, I have got time."

The SS woman said. "We can wait the whole day until this woman comes forward." My mother then went forward. Erika said, "Get down!" I rushed forward and said, "Do this to *me*, spare my mother."

"Well, if you want, I can do it to you as well. Get out!" And she was beating mother. "Why did you go? What did you go for?" until my poor mother could hardly get up. She was walking bent over all the time after that, coming to work like the rest of us.

Roman Halter
Polish Jewish youth, Stutthof

One of the SS had a dog which liked to bite people. A man from Lodz Ghetto told me, "This is what you have to do: when the dog comes for you and the SS can't see, you get hold of the dog with the right hand behind his head, then you thrust your other hand very deeply into his mouth as you kick him on the side. If you don't do this, he will tear you up."

One day the dog was set on me. I ran over the brow and put my hand very quickly deep in his mouth — here is the scar, made by his big tooth — and kicked him, he let me go and ran back and never came for me again. I wasn't seen, otherwise I would have been shot for kicking a SS man's dog.

Jan Imich
Polish Jewish youth, Dora

We were told to go down to the coal storage place, load up the coal to be taken to the crematorium. Dora camp was built on a hillside and the crematorium happened to be at the top of the hill. I remember pushing the wheelbarrow full of coal, up this slope towards the crematorium, arriving there and actually walking into the crematorium and seeing it in action — seeing the bodies lying there, waiting to be put into the ovens and seeing bodies in the oven being burnt. I did that a couple of times, and by the third time I was very weakened and so tired. I was halfway up that hill pushing that enormous load of coal and I just slumped onto the ground and started crying. It so happened

305

there was a SS man nearby and instead of taking out his gun and shooting me, which he could have done, he looked at me, smiled, and told the *Kapo* to let me go. Funny, isn't it? He could just as well have killed me, because that's what they used to do if you didn't do what they ordered.

Premysl Josef Dobias
Sudeten Czech inmate, Mauthausen

One day this SS, who was not a doctor, but wore a white coat like a doctor, called me, gave me some cards and said, "Bring these prisoners in a group and bring them in one at a time." I had no idea what was happening, but I brought the first one in. He was asked to strip and to lie down. I did the translating. The SS told me, "What you are going to see, you are never going to talk about; if you do, you are a dead man."

Then he opened a little cabinet, took out an injection tube which held half a litre, opened a bottle of gasoline and filled it. The SS pushed the needle between the prisoner's ribs and pumped the gasoline into the heart. Then the SS waited, tried his pulse and the prisoner was dead. The orderlies, also prisoners, were called to take the body out and throw it on the side. Then he asked me to bring the next one. On that day he killed about three dozen people. I could not sleep, I was so upset, terrified, horrified how a man could kill in cold blood. The SS man's demeanour was actually nonchalant, just like he was baking bread — couldn't care less, even joking about it — "That will do for today." The prisoners who came in had no idea what would happen. They thought — I have no doubt about it — that they were being examined by a doctor.

Leon Greenman
British Jewish inmate, Buna-Monowitz, Auschwitz-Birkenau

One day when I was in the hospital, I was taken by a doctor and placed in a chair, and the doctors started strapping my hands and arms to the chair, and spreading my legs out, also strapped to the chair. The lights went out, there was a very small light burning and they were getting a tube. It was as thick as a ball-pen and about eighteen inches long.

The doctors started pumping what they said was water into my bladder and said, "Don't let it go, hold it." I said, "There's nothing wrong with my bladder then?" They didn't reply and went on. They placed this instrument in the front of my body and twisted it around and around and then they pulled it out and adjusted something, then they put it back in again. I was feeling very uncomfortable and they started hurting me. I don't think they were succeeding in what they wanted to do. For the next week, whenever I had to answer nature's call I urinated blood. All the fifty or sixty men next to me underwent the same thing. I daresay it was an experiment.

Zdenka Ehrlich
Young Czech woman, Auschwitz-Birkenau

The guard took me out of the block to another block which was completely empty. He pushed me and said,

"You lie down." I had to strip. But it wasn't what I thought it was going to be. He actually wanted blood. He put a syringe into my vein and asked me to pump by squeezing with my hand. And as I was still strong and healthy, coming from Theresienstadt, the blood was just pouring, pint after pint. After a while I stopped squeezing and he slapped me across my face and said, "Keep going."

When it was over, he said, "Get out!" I must have given him a few pints of blood. After the war I learnt that they had used it for soldiers on the front.

Dennis Avey

British prisoner of war, Buna-Monowitz, Auschwitz-Birkenau

I must admit that we were a lot better treated than the "stripeys", a lot better. The SS used to turn their backs on us nine times out of ten. The *Wehrmacht* used to treat us as well as could be expected although they had their moments of course. I used to work with the political prisoners and the "stripeys" alongside us. One day at work, the roll of the cable had stopped for some unknown reason and we stood looking and one of the SS approached this prisoner immediately above me — they always had to take their caps off and stand to attention — and he stood to attention and the SS hit him right across the face and knocked him into a pit and as he fell the roll of the cable fell over him and killed him.

Like an idiot, I remonstrated with this SS man. He didn't say a word, he jumped down into the pit and hit me right across my face with his Luger. That's when I lost my eye. Nothing was said, nothing at all . . . My trouble in Auschwitz is that part of me died there, without any doubt at all. You were under-ridden by this ghastly twenty-four hour stench from the ovens and the chimneys — twenty-four hours a day this sickly smell. And do you know, to this day I can still taste it. And then these dreadful situations with the political prisoners and the "stripeys". It was ghastly, absolutely *ghastly*.

Leon Greenman

British Jewish inmate, Buna-Monowitz, Auschwitz-Birkenau

The SS had a small place with animals and rabbits. One day I looked out of the window and saw a SS man cuddling a rabbit. I thought to myself, "Look, he's cuddling the rabbit and at the same moment he could kill me." That was the mentality.

Marsha Segal

Young Lithuanian woman, Rendaels

The last camp was Rendaels, that was the hardest. Here we started losing people every day. It was November/December 1944 and the soil was hard frozen and it was snowing. We had very little clothing and very little food. We were away from everybody, it was from nowhere to nowhere. Even the SS suffered cold and they used to put newspaper under their very heavy greatcoats for insulation. If they saw us with it they used to rip it off. They made us exercise to keep us fitter and warmer,

309

but we couldn't get warm because we had no clothing. Then they gave us the spade and pick and sent us out to dig trenches. They made fires for themselves, but wouldn't let anybody near them. We could never get rid of the cold, we had no heating, only one thin blanket. We slept tight together so that each body warmed the next one.

That was the most miserable camp because we didn't have hope any more. In this camp we had a lot of dysentery, the whole camp was dirty because some women couldn't manage to run quickly enough to the dugout holes. And next morning when they found it dirty, the SS used to beat up the whole camp. And we started to be infested by lice which we didn't have before, because we tried as long as we could to wash our hair in the coffee-water, and we tried very hard to keep clean as much as possible, but there it was so cold, nobody could take off their clothes. We knew that if we saw somebody with lice, and if we saw a woman who didn't lace her shoe, that she's a goner — that was a sign of apathy, a sign she didn't care.

Helen Stone
Young Polish Jewish woman, Auschwitz-Birkenau
I had contact with my husband through other people. Something I don't understand, because there couldn't be a more loving husband than mine, was that he said he only wanted a few words from me on paper, he didn't want to see me. He *didn't* want to *see* me! He could have pretended he was an electrician coming to our part of the camp to do some repairs. He never

came. My brother came one time and he must have told my husband how I looked because I looked really terrible. At that time I was a typical *muselmann* (camp slang for someone on verge of death). After typhoid fever, I couldn't walk, I couldn't hear, I was really just bones — bones and boils. I knew I was a *muselmann*. I didn't wash, the place where we could wash was far away and I had those ten toes with chilblains full of pus. I used to pee in the same bowl I ate from. How did I do that! I didn't kill the lice any more, there were too many. I was a *muselmann*. It would have been a blessing if I could have gone.

Michael Etkind
Polish Jewish youth, Buchenwald

I was in Buchenwald, end of 1944. I was separated from most of my friends. I wasn't worried, in fact it was quite interesting because I was not only among Jews, I could look around and see Russian prisoners, Germans, later I found American and French, Dutch, Belgian — you name it — and that made me happier. I felt, "I'm not the only one suffering unjustly." Maybe because we arrived soon after the bombing raids, things were more disorganised and so there was more freedom. I could wander through the camp. There was a cinema and anybody could go there, there were very long queues outside and they were saying that the D-Day invasion was shown. It was a wooded shed structure which accommodated over five hundred at once. It was very strange to have it there. There was also a brothel for the SS and some of the *Kapos* if the

311

SS liked them and took them there. Apparently there were women from all over Europe in the brothel.

Leon Greenman
British Jewish inmate, Buna-Monowitz, Auschwitz-Birkenau
At Monowitz a barrack had been put up and we heard that there were women there. *Kapos* and some of the under-*Kapos* could get tickets from a head *Kapo* and they could visit the women in that barrack. One day one of the boys next to me said. "Well Leon, wouldn't you like to go in there?" I said, "No, I hope my wife is not in there." I was still thinking that my wife was alive. In any case, during my years in the camp I always had my family on my mind and I was far too busy thinking how to get out and stay alive, fighting hunger and other things, to be thinking about sex. That didn't trouble me.

Michael Etkind
Polish Jewish youth, Buchenwald
Buchenwald was a transit camp; inmates from various Polish camps would come there for a week or two, get injections, and then were sent out. It meant that anyone who had a grudge against somebody could complain to the camp's leaders, mainly the politicals, and there would be a sort of kangaroo court, a trial and people would be executed if found guilty. I witnessed a number of these trials and executions. There was the case of this SS man. He must have murdered someone other than a Jew, Russian or Pole and was sent to

Buchenwald. Being a German, he got the best job which was in the kitchen, he got plenty of food. Suddenly, a transport of Russians came and he was recognised as the German who had murdered many Russians back in the Ukraine. He was the one handing out soup for our camp. They sent a Russian who could speak a little German to complain that the soup was only water, there were no potatoes or anything else — this was in order to entice him into our barracks, and it worked. He became furious with the complaint but the Russian said, "No, it's only water, you come and have a look."

I was on the top bunk looking down. When he came into the middle of our barrack, he got the big spoon and started looking down into the cauldron of soup and he was just about to take these potatoes out when one of the Russians hit him over the head, not very hard. As he lifted his head he was surrounded by the Russians and they were smiling and he went pale. He realised suddenly he was in danger. Then the Russians reminded him: remember such and such a camp? Remember how you were hanging so many people? Remember how many of our friends you've killed? Now you're being tried. He shook his head, "No, no, no! I must go."

They were very quick. A rope was found and they told him, "For what you have done you are sentenced to death and you will be executed right away." They tied the rope to the posts supporting the bunks, which are sort of four inch square timber posts. They tied the rope to his neck and to the opposite post, two of the strong men grabbed his legs and they pulled him horizontally and hanged him horizontally. Then they took his body and threw it into the latrines.

Anna Bergman
Young Czech woman, slave labour, Freiberg

We couldn't understand what we were doing. We were riveting what looked like aeroplane tailpieces, only they were much smaller. The workmanship was such that we thought: they can't put a living person in this, it won't hold. With hindsight we knew they were the tailpieces for V1s, or "doodlebugs", and were needed for just one trip. By then my pregnancy was showing and they couldn't send me back to Auschwitz because the Germans had left on 18 January 1945. We were standing twelve hours at a time at these machines. I was working across from my friend — it was very heavy work, but we didn't have to think much about it.

We occupied ourselves by cooking, in our minds, cakes with twelve eggs and four pounds of butter! The hungrier we were, the richer the cakes. One of my friends, who normally wasn't worried about food, once said, "Well, we have made all these cakes, now I fancy a banana with jam and chocolate icing all over it." By then I would have been five months pregnant — a pregnant skeleton, with the baby moving inside me. I was given lighter work; they gave me the job of sweeping the factory, three storeys for fourteen hours a day. In comparison, an easy job, but fourteen hours a day with broom and bucket! I did it automatically. After work we had to walk through the town looking like God knows what, and with the people shouting and spitting at us.

Gertrud "Trude" Levi
Young Hungarian Jewish woman, Hessica-Lichtenau concentration camp

We worked in this munitions factory, we were producing grenades and mines. The grenades were pear-shaped, with a round rod with seven wings. Some of us organised a sabotage group. We were a thousand Hungarian women and they knew our professions. They took the chemists and put them where the explosives were mixed. We worked round the clock in three shifts: ten hours, then two hours walking there and two hours back, plus the work in the camps and the *Appells*, so we didn't have much time to sleep. I was put on a conveyor belt where the grenades were lying flat and I had to screw on each bakelite cap very tightly. When there was no supervision, I did it very loosely on the slant. But the sabotage started in the mixing room: we increased the production to two and a half times what it had been, and the foremen thought these stupid Hungarian women are so frightened they work so hard, we don't have to supervise them so strictly, and once that happened they could alter the mixture so that the grenades couldn't explode.

Hugo Gryn
Ruthenian-Slovak Jewish youth, Lieberose

On one occasion, at Lieberose, I was party to the killing of a guard. He was Ukrainian, very dangerous, very vicious, a terrible menace, only about eighteen or nineteen. On one detail four of us went back with this guard to fetch the soup. We stopped for some reason and he sort of leaned with the gun next to him. I was one of those who held him with another, and another man hit him on the head with that gun and he was killed — he wasn't wearing a steel helmet, just a cap. We buried him there. We were able to sneak back into the work area, unobserved, and just mingled in. I don't think they missed him until the end of the work. We were made to stand outside for hours that evening, we knew why. I was in great fear for many days that one of the others might own up.

Abraham Zwirek
Polish Jewish youth, Skarzysko-Kamienna, Schlieben, Buchenwald and Theresienstadt
I didn't know what the next hour would bring but I closed my mind to that, you had to. Those people who didn't, who were living with the thought — oh well, what's the good of living, they're killing us, they're shooting us — those people had no hope. But I lived in hope and we cheered ourselves up whenever we could. In every way of life, however extreme life is, and hard and unbearable, there comes a time when you make yourself happy. When it came to evening, everything was calm and you went to a neighbour or a neighbour came to you. We sat down and talked and maybe had a sing-song and we'd try to forget the bad times, which was a very

good thing. We knew what was happening all around us but we tried to cheer ourselves up with the hope that it can't last forever and that was a very, very great help. This helped me right through the war. I believed, and I hoped, and I *willed* to survive.

Roman Halter
Polish Jewish youth, Stutthof
I usually used to summon members of my (murdered) family around me before going to sleep, to have a quiet communion with them, and to think that so many hours had passed and I was still alive.

Michael Etkind
Polish Jewish youth, Buchenwald and Sonneberg
When we were in the camps, although the situation was very grim, there was a sense of humour: people were joking and singing, and at night when we lay on the bunks one of my friends would be singing. I didn't know the tune, but he had a good voice. After the war when I heard Pagliacchi's "On with the Motley", I recognised the tune, but the Italian words were of course different from the Polish. He didn't survive. There was friendship, a sense of humour, there was singing even in the most terrible moments.

Leon Greenman
British Jewish inmate, Buna-Monowitz, Auschwitz-Birkenau
I got the chance to sing to the *Kapos* in the barracks for extra soup. I would sing songs like "Ave Maria", "The

Lambeth Walk" or "Underneath the Arches" — four or five songs as best I could. There was one occasion, in Barrack 14 I think, and the *Kapo* was a pro-British man, a German. He heard me sing and gave me a portion of soup.

Then he said, "Sing 'God Save The King'."

I said, "I dare not because the SS guard is outside."

He said, "Sing it."

I thought to myself: well, it might bring me a piece of bread or some soup. So up goes Leon on a chair and I started singing, "God save our gracious King . . ." And they applauded. Of course the prisoners were listening as well as the *Kapos* and *under-Kapos*. I thought to myself: what a blooming cheek that they asked me to do that!

The same man said, "Now then, you come here every evening for a portion of soup because singers must be fed, singers must be strong. And Christmas time, you come and sing for us then."

And every evening I went there and I got my portion of soup. Apart from that I still went singing around four or five other barracks as well.

Ezra Jurmann
German Jewish youth, Burggraben labour camp
One day, towards the end, a group of *Hitler Jugend* came to the camp to fight the Russians who were advancing. When they saw me in my prisoner's pyjamas, working and fiddling around with the stove, they were consumed with curiosity: what was I doing there? I could have so easily been one of them.

One asked, "Why are you here?"

I said, "I am a Jew."

"Hmm, that can't be true," he said.

"Well, why not?"

Then he said, "You are too young."

I said, "What, to be a Jew?"

He said, "No, to be a prisoner. Anyway, come and have dinner with us tonight, I've longed to hear the Jews' point of view."

So that evening I duly trooped in and we had bread and jam together.

I told them, "Well, I'm here because I am a Jew, there is no other reason."

They said, "You must have committed some crime."

I said, "Well, how old would you say I am? What crime could I have committed?"

The response was, "Our *Führer* wouldn't do that."

That was the kind of thing one heard before the war, time and time again. I suppose it's as good a defence mechanism as any. Then he went around and looked at me from the back and said, "In any case, you are not a Jew, the back of your head is pure Aryan."

Now this man sported a nose that according to the Nazi race experts could only be Jewish. So I felt sufficiently bold then and said, "Well, what about your nose then?"

He said "It's pure Roman."

So I said, "Right, pure Roman it is."

I'm only mentioning this to try and transmit some of the *Alice in Wonderland* flavour of the time.

Stanley Faull
Polish Jewish youth, Buchenwald

He was a retired general from the First World War who came to Buchenwald camp. He pointed to me and three other young men, wanting to take us with him to his home. The guards said, "No, if you want to invite someone, take the German political prisoners in the same group." But the general picked out four Jewish prisoners with the Star of David. The guards said "No, you have to go to the superior officer." The superior officer came down and they had an argument. He (the general) showed him what rank he was and permission was given for us to go to his home. It was a freezing cold day, February 1945. He took us to a beautiful, very old-fashioned house. On the very large mantelpiece there were three photographs of three *Luftwaffe* men, his three sons, with black ribbons across. His wife was crying. She explained to us that the three of them were lost on the Russian front.

Rena Quint
Polish Jewish child, Bergen-Belsen

I don't remember very much about my time in Bergen-Belsen. I don't remember what we did except seeing all those bodies. And I have asked people, "What did children do?" and they said, "They didn't do anything, they just tried to keep out of the way."

There were two women guards and every time they came in, people would start shivering because they were really mean people with whips.

I was not affected by the sight of dead bodies, in Bergen-Belsen there were bodies all the time and I don't think it even bothered me. I mean I didn't know this was not normal as I had been in this situation for most of my life. I remember saying to myself, "I'm never going to cry, I'm not going to call for my mummy or daddy because they're not going to come." There were other people I could call, but they were always new people. I remember a lot of survivors say that everybody was out for themselves. I don't remember that at all. Somebody always took care of me. As a small child, without having someone there for support, I could not possibly have survived.

Anita Lasker-Wallfisch
Young German Jewish woman, Bergen-Belsen
Belsen doesn't compare with Auschwitz at all. You see the difference between Auschwitz and Belsen basically is that Belsen was a *nothing* place. It was in the Lüneberg Heath, we went straight into tents. It was a very small camp which had all sorts of functions. It was never an extermination camp, there was no actual extermination plant there, but they didn't actually need it because conditions were such that you just perished there. Auschwitz was a place where you got killed. Belsen was where you perished.

That is perhaps the basic difference. People just sat and waited to die.

Steven Frank
Young Dutch child, Theresienstadt

I remember one morning, we in the children's home were made to get up and get dressed, and we were taken in file to the crematorium of Theresienstadt which was underground. We were made to stand in one great long line in this brick tunnel with bare bulbs lighting up the tunnel. Then from the right a little box would appear, big enough for a child to hold. So you went to your right, picked up the box, turned to your left and handed it to the next child, then you turned to your right, picked up the next box and so it went on for a long, long time. Each box contained the ashes of the dead of Theresienstadt and in traditional German fashion, each box had the name of the person whose ashes it contained, date of birth and when they died. I remember from time to time, either upstream or downstream, you would hear quiet little sobbing, not hysterical crying like when children were taken away, but subdued grief as somebody held the ashes — of their mother or father, of brother, sister or friend — briefly in their hands before passing it to the next person. We heard later that all these ashes were thrown into the river, all part of the removal of evidence towards the end of the war.

322

Anna Bergman
Young Czech Jewish woman, Freiberg
The bombing of Dresden was the most marvellous theatre I had ever seen in my life. We were only about ten miles away so we saw the incendiaries pouring down and the lights and everything; it was music to our eyes and ears. The Germans locked us up where we made these V1 parts, and they went into a shelter. We prayed the bombs would drop on us, we would have gladly died. And the next day when the workmen came back with those dreadful stories, our faces were all smiles.

REVOLTS

Some Jewish underground organisations managed to operate in a number of concentration, slave labour and death camps, including Auschwitz-Birkenau. In 1943, before the closure of Treblinka and Sobibor, two large revolts had succeeded. Jews in Treblinka, on hearing of the Warsaw Ghetto uprising from a transport brought to the camp, revolted on 2 August 1943, with as many as 200 escaping to the nearby forest, and approximately twenty men surviving German efforts to recapture them. This was followed, on 14 October 1943, by an uprising in Sobibor during which 300 prisoners escaped and 11 Nazis were killed, including the camp commander; nearly 200 managed to avoid capture but only a small number survived the war.

323

In Auschwitz-Birkenau, on 7 October 1944, in a daring act of desperation, a group of *Sonderkommando*, using dynamite smuggled by the Underground from a nearby munitions factory, blew up one of Birkenau's four crematoria. Six hundred prisoners escaped, but all were either recaptured or killed as they fled.

Kitty Hart-Moxon
Young Polish Jewish woman, Auschwitz
While I was sorting clothes in *Kanada*, we gathered an enormous amount of jewellery and money. Money was of no value to us, we used it as toilet paper, but the jewellery, we realised, could just come in handy for the Resistance movement. We didn't know who they were, but we figured it must have been most of the men; we didn't realise that some women were also involved. On one occasion I had a whole pile of diamonds and jewellery which I was determined not to hand in. It was too dangerous to take it into the main camp, so when I heard that a group of men were coming round to do some work, I managed to pass near them and drop them into the bucket of soup they were carrying. At the same time I tried to indicate that there was something at the bottom. They nodded so they did realise there was something there. Explosives had to be purchased and much of it was purchased by the loot that we managed to pass to the men who, in turn, passed it to the Resistance who, in turn, passed it to the girls who

worked in the munitions factory and they smuggled explosives back into the camp.

Eventually something did happen, transports were no longer arriving and there was a rumour that the whole area, especially the area around the crematoria, was going to be razed to the ground. So we knew our days were numbered. Now the men of the crematoria, the *Sonderkommando*, they knew that their time was up, they were always killed off when a new *Kommando* was formed, and the news leaked out that the Russian front wasn't all that far away. It happened on 7 October 1944: we heard a rumble and our first thought was that we were being bombed and we threw ourselves on the ground. But in the very next moment, from our hut we saw the chimney of Crematorium 4 topple to the ground. We couldn't understand this at first, and then we heard shooting from all sides and there was a command to lie spread-eagled on the ground.

Then a motorised division of SS moved in and we realised that it wasn't a bombing, it was an uprising. And of course it saved an enormous amount of lives because they could no longer continue the programme of killing, it had disrupted their routine. But of course they killed all the people involved. There was a huge interrogation, they came up to *Kanada* and we were all interrogated. When my number was called I thought some evidence had been found of my handing this jewellery over to the Resistance, but in fact I was told that I was to be

325

transferred back to Birkenau and be put on a transport with my mother.

Ignacz Rüb

Jewish Hungarian electrician, Buna-Monowitz, Auschwitz-Birkenau

We started hearing shooting every night. I had some contact with a SS man who came to see what we were doing and I asked him: the Russian front is not far away, what will happen now. He said, "I'm sorry but the camp is mined and when we have to leave from here, the whole camp and the people in it will be blown up." Can you imagine: after four and a half years, to die like that, nowhere to go, nowhere to hide! So I thought I must do something just to compensate for what I'd suffered. They had electric motors to drive the anti-aircraft guns and I thought if I changed these fuses, they wouldn't be able to shoot with the guns. So I took all the tops off and changed them so that when all the motors started, they would break down.

For a week or ten days, I couldn't sleep, it worried me so much that they'd find out what I had done. But suddenly one day, about half past ten in the morning, the Allied planes came and in a few minutes the factory was bombed and destroyed. Of course the Germans came to see what had happened and I gave a good explanation of what could happen if all the motors were switched on at the same time, and they started to rebuild the factory. But it was so badly damaged that they had to leave when the Russians were near in January 1945.

John Fink

German Jewish man, Auschwitz-Birkenau

By the time the winter of 1944/45 had come, we knew the Russians were advancing and in January 1945, we could hear the bombardment of Krakow which is only about 55 kilometres from Auschwitz-Birkenau. When we heard the increased gunfire we thought: well, that's the end now, that they would take a machine-gun to us. But on 18 January they told us not to go to the work station and in the afternoon we were assembled and told to march out in all the ice and snow. Nowadays, those marches are called "death marches".

1945

DEATH MARCH

We devised a way that the five of us were supporting the girl in the middle who was hanging on asleep with her feet and legs still moving. That way you could actually relax and get some kind of relief; and we changed so that everybody could have a go and sleep while walking — a different kind of sleep walking.

By August 1944, the Red Army was at the gates of Warsaw; simultaneously, the Anglo-American forces were liberating large parts of western Europe. As well as trying to obliterate all evidence of crimes in the western Soviet Union and Yugoslavia, the Nazis acted to ensure that no living witness would fall into Allied hands. As battlefronts approached the concentration camps, these were liquidated and inmates were forced out on death marches deep into the Third Reich. In the spring and summer of 1944, the camps in eastern Europe were the first to be dismantled with the inmates driven in a westerly direction away from the approaching Red Army.

As the noose around the Reich began to tighten in the winter of 1944/45, inmates by the thousands — Jews and non-Jews — even within the *Grossdeutsches Reich* itself, were sent on forced marches in various directions to concentration camps such as Bergen-Belsen, Dachau, Buchenwald,

Mauthausen, Sachsenhausen and Ravensbrück. Even this was not the end of the agony as the newly arrived inmates — in Ravensbrück, Sachsenhausen and, finally, Mauthausen — were pushed out again on further ordeals of marching as the Western and Soviet forces drew closer.

Without supplies, starved for days and weeks on end, hundreds of lightly clad, ill-shod prisoners literally froze to death in open fields where they had been forced to stand or lie all night. Others were crowded into draughty barns. Thousands died from exhaustion, diphtheria, typhus and other diseases and most suffered from crippling frostbite. Any prisoner lagging behind the columns, or caught trying to escape, was shot. Of 66,000 evacuated from Auschwitz from 18 January 1945, 15,000 died. Long columns of inmates from different camps trudged along, merging, separating, merging again in sluggish columns of increasing misery, leaving corpse-strewn paths behind. Finally, many SS guards abandoned their pitiful columns, leaving the exhausted, frozen and starving men and women to their own fate. In the last two months of the war, 250,000 prisoners were sent on death marches which continued until the last day of war in Europe, 8 May 1945.

John Fink
German Jewish youth, Auschwitz to Bergen-Belsen
When we were marched out of Auschwitz-Birkenau on 18 January 1945, we didn't know where we were going.

The only ones left behind were the sick prisoners, about eight, nine hundred of them, including Primo Levi; we thought they would all get killed because we couldn't imagine that they would let anybody live.

So we marched. Well, the weather was terrible and anybody who dropped back was shot in the back by the SS; so many. They were just left lying there, and there were already dead people lying there who had marched before us. These were the people who really couldn't do it because most people didn't even have shoes; they only had those wooden clogs and you couldn't march in those in that terrible frost and snow. I had a pair of shoes, but the right and left weren't the same. When you could keep your feet in order you had a chance of life; so many died because of their feet, many got water in their knees and the pus would come out of their bodies.

Anyway, we marched during the night and in the morning they put us in an empty tyre factory. We rested there for a while, then we were ordered to march again. In the afternoon we must have reached the former German border. We marched through the streets of Gleiwitz, there were street cars running and civilians about. The SS weren't around us there and we were so desperate for food that we asked people where there was a concentration camp — can you imagine the mentality! We stayed two days in an overcrowded camp; no order there, nothing.

After a day or two we were ordered to the railroad yards. We were put on an open train: every car was filled with prisoners, you couldn't sit down. We went on

333

through the days and nights, the train would stop every so often because of the bombings. People died. We would just throw the dead out of the cattle cars to make room to finally sit down. We came through Czechoslovakia and at the railroad stations we would have to take the sick out and leave them on the platforms where the *Gestapo* would kill them in front of the civilians of those towns in Czechoslovakia and Austria. Then they took us to Mauthausen. By then the camp was so overcrowded that its *Kommandant* refused our unloading, so the train went on and on.

Suddenly we came to Berlin. I knew Berlin, I saw the famous radio tower — that was 28 January 1945. We were unloaded in the big, old concentration camp of Sachsenhausen. Then back on the train again to Flossenburg, another overcrowded camp. Since the Americans were coming from one side, the Russians from another, and the British from up north, the noose was tightened. But they never got rid of the prisoners for some reason, except those who got killed or died on the way. Then I was loaded on another train and now we were sitting on the dead. We weren't human any more, we weren't supposed to *be* human anyway; that's how I came to Belsen around 8 March 1945.

Helen Stone
Young Polish Jewish woman, Auschwitz to Ravensbrück via Gross-Rosen

That march from Auschwitz in January '45! Half of the people were naked, well not exactly, but what *did* we wear? *One dress*. Some had no shoes and we walked in the snow for twenty-one days! I was wearing a dress. Do you know, I walked, I marched, and I *slept* while marching. We passed a few camps; what I liked was going through villages where we saw that *life* was still going on. Really, you didn't know that people could live a normal life with electricity in the rooms.

Anyway we came to Gross-Rosen. They couldn't let us in: no more space. But from there we got on trains, open trains, and it was *freezing* cold. I remember the Italian girl next to me, she must have done a wee and she froze to the floor and couldn't get up. On the way we saw another train with men; these men — oh, they looked terrible and so hungry! In my headscarf I had just crumbs of bread, and I threw it to them and they were tearing it up just like animals. They looked like animals, much worse than the women.

We were rather quiet, didn't talk much so as not to lose energy. Everybody who had a little piece of something threw it to the men because they looked *terrible*, really *terrible*. We drank snow, when the train stopped we ate frozen beetroot from the fields. Then we came to Ravensbrück where I spent two weeks on a bucket because I had dysentery.

Harry Lowit

Czech Jewish child, Auschwitz to Ebensee, via Melk

We walked out from Auschwitz in January 1945. It was cold and a lot of people didn't have adequate clothing. I still had my boots, my breeches and my jacket and was possibly warmer than most. I seem to remember the first night we stayed on a farm, in stables; it was warm there. We were marching five abreast. At the end of each group were those who couldn't walk and they were shot; the result was that when we got to Mauthausen we were only three thousand out of the ten thousand who had started off. For the last part of the journey to Mauthausen we were eventually herded into open wagons. It was winter and there was no roof, about one hundred to a wagon and we were standing. So probably that was the most traumatic of transportations for me. Again I survived, but it was more difficult.

When we got to Mauthausen, that's when I had my hair shaved off. I seem to remember remonstrating that I was the messenger of Kramer and Höss and how *dare* they do it. From there we went to Melk, this was in Austria, near Vienna. This was a much more relaxed camp and it was manned by the *Wehrmacht*, not the SS. They were much nicer people. I was there for a couple of months and was the messenger for the *Wehrmacht* man there. Then finally we went to Ebensee. This was a place not far from Salzburg. It was the last camp I was in and it was high up in the mountains. That is where I saw cannibalism. Yes, people were slicing meat off the dead. I was once more the messenger for the *Kommandant* there.

While the SS were still there, I heard that they were going to liquidate the people by putting them into the salt mines and blowing them up. I thought: well, I haven't really striven for three years to go this way. A friend of mine was a driver and was bringing in supplies from Ebensee. I had a chat with him and we decided that we should both try to go into the town and try to disappear while the coal was being loaded. And that's what happened.

Fritz Moses
German youth, Austria, witness of death march from Melk

We left Strehlen on about 16 February for Austria to stay with my uncle who was a state-certified state farm manager. An order came in April to move his farm into the Alpine fortress area. We drove the cows and horses every day on country roads for twenty kilometres in the direction of the Alpine fortress area — just like the Wild West! In the process we saw something terrible. Along the route we took was Melk, a sub-camp of Mauthausen. One time we travelled on a different route and the concentration camp inmates passed us; it was night and we saw these emaciated forms in striped clothing, black-blue and black-white with a Jewish Star. Sometimes you heard shots and when we passed them, there, lying on the side of the road, were blue-grey blankets, and when the Hungarian-Germans removed the blankets, we saw corpses of people who had been shot.

Later (after the war) there was a trial of a SS named Kreischner who was charged with crimes committed against this column of people. In other words, the man was called to account for it.

Ignacz Rüb
Hungarian Jewish man, Auschwitz to Landeshut

One night they put us in a factory that had been evacuated for some time and this had a kitchen. I was always looking for something to eat and I found a store for vegetables with some half-rotten carrots. I took some up to my friends upstairs. People used to watch where I went, knowing that I was always looking for something. They saw me going back and coming up again, and they went after me and found them. It didn't take more than half an hour and all the rotten carrots were gone, eaten up. The next day everyone got diarrhoea. It was very cold, freezing, and as we marched along, all this mess was frozen in our trousers and made a noise like cow-bells as we went. The SS laughed their heads off. You can imagine: diarrhoea frozen into ice! It was *terrible*.

Helen Pelc
Young Polish woman, Kurzbach to Bergen-Belsen

We marched and we marched and eventually we marched into Bergen-Belsen. We were crying, "Oh God, we want a roof over our heads and something to eat." About four hundred out of the thousand survived that march. My mother and I wanted to survive, we would talk about how we would survive and I remember her saying to me in Yiddish, "For you, my child, I am still with you. I'll see you through." When I look at the map now, can you imagine it! — Kurzbach to Mauthausen, then Gross-Rosen, then Bergen-Belsen! Because the guards needed rest, we got some, but no regular food, no bread, only what we picked up in the snow. No drink. Nothing.

Marsha Segall
Young Lithuanian Jewish woman, from Rendaels
We marched from one barn to a second one where they decided to stop. This was a barn which was both tragic and happy. The happy thing was that I was picked with another few to bake potatoes and that was inside, next to the oven. We hadn't had any food for six or seven days. So I was in a warm place and I could get some potatoes for my mother and sister. What was tragic was that the two women next to us stole our little bit of margarine and the gloves we had made. That meant death because we didn't eat the margarine, but rubbed it into the hands as protection. That was gone.

The next day was a blizzard and they decided to march. I don't know whether you've experienced a blizzard, but it hits you in the eyes and you don't even feel the cold because you try so hard to see. At the end of the march, when I tried to help my mother, I realised that I couldn't bend my fingers because I had no margarine to rub in them and no gloves. Mummy also had frostbite, we had it everywhere on hands and face.

When I came to the next barn there was all this whimpering — the crying and the misery was something unbelievable. I was sure that was my last day. And from there I marched one day with frozen feet and hands. At the beginning you are numb but then the flesh gets black and it smells of pus and starts to get painful. Next day, someone came up to me and said,

339

"Look, I think we ought to escape because you won't make it another day, you've got nothing to lose." My mother and sister urged me to go and four of us crawled from this barn and went into another and hid in huge stacks of straw until they marched off — that day they couldn't count because they had lost three-quarters of the women. I was told after the war that my mother and sister died of typhus at the end of that march.

After this I managed to pass as a German refugee and was given medical treatment in Gdynia. By that time gangrene had started to set in and my feet had started to shrink. When the doctors came to check my feet it was the first time I had seen them and I just can't forget it. They uncovered a bit at the end and the doctor just scraped the flesh which was like burnt sticks . . . I thought I'd never be able to walk; and my hands — the skin just came away from the bone . . . I was taken by a pocket battleship, the *Deutschland* (re-named *Lutzow* in 1941, but still known as the *Deutschland* in the Baltic area), then by a small hospital boat, to Bergen on Rügen Island, for the operation. They did a *marvellous* job, they saved everything possible.

Ignacz Rüb
Hungarian Jewish man, Auschwitz to Landeshut
We came to a town and in the night they put us into this space in a stone quarry. After about two hours we had used up the oxygen in this stone quarry place. Somehow I managed to get within a couple of metres

of the door, many were knocking on it because we were starting to suffocate. I remember I saw my life coming before me and I thought this was the end. In the morning they opened the door and were terrified that there were so many dead; they called for ambulances and started to carry the people out. I wasn't entirely dead and I survived. But I want to tell you how hungry I was. I had no knife, only a tin and I thought I would go and try to cut a piece off of one of the dead. I *had* to have something to eat. I started to move on all fours, and just then they started taking them away. I mention this to show how terrible hunger is. Had I done it, cut from the dead, meat, I don't think I could have lived with myself, but at the time . . . hunger is the most *terrible* thing. Only someone who has experienced it can understand. It can make a man do the most unbelievable things.

Jan Hartman
Czech Jewish youth, Czechowice to Buchenwald
This march was something *unforgettable*: the Polish countryside was under snow, freezing cold, January, the temperature must have gone down to thirty below zero or more, *very* cold. One of the things which would have meant death was if you had picked up paper cement bags to put under your pyjamas — they hit you with wooden sticks just to feel if you had them under your clothing, and if you did, it didn't end up very well. My brother dared several times, but I didn't. We were driven along by the SS, and along the way there were little heaps, mounds that were full of the dead of

341

the preceding transports, and behind us occasional shots — those who couldn't walk any more. That took a full day and at night we got into a barn. It was a formidable temptation to try to get away because the hay was a huge mountain. My brother and I were hesitating: if they catch us, we are executed. We both decided not to escape.

So then it went on, another full day until we got to Bielsko which was a huge junction, enormous. You know I had seen so many dead before, but you see just *one* and it hits you, and there was a person between the railways with all this blood, he had just been killed and it struck me — almost like a joke — it's becoming *serious*. But then we got onto the open wagons on our way to Buchenwald. I don't know how long it took: three days or it may have been six, I just don't know. But we were on those open wagons. It was freezing. And I remember at one moment someone near to me tried to kill me. It was a man I knew called Fischel. He was a very nice man, father of a boy I knew, and he took me by the nose and literally tried to tear it off and strangle me. People were already crazy, losing their minds.

At one moment along the railroad there were little houses approaching a town, and in front of the houses the Germans saw us coming by and were throwing cigarettes at us. People were dying of *hunger*, but it was a good action. Then there is a complete void, I just remember suddenly waking up on a layer of dead people, frozen like stone — many layers of them, three, four, five layers high, and just under me was Fischel, dead. But, "*Raus! Raus! Schnell! Schnell!*" — "Out! Out! Quick! Quick!" and somehow I got into this *Grosslager* (big camp) as it was called, the new part of Buchenwald, where I was separated from my brother George because somehow he was in the *Kleinelager* — the small, political camp.

George Hartman
Czech Jewish youth, Czechowice to Buchenwald
I remember different circumstances on the train from my brother. There was a man who had this metal pan, and he started hitting me; I still have a depression here on my head where he kept hitting me with the edge. He was going to kill me, so I sat on him, and sat on him until he stopped moving. I sat on him so that I could survive.

Barbara Stimler
Young Polish Jewish woman, Pirschcow to Niederschlesien
One day we stopped in a village; they took two wagons, put the ill girls in the wagons and we had to push them into the forest where they finished them off. It was better for them, believe you me.

Zdenka Ehrlich
Young Czech woman, Kurzbach to Bergen-Belsen
One day we came back from our hard labour in the forests at this place called Kurzback and instead of going back in the barrack, the *Kommandant* said, "We have to clear out of here, tonight we start a march." That was 21 January 1945. About half an hour out of

343

the camp, we heard a strong explosion and the news was that the sick bay had been destroyed, so anybody in there was killed. We marched a fortnight, day and night, along the flat, windy and icy cold countryside. One night it must have been thirty-five degrees below zero. I have never seen it before but we all had completely white noses like pieces of ice, completely frozen. And we learned something that I didn't know was possible — you could walk and sleep at the same time. So we devised a way that the five of us were supporting the girl in the middle who was hanging on asleep and the feet and legs were still moving. And that way you could actually relax and get some kind of relief, and we changed so that everybody could have a go and sleep while walking — a different kind of sleepwalking.

Barbara Stimler
Young Polish Jewish woman, march from Pirschcow to Niederschlesien
A Pole said to Irma and me, "I will hide you," and he put us in a loft and said he was going to bring us food and was going to help us. And in the night two soldiers came and they raped us, and then they threw us from the loft and we had to go again from place to place.

Zdenka Ehrlich
Young Czech woman, Kurzbach to Bergen-Belsen
Funny, human things always happen. Before we left, somebody found a store of raw potatoes, and we stuffed these in our clothes and we were eating them raw like juicy apples and they sustained us because of the

344

starch. As we marched, behind me was a milliner from Prague, and she tapped me on the shoulder one day and said, "Excuse me, do you think you could lend me a few potatoes, I'll return them after the war." Things like that sound funny now, but they didn't then. She didn't survive, even *with* the potatoes.

Alfred Huberman
Polish Jewish youth, Rehmsdorf to Theresienstadt
One remarkable incident: we were walking towards the Sudetenland inhabited by Czechs and when we got to a suburb of some town, it was like a mirage. On the verges, big slices of bread had been put there; the Czechs must have seen us passing by and saw how emaciated we were. There were no people about. I just flew for it. It was dangerous because I could have been shot, but I got some for myself and for a friend who had no shoes and couldn't rush and shove for it. We walked on and when we got to where there were houses, hands kept coming out with bread, cakes, cigarettes — no faces, just hands throwing these into the road.

Zdenka Ehrlich
Young Czech woman, Kurzbach to Bergen-Belsen
Eventually, they loaded us in open coal trucks — a transport of death. Always we thought: whatever comes next will be better; but it was always a shade worse, much worse, closer to death. You were really moving towards the end. It was so crowded you could stand only on one foot. I hung on for five days, five nights

345

inside the truck. Every now and then hysteria broke out and those who didn't have enough strength virtually fell to the ground and the mass of bodies just closed over them. I lost my footing and fell backwards and for a whole night I was sitting on a dead woman's body and the only space for my hand to support myself was on her open mouth, on her teeth.

After that it was a stay in Mauthausen, then off again. This time it was a normal, absolutely luxurious train for people, not animals, not for coal, not for goods, but for people. We went west through Rokycany. The next stop was Pilzen, behind the Skoda works. The workmen were fantastic. They all came to the fence and started to shout, "Why don't you run away? We'll hide you." I left the train — as if mesmerised, and ran to the fence. I said, "You have bread?" They brought two huge loaves of bread which they threw over the fence and I took it back to the train and of course we had a feast.

Ruth Foster
Young German Jewish woman, from Sophienwald, Pomerania
By that time we were like zombies: we had nothing to eat, nothing to wear, we were cold, we were humiliated and we couldn't care less about what was happening to us. We had lost everything and life wasn't worth living. We were marching at night and during the day they would rest us in a forest or in an old barn. At one time, my two friends and I couldn't walk any further. There was a ditch in the road and we said: we'll stay here, at least we'll be buried together when they find us. A

German soldier or SS man passed us. "Oh," he said, "they're not worth a bullet," and he just walked away.

Roman Halter
Polish Jewish youth, Pirnau to Dresden area

The progress from Pirnau was very slow, we did something like eight or nine kilometres a day — this was February 1945. We were in our striped outfits and, before we left, everybody had a strip shorn in the middle of his head so that if we escaped, we could be easily recognised — so really we were the first punks! Once we were stopped in an area and asked to sit down in the market square. The German population came out and the SS wanted to show what beasts we were, so they cut up bits of turnip and carrot and threw them in the middle so that we should fight over them. But our leader said, "Don't fight, keep your dignity." We looked up to him and so we listened. The SS were disappointed so they started kicking those on the outside of the circle, but we didn't perform. Very few of the people who came to stare had any empathy with us. They shouted insults and said that we were responsible for the bombing; it was terribly disheartening — they were supportive of the SS. And so like poor starved souls, eventually we were put in an agricultural implement shed. By that time the SS were also tired and thought we wouldn't run away and they left only four people to guard us. That is when, with a small group of those who came from Auschwitz, I managed to escape . . .

Michael Etkind

Polish Jewish youth, from Sonneberg

We saw a group of German civilians with swastikas on their arm bands; they were older Germans, like home guard, with guns. They had captured a group of American soldiers and were taking them into the forest. The Americans were waving to us and calling, "*Hitler kaput*" (Hitler is finished), and smiling. They were taken into a small birch wood forest and then we heard shots and they must have been killed. We could read from the grim expressions on the faces of the Germans what they were going to do. But the Americans didn't realise what was going to happen to them and that, of course, was very upsetting for us because we were so near liberation.

Zdenka Ehrlich

Young Czech woman, Kurzbach to Bergen-Belsen

At the next stop we experienced air-raids for the first time; these were phosphorus bombs, they went: "Eeeeeeshzh, boom!" and it was music to our ears. We thought: well it can't be too long before the end of the war — this was February 1945 — any day, from now on any day, don't lose courage, keep going, it can't last, there will be an end soon. But as I said before, every stop was worse. After about five days, the train stopped and it was Bergen-Belsen. My very first impression was: this is *beautiful*. It was all forest, trees, birch trees, nothing menacing, no guards, no barbed wires, lovely countryside.

Kitty Hart-Moxon

Young Polish Jewish woman, from Gross-Rosen area to Salzweden

I don't know how many days we were on this march in February, it seemed endless. One day there was a lot of commotion and a cart with potatoes went by. I threw myself at this cart and of course the next thing I knew, I was hit by a rifle butt from behind. I believe I was knocked out and was carried by my friends until I regained consciousness. It transpired that I had a fractured skull, nevertheless I continued my death march the following day.

At one time we had to march towards a mountain range and the only pathway open to us was a very narrow path over the top of the summit and down the other side. I think it must have been something like a thousand metres. When we got to the top there was a most amazing sight. It was a plateau and there were hundreds of German civilians in their carts, still asleep because it was early morning, with hoods over their carts, and they had sausages and all kinds of things hanging all over the carts. There were lots of cows. I remember I threw myself at one and started milking; unfortunately it was a bull and I was thrown to the side.

The next thing, we started raiding the Germans. They didn't know what had hit them! About ten thousand women suddenly overran this area and the soldiers couldn't shoot because of the civilians around. So we managed to grab quite a lot of food. At one point I managed to dislodge a bucket which was hanging from one of the carts. When I looked inside it was just a bucket of lard, but my mother was overjoyed because so many of us had frostbite on our toes and hands and so we smeared ourselves with this: our hands, face and hair, and passed it down the column and it protected us from the cold.

Well, we were transported from one camp to another, shunted from one place to another and a lot of people died. Just before liberation we were placed in what was probably the worst experience of the whole war: we were locked in an air-tight truck. Many of the girls began to faint. I believe the only way my mother and I survived was because I had a knife and I enlarged a crack on the floor of the truck and my mother and I took turns to breathe.

We had been bolted in that truck on a siding outside Belsen. For some time muffled sounds could be heard from the trucks next to us. But eventually there were no sounds at all and we realised that all these people were by now dead. Suddenly we heard footsteps and with all our might we began to scream and bang against the doors of this truck and suddenly they opened and we simply fell out on to two or three men. One was an officer. I think they were surprised at what they'd done. And my mother said, "You can kill us here, but we are *not* going back into that truck. We demand to be taken to a camp."

And these men conferred and one went off on a bicycle and came back and said, "The *Kommandant* of a nearby camp agrees to take you in." And that is how I came to a place called Salzwedel.

Anna Bergman

Young Czech Jewish woman, Freiberg to Mauthausen
On 4 April the factory was abandoned and we were evacuated and put in sooty, open coal wagons. It was raining — it was really apocalyptic. We were sent off across the Czech border and we were hoping to return to Terezin but instead we turned south. Before that we stood in a siding for about a fortnight with no facilities: nothing to wash with, we were dirty with the soot, it was raining and muddy, no food — it was a catastrophe, dreadful. Going slowly south in Bohemia the train stopped for some reason. I stood at the open door, a pregnant skeleton, a passing Czech farmer offered me a glass of milk. The SS standing near me raised his whip as if to strike me. I have never seen a face like that Czech farmer when he saw what that SS was going to do! I thought he was going to die, but he gave me the milk and the SS didn't hit me.

As we arrived at Mauthausen, I started to have the baby. The camp was on a hill and I was put on a cart with some others and when we came to the camp I had to change for another cart and this is where I gave birth — changing from one cart to the other. There was a Russian doctor there and I begged her to help me, but no. Then down the hill on this other cart, with the birth pangs, with twenty women in the last stages of typhoid fever and lice running all around. The baby started to come out and I must have screamed a bit because a SS passing by said, "You can scream as much as you want!" I never knew if he meant it kindly or ironically; halfway down the baby came out without moving, without crying, and I was totally indifferent because of these other women dying on the cart and all the lice running around in millions, and something here between my legs.

For five minutes we were going down and nobody helped me. And when we arrived in the *rivier* — the camp hospital — they called a doctor who happened to be a gynaecologist from Belgrade and he smacked the child's bottom and it started to cry. I was told it was a little boy and he was wrapped in paper because there was nothing else, and I was very happy. I was given my own bunk — a miracle! The Germans had changed from being murderous to being very, very good-hearted people — they knew the war was lost — and they brought me some bread and macaroni. I had so much milk for the baby that I could have fed five.

Michael Etkind
Polish Jewish youth, from Sonneberg camp
Towards the end of April we were in a barn and there was a rumour that Hitler was dead. We were lying on the straw and it was about seven in the evening, not yet dark. The SS were standing outside the big double doors and the guards were sitting on stools in the doorway, they all seemed sad. Suddenly, someone whispered, "Hitler is dead. Hitler is dead!" It was a kind of electrifying situation — Hitler is *dead*. Suddenly, the man we called "The joker" — he was always telling jokes — suddenly, he leapt up and started jumping up and down in the barn shouting, "Hitler is dead, I have survived, Hitler is dead, what else do I

need? I am happy." And he started dancing. He was a tall man with long arms and long legs, and he ran out through the double doors into the field singing and dancing. A German lifted his gun and shot him. We could all see: he sort of raised his arms, turned round and collapsed like a puppet on a string when the strings were cut. It was very strange. There was silence, we were very sad. We thought: the war is virtually over, but what will happen to us?

Gertrud "Trude" Levi
Young Hungarian Jewish woman, from Tekla camp near Leipzig

I got myself into this barn; already there were two of my camp-mates there, a young girl and her mother from my home town. It was April 1945. We were very weak and didn't know what was going to happen to us. During the night, the door opened and five men came in with torches and with knives and revolvers in their outstretched arms. They were Russians and seeing we were women, came nearer and lay down next to us, wanting to do something to us. Then they decided that we were not appetising women and left us alone. It was quite obvious to them who we were and that we weren't quite human. A couple of them stayed and the others came back with a German-speaking officer who looked at us, told them to go and bring stretchers and take us to the farm. These men were ex-prisoners of war, they had come to the farm to look for farmers who had treated them badly, expecting to find them in the barn, but they found us instead.

Stanley Faull

Polish Jewish youth, Buchenwald to Theresienstadt

That journey from Buchenwald to Terezin, April 1945, was the worst for me because I was at a very low ebb. How any of us survived, I don't know: freezing bad weather, no organised control, lack of food, lack of sleep, ice, no sanitation, no water to drink apart from rain and snow. People were dying, and the dead and the very, very sick had to stay where they were, because there was no way of moving them. Survival was a *miracle* — ten days to two weeks this lasted!

We had no idea where we were going, we stopped in sidings and other trains would go past. We were unguarded but nowhere to go. I always remembered what my father said: "Now that America is in the war and Britain is on our side, we're going to destroy this man; our job is to wait it out and survive this period of time." This stuck in my mind all the time: it is an abnormal time but it will pass, maybe it will take weeks, maybe several years. I now think that somebody used to look over me, direct me — call it what you may — in order to make sure that I would survive. I feel to this day that there was another being there looking over me. Why I was chosen, I don't know. But I was, and the result is that I am now getting on for seventy years old, and I'm still here.

1945

LIBERATION

To be free was a circumstance that was completely strange. To be able to wake up and know you could go outside the perimeter of wherever you were and nobody would challenge, "Where are you going?" It's the most wonderful feeling of all — freedom!

The liberation of the camps started with the advance of the Soviet Red Army from the east. Majdanek was entered on 24 July 1944, Auschwitz on 27 January 1945 and Stutthof on 1 May 1945. In all these camps the SS had fled before the advancing troops, leaving behind pitifully small, barely alive remnants of the camps' populations, very few of these having the physical strength to survive liberation. Soviet forces went on to liberate: Sachsenhausen, 27 April; Ravensbrück, 29 April; and Gross-Rosen, 8 May.

The Western Allies had liberated a number of camps during the summer and autumn of 1944, but it was not until 4 April 1945, when the American forces discovered the small camp of Ohrdruf with its heaps of emaciated corpses, that the grim reality began to hit them. Buchenwald and Nordhausen were freed on 11 April; Dachau on 29 April; Mauthausen and Ebensee on 5 and 6 May. Belsen was liberated by the British on 15 April 1945. The Red Army entered Theresienstadt, the last camp to be liberated,

357

on 9 May. Shocking sights greeted the young Allied soldiers who reacted with horror and outrage. In almost every case, the liberators forced local Germans to view the sites.

As well as these more notorious camps, hundreds of others, holding tens of thousands of victims of all nationalities, races and religions, were also liberated by Allied forces just before the total collapse of Nazism. As the Allied armies swept across Europe from east and west, Jews in hiding started to emerge.

Jerry Koenig
Polish Jewish child, Kosow, Poland

The front line on the Eastern Front was moving in the right direction. I'd hear the sounds of the artillery, bombs and shooting all coming from the east. One day it sort of rolled over and started coming from the west. Mr Goral opened the trap door, "They're gone." That was the day of liberation. We left the bunker and were just so absolutely grateful to the Soviet troops. It was late summer, early fall '44, a very hot day. We were just sitting in amazement, watching all these soldiers march by. And they were looking at us, probably more amazed than we were looking at them. You can just imagine what you look like when you haven't seen the sun for longer than a year and a half! We were completely white.

Lili Stern-Pohlmann
Polish Jewish child, Lvov

When the Russians re-occupied Lvov, we were still lying low. It was July 1944 and by then (with the

358

assistance of the Metropolitan Andrej Count Sheptyckij) I was in a Ukrainian orphanage, with my mother next door in a convent. For a day or two Lvov was an empty city, very eerie because there was such complete silence: no shooting or bombing, nothing moving, everybody was taking cover. The Polish and Ukrainian populations were afraid of the Russians and if there were any Jews in hiding, they stayed hidden because of the uncertainty. Then one fine day, suddenly a Russian soldier on horseback entered our part of town, with a tank close behind him. People started rushing out and kissing his boots; one Jewish man rushed out from his hiding place shouting, "Thank you for coming and saving our lives." He was shot on the spot by the Ukrainian underground — he ran out too soon.

The town was then in upheaval and disarray; but for us, of course, we were *free*. Within a few days we could go out and thank those who had helped and saved us. *Everybody* was looking for their families. A Jewish committee was formed, but there were literally only a few Jews left.

Halina Kahn
Young Polish Jewish woman, Lodz Ghetto
When the last transport left the ghetto in 1944, just seven hundred remained and we worked there from August 1944 until 18 January when the Russian Army came. Just before the end, when the order came that we all had to go down to *Appell*, people just ran and hid in cellars, wherever they could. My husband was from Germany and didn't know where to hide, so just

359

twenty-nine of us, mainly Jews from Germany, went down to the empty *Appell*. They took us down to the cellar in the prison.

Then after twenty-four terrible hours without food or water, we heard knocking on the door. Our people said, "Don't answer, it's probably the SS and they're drunk." But the banging was louder and then the locks were shot and Poles came in and said, "We are free, the war is over, the Russian Army is coming in." The Russian Army arrived. That was a terrible agony: they were Cossacks and they had been on the front for three or four years, dirty and black, and they saw women for the first time and would take the women and girls to the barracks. They raped these hungry women and left them like little heaps of rubbish.

We were hiding. I didn't have any hair, I was wearing a little red scarf over my head and I was dressed in men's clothes. My husband painted us in different colours making out we were ill and when they came to us, we screamed in Russian that we were very dangerously ill, so they kept away from us.

Ezra Jurmann
German Jewish youth, Burggraben
Little by little the thunder of the guns was heard at night — a sort of rolling, rumbling noise in the background, continuous. At night, when it was dark, one could see fires on the horizon. I stayed in the cellar from then on. Then one early evening, there was suddenly a shout, "Russki! Russki! Russki!" I rushed up the cellar steps and saw the camp was full of Russians.

I went back to my bale of straw and I cried for the next two hours or so.

This was just before my sixteenth birthday on 20 March 1945. When you read in novels about leaving prison, the prison doors always seem to clang shut. Well, this gate was hanging at a crazy angle and we just walked out of the camp. Soon the two girls I was with had to support me on each side; I couldn't walk unaided any more. We were picked up by a Russian first-aid post. The first thing they did was to try feeding us. I couldn't eat anything: my first real meal in freedom and I couldn't even eat it! Those Russians were very kind; they were junior officers and medical people.

John Chillag
Czech Jewish youth, Buchenwald

I was in the "infirmary". I don't know how some of them crawled up to the upper two levels where the weakest people were, but certainly once up there, no way could you come down for food or anything else. I was on the second level which wasn't that bad, apart from getting all the excrement and everything from the top. My disease was extreme, final weakness. We were just lying on those bunks, too weak to do anything, and I wouldn't have survived more than a day or two.

The camp was liberated in two ways: some of the longer-serving prisoners over the years had made, or acquired, some guns and ammunition and when the Americans were a mile or so away they started to self-liberate. With a clandestine radio they encouraged the Americans to move a little bit faster and they turned up in half an hour or so. This was the first big camp liberated by the Western powers — the Russians had got to Auschwitz and some other Polish camps earlier, but Buchenwald was the first liberated by Western powers on 11 April 1945. It was the first time that anything like that was seen. And the American soldiers were trying to give us everything they had: chewing gum, bully beef, and of course that, unintentionally, caused the death of many people. A week after liberation I weighed fifty-six pounds.

Jan Hartman
Czech Jewish youth, Buchenwald

Arriving in Buchenwald, I was among the *Muselmänner*. I was taken to the *rivier*, the hospital of the *Kleinelager*, where they were cutting my frost-bitten toes like mushrooms. I must have got back to the *Grosslager* where I was mixed up mainly with Russian POWs who were dying like flies. They were completely starved. One thing I remember well: there was a dying man who was alone, he was given some porridge stuff and as he was dying he spat out this big red stain of blood in the middle of it. I don't remember whether it was I who ate up this food with the blood, or somebody else. Then it was complete darkness in the barrack until one day, in the sunshine at the end of the barrack, there appeared a smartly dressed American soldier. It was liberation.

Then I see myself in this sunny place with the Americans, and they were interested in me and my brother because we could speak English and discuss things with them. It was wonderful for them, it was *wonderful* for us. I will never in my life forget what we got to eat, because among everything there was peach compote. It was like a miracle. That would be my recollection of Buchenwald except for one thing: even in Auschwitz I hadn't seen so many dead. Here they were massed everywhere, several metres high, not human any more, just dry bones. That is my recollection of Buchenwald, liberated on 11 April. I think Roosevelt died the following day.

George Hartman
Czech Jewish youth, Buchenwald

I heard a rumour that the Americans were coming to liberate Buchenwald but how the whole camp was dynamited and it would be destroyed before they came. I thought, well, what can you do? Nothing. The guards were still there. Then the liberation suddenly happened. And there was this sudden chaos with people running around and rounding people up. I remember somehow I was at the officers' swimming pool which was covered with ashes — in Buchenwald they were also burning people and it was spewing ashes — and in the water were these SS swimming. The prisoners threw them in and as they came to the edge, we would kick them back in until they were all drowned. None of them survived. We didn't drown them, we just didn't let them get out.

Then there was total chaos: the fences were broken and people started running outside the camp. I was in a horrible shape but I went with this running mob. And I remember I went to this Ilse Koch's house. People were

363

taking things: furniture, lamps — whatever they found. I didn't take anything. I was too sick and I decided I wanted to get out of that, I couldn't stand it because I was going to be trampled to death — it was mania. I decided to wander away from the camp and came to a nearby farm. There was a German farm woman, scared to death of me, telling me that she didn't *do* anything, she didn't *know* there was a camp — and she was about two thousand feet away! — and that her husband died on the front. She gave me a raw egg, it was the first food and it nearly killed me, it was the most disgusting thing.

I stumbled out of that place. If I had been a little more alive, I would have raped that woman, but at that point there was nothing. Here I had been trying to survive in order to have sex, never having made love in my life, and here was a single woman, not yet thirty years old, but I had no thoughts of that at the time. I decided there's no way I'm going to survive much longer, the only chance is going back to the camp, so I went back; I don't remember the details, but somehow I got reunited with my brother.

Josef Perl
Czech Jewish youth, Buchenwald
When the Americans came in, I was three-quarters dead. I opened my eyes and everything was moving, I couldn't quite see their faces. Then all of a sudden I saw a smiling face, and he sort of took my hand and lifted me up and I looked around and thought: I'm dreaming. He gave me a bar of chocolate. All the

youngsters from our block and some other blocks went to live in the SS quarters. We had wood; I used to make the food, we would share it.

I built myself up. We youngsters had a different perception of life, the will to live was so strong; we only needed a bit of space to move and there were plenty of fields with cabbage, carrots, beetroot, and if anyone wanted to stop you taking the things then you threatened to kill them.

Some German boys came and told us there were four SS hiding on a nearby farm and they would take us to them. So we went up to the farm with guns, picked them up and were marching them to the Americans, but we were stopped by a Russian officer. He said, "What's this?" We told him we were taking the SS to the Americans. He asked if our guns had bullets, we said: yes, sure. So he took a gun from one of the boys and went bang, bang. He said, "You are fools, what do you think the Americans will do? They will pat them on the back and say, 'Don't be a naughty boy.' " He shot them, no hesitation.

Stephen Dale
German Jewish refugee, SOE, prisoner of war, Oflag 79, Querum, Germany
On 12 April 1945, American tanks rolled into the camp. They were very depressed as Roosevelt had died that day. But it was a great moment, they were marvellous to us and as victors they were on top of the wave and gave us everything they could do without. It really was a fantastic moment. For me it was significant

in one respect, because the constant fear under which I had lived from the moment I was taken prisoner suddenly didn't exist any more. I was always terrified that they would discover my background as a German Jew: that would have been enough to spell the end. That was a *phenomenal* relief.

Helen Stone
Young Polish Jewish woman, Zwodau

They put us six Jewish girls in this cellar without food or water. And then one day in April we heard a terrible noise outside, but we still sat in that dark cellar; and then somebody opened the door and light came in, the sun was so strong that we just couldn't keep our eyes open. They said, "There are soldiers here and the Germans are running away." And we came out and kept our eyes shut at first, but I wanted to know who the soldiers were. I saw tanks with a star, but I wasn't sure whether they were Americans or Russians.

I was wearing a belt which I had found in Auschwitz, the belt had an inscription on it in Hebrew. I had put a little rag around the buckle and I took off the rag. I was facing the sun and that buckle must have caught the eye of one of the soldiers and he walked towards me and asked me, in very bad German, "Do you know what that is?" — pointing to the Star of David in the middle of the buckle — and, being Jewish, I answered with a question, "Do *you* know what it is?"

"Yes, it is the Star of David."

I thought: maybe he is a Jew, and very, very quietly I whispered, "I'm Jewish," and he said, "So am I."

And from that moment on they really took care of us.

Antonie Krokova
Czech gypsy child, Wittenberg

The Russians came, they brought cows and horses and put the old people and children on carts. I couldn't walk either; we had swollen legs, inflamed. One Russian gave me a piggy-back and carried me for almost three kilometres, saying "Good girl." They took us to a village and said, "Which house would you like?" And the women would say, "Wow, that's a nice house." And they chased the Germans out and we moved in. The Russians said, "Take whatever you like, dress up." We spent about a month there because some of us were ill and the old people were weak, starved. The Russians killed whatever they could — pigs, chickens, geese, anything they came across. There was abundance. Sometimes people ate a lot and then, poor guys, they died. They had weak stomachs so they couldn't cope with that.

Jan Imich
Polish Jewish youth, Nordhausen

The camp was in the industrial part of Nordhausen. When the first wave of bombers passed, we ran out. The wire had gone so we all ran into the open fields, hoping to hide there. The American fighters, of course, saw us and, thinking we were Germans, started strafing

367

us. But we couldn't run far because the Germans started rounding us up and eventually we were taken back to the hangars and left there. It was like *Dante's Inferno* — everything around us was burning, with charred bodies lying all over the place. Inside the camp hundreds were killed by bullets, bombs and shrapnel. The next day the same thing happened, the Americans came back with a vengeance and bombed everything in sight. I survived without a scratch — a miracle because there were hundreds, if not thousands, killed. After that for two or three days, German activity was intense, they were all around, shouting, screaming, and everybody just tried to lie low pretending to dead. And all the time you could hear the sound of war — the artillery — coming nearer . . .

One day there was silence in the camp; we couldn't hear any guns, nothing, just silence. A group of us were just lying there on the straw, and from a distance you could hear footsteps, very distinctly from long afar, on these concrete floors. They were unmistakably footsteps of soldiers. Everybody froze because we thought perhaps the Germans were coming back. We all lay there, very quietly, not moving, pretending to be dead, and these footsteps coming nearer and nearer, and then all of a sudden they stopped. So after a few seconds we began to raise our heads to see, and there in a doorway we saw this man, quite a tall man — or he appeared to be tall — in an unfamiliar uniform, with a helmet with a big red cross. And all of a sudden we realised he was an American.

It was such a moving experience — you have no idea. We all got up and started shouting — in all languages — "Hooray, America!" And this soldier looked very bewildered; he looked around and smiled and told us to stay where we were. And about maybe half an hour, two hours later, we could hear the sound of trucks, and all of a sudden there was a swarm of Americans and Red Cross people — also a film unit. Before we were moved, we were filmed outside the barracks of Nordhausen Camp, 11 April 1945.

BERGEN-BELSEN

Ghastly conditions horrified troops of the 63rd Anti-Tank Regiment of the Royal Artillery when they liberated Bergen-Belsen on 15 April 1945. During the first ten days, the British buried thousands of dead. Despite heroic efforts by army medical personnel and a group of volunteer British medical students from London teaching hospitals, a mass outbreak of typhus occurred between 19 April and 5 May, and nearly 11,000 of the 60,985 inmates alive at liberation died of typhus. A Friends Relief Service team of seven women and five men — RT 100 — moved to Belsen soon after liberation, under the auspices of the Red Cross Commission. They stayed for six weeks helping to clear the camp, repatriate able-bodied survivors and provide much-needed humanitarian assistance to the majority remaining within the camp.

369

Michael Lewis
British Jewish NCO cameraman, Army Film & Photographic Unit, Bergen-Belsen

Captain Evans came and said that he had been told that the Germans had a camp ahead with what they called "political prisoners", that there was danger of disease and they wanted to hand this over to us; would we go and cover it? It seemed a bit vague and rather dull, but certainly safer than following the front up. We drove in a jeep through dense pinewoods to a wired gate. That place was Belsen. There were people standing behind the wire at the entrance to the gate, pressing their faces against the wire, eating us up with their eyes. They were not political prisoners, this was a concentration camp. They couldn't believe their eyes at our khaki colour and our British voices. We began speaking; I could understand a bit of German and I said that I was Jewish. And one of them said in a voice of wonder: "You are, and you are *free?*"

John Fink
German Jewish youth, Bergen-Belsen

Confusion started really in earnest because the SS disappeared, only certain troops were left behind, *Kapos* and the privileged prisoners disappeared. That was on the 13th and 14th of April. By that time I was almost a skeleton, I was about eighty pounds by that time, and there was nothing but dirt, filth, lice and bed bugs. On the 15th, in the afternoon — a sunny day, I understand it was a Sunday — we saw different military vehicles and then a loud-speaker car; and a field ambulance truck came into Bergen-Belsen and they told us that we were free.

The English troops came in, the simple English soldier — some of them I met couldn't even write — but they would give away *all* their rations. There was no British Red Cross yet, only the soldiers and they meant so well. They gave us their milk, their chocolate, their emergency ration; and you know you would take this and eat it and it would come right out because you couldn't hold any food. And people were sinking on their knees before the soldiers and kissing their hands and those who spoke English would tell what was going on. The British saw what the situation was, they tried hard but they weren't prepared for it. This was their first camp and their first experience and they did the best they could.

Anita Lasker-Wallfisch
Young German Jewish woman, Bergen-Belsen
I remember the liberation of Belsen very clearly. I wasn't very well at the time. I kept hearing rumbling noises and we heard there was something going on. Quite a lot of people thought it might be liberation. I got very annoyed about it because I didn't want to believe it. I remember getting furious when somebody said, "I think these are British tanks outside." I didn't want to know. But I remember — I can see the tank now, coming in with a loud-hailer, saying that we should keep calm, that we were liberated, but we should stay where we were. We were quite a formidable mass of people. The British didn't know what to do

371

with us: how to feed us, what the next move should be — it must have been a very difficult situation for them, apart from the fact that what they saw was so hideous. The smell was unbelievable, we didn't smell it, but people who came in did — there had never been *anything* like what they found in Belsen.

At that time I had been there for the best part of six months. I remember that a lot of people died because they suddenly started to eat. How I escaped that, I really don't know; somehow I managed not to fall into that trap. I remember Patrick Gordon Walker coming in with a BBC van and I was called to sit in this van and talk as I am talking to you now, but in German. They wanted to send messages to find out if people had any family. In England, for instance, they would play it on the BBC. I had a sister here in those days and an uncle in America, and the message was broadcast, "This is Anita Lasker speaking. I have a sister. I am still alive," and that's how my sister found out that I was still alive.

Rena Quint
Polish Jewish child, Bergen-Belsen
When the British liberated the camp, I was taken with the other children and I remember getting some milk and bread. I was brought into what looked like a tent, I guess it was a hospital and I started being nursed back to health, and there were sheets and beds and so it was a different kind of life. It's amazing how people adapt, life had changed and we accepted it. All that time I was

sick, and I was so lucky that I was sick because I was one of the first people to be taken to Sweden.

Leslie Hardman
British Jewish chaplain with VIII Corps, 2nd Army, Bergen-Belsen, April 1945

We moved and eventually came to the headquarters in Celle. I went to the mess; it was like a morgue, nobody would look at me. I spoke to the education officer, a lieutenant.

"What's the matter?"

He said, "Hardman, go and see the Colonel."

I go to see the Colonel. His face! — green, yellow, *miserable*.

"What's the matter, are you ill, sir?"

"Sit down, have a drink."

"No, I don't want one, what's wrong?"

"We've just uncovered a concentration camp and it's hell, it's ghastly, it's foul. I think most of the inmates are your people and I think you should go and have a look."

"Shall I go now, sir?"

"No, go tomorrow morning."

So I went on the morning of the 16th. I went to the gates. First the soldiers wouldn't let me in. I think they were terrified, poor fellows. Eventually I got in. There was a young woman at the gates. She saw the *Mogen David* on my uniform and knew I was Jewish and wanted to rush forward and hug me. She looked so repulsive, but I knew if I moved backwards as she moved forwards, she was liable to fall. I managed to control myself and kept her on her feet.

A few yards further on there was a group of about eight or ten people lying on the ground.

I said, "Why aren't they in the huts?"

She said "They're dead and we'll all be dead if help doesn't come quickly."

Then I started to learn about the gruesome things the Nazis did . . .

Bill Essex
British soldier, Royal Engineers, Bergen-Belsen
The first sight of Belsen was this big German barrack, spotlessly clean and we thought: blimey, they must be living in luxury! But that was the first camp; there were three more beyond that and that's where all the dead were. We went into number two and three camps, there were about fourteen/fifteen thousand dead I would think, and we had to bury them all. We dug trenches by the sides of mounds of bodies, down about eight or ten feet and about eight feet wide. We wanted to lay the bodies in so that they would have a decent burial, but we couldn't handle them at all — if I caught hold of an arm, I finished up with it in my hand. So, as they were rotten, we used the tractor to scoop them up from the square and pushed them all in. It wasn't easy, and when you disturbed the bodies there was a terrific smell. We wore masks and changed our clothes every night. I was working when the BBC came and they filmed me on that tractor in the camp. This work went on for three weeks.

Michael Lewis
British Jewish NCO cameraman, Army Film & Photographic Unit, Bergen-Belsen

The smell was terrible. I soaked a handkerchief in petrol and put it over my mouth as I sat in front of the bulldozer filming. I couldn't bear the smell of petrol; I didn't know whether to try to bear the smell of petrol, or to take it off and stand the smell of death.

I'd heard stories of cannibalism: they were so hungry they cut the livers out of the corpses that lay there and ate them. I remember one scene in this mass of bodies which comes back to me: there was a spade there with a cross-piece in it. It was just on the part of earth where those corpses were buried. It was a grey, dreary, depressing scene, and it suddenly came to me that this spade looked like the cross. And I put it into the foreground of my pictures. I believe it was used like that.

Leslie William Clarke
British medical student, Bergen-Belsen

I gather that most of the guards had disappeared down into the mass graves as they threw in the bodies. They were, I think, burying the dead at the double and I gather that many of them fell in with the dead and couldn't get out again. I don't think anybody tried to help them out. They were not deliberately thrown in, they fell in from exhaustion from the edge of the graves on top of the others; they went on chucking more bodies on top of them and that was that.

Bill Essex
British soldier, Royal Engineers, Bergen-Belsen
We did find one woman alive. She was in about four feet of bodies. How she remained alive or how we came to find her, I don't know. It was only that we had shut the tractor down for something when we heard a murmur; but we couldn't make out where it was coming from, we listened and then got her out. She was just about dead, but we managed to save her. When we left she was up and about.

Jane Levy
British Jewish member of Friends' Relief Service team RT100, Bergen-Belsen
Leslie Hardman stood at these mass graves and recited the *Kaddish* (the Jewish prayer for the dead) over and over again. It must have been terrible for him and for the Anglican and Catholic padres who followed him. One of the dreadful things was that there were no records of who the buried were.

John Roger Dixey
British civilian medical student, Bergen-Belsen
Having got rid of the dead you then looked around to try to do what you could for the remainder, the vast majority of whom had diarrhoea. They all had the most appalling coughs and the most dreadful skin diseases. They were all filthy dirty and absolutely skeletally thin. What could we do? The total amount of our medication amounted to aspirin and some tincture of opium. I don't think we had any cough medicine, we just dished

out pills. If you gave a pill to anybody, you had to give one to the next person too because they thought you were showing favouritism. I'm quite certain we did little good medically because we all knew that we were dealing, not only with extreme malnutrition, but also with tuberculosis as the prisoners were coughing up bloodstained sputum. But the main killer was typhus. So we didn't really do anything about curing them, but let's hope we did something about showing that somebody minded.

Jane Levy
British Jewish member of Friends' Relief Service team RT100, Bergen-Belsen
The "human laundry" was an extraordinary experience: there were rows of Queen Alexandra's nurses by the sides of these sinks and they were bathing people who had been brought from the concentration camp and were going to be put in the camp hospital. They were just like skeletons and looked so small, just like children; and these marvellous nurses were bathing them very gently, drying them and putting blankets around them, and then they were carried off to ambulances which took them to the hospital blocks.

Norna Alexander
British Red Cross worker, Bergen-Belsen
There was a doctor who thought he'd like to do a post-mortem and I helped. I fetched and carried as he did the operation, but I remember seeing it. You know that flower, honesty, that's sort of silvery? Well, the

bowel was just like that, almost transparent. He took it out and it was almost falling apart, it had dehydrated because this person hadn't had food, drink or anything.

Jim Wheeler
British private, 11th Light Field Ambulance, Royal Army Medical Corps, Bergen-Belsen

Shortly after the British Red Cross arrived a very large quantity of lipstick came. This wasn't at all what the men wanted — they were screaming for hundreds and thousands of other things. Nobody knows who asked for the lipstick, but in the event it was sheer genius on the part of whoever thought of it. It was obvious that nothing did more for these internees than the lipstick. Women lay in beds with no sheets, no nighties, but with scarlet lips. You saw them wandering about with nothing but a blanket over their shoulders, but with scarlet lips. One saw a woman dead on the post-mortem table, clutched in her hand was a piece of lipstick. It was an attempt and a method to make people feel like individuals.

Charles Salt
British Jewish soldier, Corps of Military Police, Bergen-Belsen

Being Jewish made all the difference, no one wanted to speak German — it was a taboo language — most of them spoke Polish. The only other language was Yiddish and I was the only one that spoke it. So when they wanted something, I could talk to them.

Jane Levy
British Jewish member of Friends' Relief Service team RT100, Bergen-Belsen
They were absolutely thrilled to see my *Mogen David* which I wore; they clustered around me, shouting with pleasure, they pinched my cheeks and said how lovely to see a plump girl.

Leslie William Clarke
British medical student, Bergen-Belsen
The people who did even more than we did for their benefit were the Quakers. They laid on fresh water to Belsen. And they seemed to have no fear; they didn't mind what they did and they worked very hard; I have great respect for them. And of course water was probably more important than food, and it did provide some minor sanitation; they could go to the end of a hosepipe and at least get some water to wash with.

Zdenka Ehrlich
Young Czech woman, Bergen-Belsen
My sister was dead, all my friends around me were dead. I was one of the three hundred on the floor, some were alive, some were dead; you couldn't tell the difference any more between who was breathing, who was not. Nobody came into the block. They left us absolutely to our devices: to perish, human refuse — who cares?

There was a rumour: the English army has arrived. How did we feel? No different. It could have been an angel from heaven, it could have been anybody. It was too late. There was no strength left even to understand the news — nothing mattered any more. So a fortnight passed until the end of April where I don't remember any big improvement. Perhaps there were more rations. All I know was that I was half dead: four and a half stones, my intestines were hanging out because I had not enough strength in the muscles. I was just like a dying animal lying there on the floor — completely left to my own devices. My lips were blue from thirst. I was delirious.

I was as close to death as one can possibly be. I couldn't stand, I had no muscles, and my arms looked like brown paper, hanging everywhere. I only had the eyes and the teeth, the rest was gone: four and a half stone, a grown-up woman!

John Roger Dixey
British civilian medical student, Bergen-Belsen
The people just lay on the floor. One of the abiding memories is that you had two or three people lying huddled together and when you removed, out of a group of four or five, two who were dead, there was absolutely no reaction from the others at all. You just removed them and they pinched the scraps of clothing off the one you'd removed to have a bit more themselves; they were totally and absolutely apathetic. And I remember when VE Day came and we went into the hut which by now was getting a bit more organised, we said in a multitude of languages, "You'll be glad to hear that the war is over, Germany is defeated, the war is *over*," there was practically no response at all — no

cheering, or waving or "well done-ing." They just looked at us: the war's over, but not for them. I think they knew there was little hope for them.

I well remember talking to a girl who was a walking skeleton. I said, "How old are you?" And with tears in her eyes she said she was twenty-six. And I was — what was I? Twenty-four. She was my age and looked eighty. And I can remember one old Polish lady — probably wasn't aged come to think of it — with nothing on except a blanket around her shoulders. She was walking out of the hospital grounds, announcing that she was going back to Poland. It was pathetic, she was determined to go home. Goodness knows what happened to her.

Charles Salt
British Jewish soldier, Corps of Military Police, Bergen-Belsen
There were a few women there that didn't look all that starved: they had cosmetics and some dresses and shoes. I asked them why they didn't look the same as the others and they said, "There's only one way if you wanted to stay alive: if you lived with a SS officer at least you had something to eat and something to wear." So in spite of everything, they still had Jewish girls as mistresses.

Ryvka "Rene" Salt
Polish Jewish child, Bergen-Belsen
When they started feeding us, my first meal consisted of a quarter of a slice of white bread topped with a teaspoonful of stewed apples. The taste is still in my

mouth today. I shall never forget that meal, never! Fortunately, by then the British knew that if people got greedy and ate a lot they would die, and they gradually gave us a little bit more until we were better.

Edith Baneth
A young Czech woman, Bergen-Belsen

I remember the first time I went out with my mother after liberation. There is a beautiful forest in Belsen — it is still there today — and we walked on the main road and crossed into the forest. It was the first time I felt a little bit better from the typhoid I'd had for three weeks. I was sitting down with mother in a meadow, and then we saw all the nature and lots of marguerites around us; my mother took one and did "I love you, I love you not" with it.

And suddenly, at this moment, we both realised that we were *free*: sitting in a meadow on our own, seeing flowers and doing what pleased us. It was then that it hit us and we hugged each other and said, "We *made* it, we are *here*, we have *survived*, we are *alive* and soon we'll go home." I had survived the typhoid, my mother didn't get it, and we were so hopeful that it's all over. The next day my mother did suddenly get a temperature and she was one of the last cases of typhoid and she was taken to the hospital.

She died on the 15 June 1945, two months after being freed. In two or three weeks we were supposed to go home and start a new life together. Going through all that had happened, it was the worst thing. She was forty then, she still had another thirty years of normal life to live.

Jane Levy
British Jewish member of Friends' Relief Service team RT100, Bergen-Belsen
I had a slight problem at Belsen: when the casualty clearing station's wonderful nurses left Belsen, British Army nurses took their place. One of the nurses, to my fury, said to me, "I don't know what I'm doing here, I came abroad to nurse Britain's brave boys, I didn't come to nurse this *scum*." I was absolutely horrified. But most of them were very good and nursed those who needed it.

Charles Salt
British Jewish soldier, Corps of Military Police, Bergen-Belsen
Irma Grese, a SS officer, came from Auschwitz with Kramer, the Camp *Kommandant* and somehow, when Kramer was taken, she escaped the net.

One day, I was in the information post when a woman inmate came in and said, "There's a SS officer going out of the camp wearing civilian clothes."

I said, "What's she done?"

"She used to make the selections at Auschwitz and would beat up people."

I said, "Did you see her do this? I need witnesses otherwise it won't stand up in a court of law."

She got down on her knees and said, "I beg you as one Jew to another."

So I told a chap standing there to take a jeep with an armed escort and bring her in.

He said, "There's no point, if you bring her in and you've no witnesses, she goes scot-free and can't be charged again."

But I insisted thinking there must be *someone* there who saw her do these things. They brought her in: smartly dressed, very young. She showed me her pass which the British Camp Commandant had given her to travel to Celle, and her SS pass. I told the woman to go and find witnesses, that we could only hold her for forty-eight hours. First day went past, nothing happened; second day, nothing.

I said to the Sergeant, "We'll hold her for another day, if no one comes for her by 4.30p.m., that's it."

I was going off duty at 5p.m. that day, by then she had been let out of the bunker; because no one had come forward she was betting on a safe wicket and had stayed behind talking with some of the fellows and having tea. She felt they had no witnesses against her.

About 4.55p.m. two sisters who spoke good English came in to discuss something with me, and I took them upstairs to the dining room to have some tea. The only empty place to sit was near where Irma Grese was sitting. So I indicated to go over there but one of them said, "No, we don't want to sit there."

I said, "Look, I can't offer you the services of the Hotel Adlon!"

She said, "But you don't expect us to sit next to a SS officer do you?"

I explained that I knew about her, but we had no witnesses, and one of them said, "Well, *I* saw her do it, I used to play in the orchestra in Auschwitz and saw what she did."

And the other one said that she too saw her as she did her job as an interpreter. So I went over, got hold of her, took her down, filled a charge sheet and sent her off to Celle.

One of those girls was a witness at her trial and Irma Grese was hanged with Kramer. She could well have gone free. Five minutes later I would have gone.

Freddie Knoller
Austrian Jewish youth, Bergen-Belsen

As I was looking for food (in this nearby farmhouse) I saw something sticking out from behind a wardrobe. It was a framed photo of Adolf Hitler. I took a knife and slashed it in front of the old farmer. That's when he came to me and said, "*Du sau Jude*" — "You pig-Jew." I had the knife in my hand and I just stuck the knife in his stomach. I don't know if I killed him or not. The British soldier said, "Come on, let's get back to the camp." He didn't want anything to do with it. I would never have done that under normal circumstances, it was just that we were liberated and that a German continued to call us "*sau Jude*".

John Fink
German Jewish youth, Bergen-Belsen

I was there that day when the famous picture was taken of the camp burnt with the flame-throwers. I was standing right behind the British officers and soldiers. Only after the last barrack was burnt was the British flag raised. It was symbolic. It was very emotional. I still get emotional when I talk about it.

Leslie William Clarke
British medical student, Bergen-Belsen

Some RAF chaps had been delegated to go round and find people suspected of being war criminals; one of these chaps came into the "human laundry" and asked me about it. Then he said, "I've been given this job of finding war criminals, I wasn't really keen on the job at all, I didn't really have much incentive — by golly, I've got an incentive now!"

Bill Essex
British soldier, Royal Engineers, Bergen-Belsen

I never saw a bird flying there.

Harry Miller
British NCO, 12th Field Hygiene Section of RAMC, liberation of Sandbostel prisoner of war camp, concentration camp section

All they wanted was cigarettes, they didn't want food because they couldn't eat as they were in such a bad state. When people talk now about how bad cigarettes are, I look back into the past and see these men taking a real good inhale and dying. The last thing they did was to have a cigarette and enjoy it, they didn't want anything to eat at all. When you've been starving for so long you can't eat.

Harry Lowit

Czech Jewish youth, liberated after escape from Ebensee concentration camp

It was nice to feel free — the first time I felt free for many years. Freedom is the most precious commodity! I'm a great advocate of freedom. I didn't have the benefit of kindness from others from 1940 to 1945 — five years of being made to feel guilty because one was Jewish! Not only by Germans, but by Czechs, and that's hard to forgive. But to be free was a circumstance that was completely strange. To be able to wake up and know you could go outside the perimeter of wherever you were and nobody would challenge, "Where are you going?" It's the most *wonderful* feeling of all — freedom!

Kitty Hart-Moxon

Young Polish Jewish woman, Salzwedel concentration camp

Everyone who was still able to run or walk just poured out of the camp into this little town of Salzwedel. The first thing we did was to rush around to see if we could find any food. Unfortunately we liberated prisoners were a little bit too late because a lot of forced labourers from the region, including prisoners of war, had been liberated days before and they had already plundered and rampaged through the town. By the time we came in there was very little left. But nevertheless I recall going into a dairy and we overturned all the churns that were full of milk, and we splashed this milk and then drank it with our hands and

387

sort of bathed in milk. Then we rushed into the houses, obviously trying to find some food, but also just to see what the inside of a house looked like — we hadn't seen one for so long. Well, we rushed from one house into another and tried to lie on the beds, even set fire to some of the places. We opened up taps. All we wanted to do was just *destroy*, we didn't want to take anything except food. We were all in rags, we were barefoot, but all we were looking for was something to eat. We loosened a bath-tub in one house and filled it with all kinds of provisions and we carted that back to camp.

Frank Gilliard
BBC War Correspondent, Regensburg camp
Regensburg had just been opened up. Two or three thousand prisoners were still alive there, they were forced workers brought in from eastern Europe, from the Russian front. They were in a terribly emaciated condition. All around the camp were great piles of corpses — like planks piled up in great heaps. The dead were not festering, not smelling because there was nothing left on them to fester; they were just skin and bone, they'd been worked until they dropped dead. You would have prisoners coming up to you unable to speak because of language differences, but they would show how they'd been castrated. And you'd get hold of an interpreter who would tell you the most harrowing stories as they related what they'd been through.

388

They had been obliged to spend the nights in slit trenches over which they had built thatch-like coverings, both to avoid observation from the air, also to give some sort of shelter in heavy rain. But with the rapid approach of the American forces, the guards had simply run around this place with cans of petrol, poured it over the thatch covers with the prisoners still in the trenches, and then set fire to the thatch. Every trench was full of the charred remains of incinerated human bodies.

Anna Bergman
Young Czech woman, Mauthausen
After three or four days the Americans liberated us and I begged a nurse to give my little boy a bath, and she said, "What do you mean a little boy? It's a girl." I was delighted as I had wanted a little girl. She was like an angel, I kept warming her little feet with my hands, she was wrapped in paper all the time in Mauthausen. In the nearest Czech place on my way back to Prague, people saw the baby and gave me so many clothes, so she came to Prague beautifully equipped.

Steven Frank
Dutch Jewish child, Theresienstadt
Things were really desperate at the time: food was minimal, typhus had exploded. People were very frightened — still this peculiar feeling of elation that war was coming to an end and this utter fear that we were going to be gassed. And one May day, my mother was accosted by some Russian POWs in the camp who

389

knew she was one of the English speakers. They asked if she would come to their house at six o'clock that night. So she went and they took her up into the attic where, miraculously, they had hidden a radio. They switched it on and she wrote down on a piece of paper — which is now in the Imperial War Museum — Winston Churchill's broadcast on the Overseas Service of the BBC announcing that the war would end at midnight that night. So my mother was probably the first person to know in Theresienstadt that the war was going to end in six hours' time.

The Germans disappeared during that night and the Russian Army came into the camp. And I remember quite clearly that they were nothing like the Russians in my mind. They were Mongolians wearing Russian uniform, unbelievably poorly equipped — it was horses and carts and World War I type of equipment. Later on mechanised forces came through and they would throw things out of the wagons and we would grovel for whatever they threw.

The camp was in complete confusion. The Russians were in, people were dying like flies. And very soon the camp elders, of whom Leo Baeck was one, issued a statement about the camp being liberated and the International Red Cross (IRC) taking it over, appealing for calm and various other things. The Red Cross came in and the whole camp was sealed off and there was this euphoria and relief — the main relief that we were not going to be gassed. The first thing the IRC did was to try to decontaminate and contain this typhus. I learned that the gas that was actually

390

used to carry out the de-lousing operation on the living quarters was none other than Zyklon B — the very gas that killed my father. We were in fact the very last place to be liberated on 9 May 1945.

Alfred Huberman
Polish Jewish youth, Theresienstadt
I looked out of the window and saw a Russian scout on a push-bike and we shouted, *"Tovarich"* (Comrade), at him from the window. Off he went and then we saw Russian tanks; the people rushed down into the street and those tanks were covered with people greeting the Russians. I didn't feel very well but I thought I must go down and feel what it felt like walking freely. I went down and walked through that big gate into the street and just walked. And there were Russian tanks going towards Czechoslovakia and German prisoners being taken to Russia, and within a matter of days, from arrogant and heroic, they looked downtrodden and dishevelled. I went over to a dead German and took his belt off and the belt had a buckle inscribed, *"Gott mit uns"* — "God is with us".

Stanley Faull
Polish Jewish youth, Theresienstadt
When I first went out of the camp after liberation, I saw this vast army on the move. And when you see tanks and lorries and kitchens and hospitals, all on wheels, and moving along and, say, one lorry breaks down and a tractor comes and pushes it out of the

391

way, this is a fantastic sight. This was the Russian Army advancing towards Berlin. We asked them to stop, we understood Russian. They used to throw cigarettes, bars of chocolate, but they couldn't stop because it's like a moving town, day and night. But they told us that the civil administration's coming. Eventually it started to arrive and taking charge. They brought their own food in, their own doctors, we got ourselves registered. It was the first time we had normality. This is when they said that anyone over sixteen had to go into the Russian Army. Fortunately I was just under this. Most of the boys just wanted to go back home. In my case I knew I'd lost everybody. I knew I was on my own, but I did know that I had a brother in England so I put my name down that I wanted to go to England.

Michael Etkind
Polish Jewish youth, after liberation
I had been picked up by the Russians and was being marched towards Prague in a line of Russian and German prisoners of war, when suddenly I fainted and they put me on a horse-driven cart. I slightly recovered after about an hour and listened to the conversation between two Russians — the driver and a Russian prisoner who had no legs. There was a silence in the conversation and I tried to break in. I said, "I am a Jew from Poland, I was in the ghetto and the camps, why am I now being taken away, where are we going?" There was a silence for a little while, then the driver, an

older man, without looking at me said in Russian, "Why did the Germans not burn you?"

Clive Teddern

German Jewish soldier, Royal Armoured Corps, Germany

In May 1945 my unit was approaching Hamburg. In fact the area where we were was very familiar to me. We entered Hamburg on 8 May — yes, the day the war finished. And I immediately started investigating what had happened to my parents. I found some people had returned (from the camps). We then moved towards the Danish border and I was then told that transports from Theresienstadt — where my parents had been imprisoned — were coming back on a certain day. My squadron commander and others in my unit were very very understanding and I was given time off and even transport to take me into Hamburg to meet that particular convoy when they came back. I went to the place and the lorries arrived, spread over a considerable period of time. Out of three thousand people, six hundred came back.

Of course, I was there asking people if they knew my parents and if they knew what had happened to them. And those from Theresienstadt told me, "Your parents were sent from Theresienstadt to Auschwitz, to the gas chambers. They're not coming back." And that's how I found out. And I remember one of my friends came with me, a Welsh sergeant to whom all this was completely . . . well, remote. But I don't

393

think it will ever be remote from his mind again. It was traumatic: took me a while to get over that.

Stephen Dale
German Jewish member of Special Operations Executive, SOE, London

When we got back to Kidlington, in England, after liberation from the prisoner of war camp, I didn't kiss the ground like the Pope did, but I patted it with great affection. I had come home.

During the day of 8 May (1945) it was announced that everything had been signed and there was this — not entirely spontaneous — jubilation, because everybody was prepared for it. But around Piccadilly and Leicester Square there were millions of people milling about and being very exuberant, climbing up lamp-posts and onto bus shelters. People were very friendly, embracing each other with much cheerful bantering going on. I was upbraided on several occasions for walking around with a miserable face. And it was perfectly true. I was naturally very happy that the war was over. But it was also, in a way, a moment for reflection: it was great that the killing had come to an end in Europe, but I suddenly felt all the awful things that had happened to my family and to me; they came very much to the surface. Therefore, I could not join in these celebrations which were, of course, perfectly justified.

AFTERMATH

When we came to the main station in Prague in the evening, it was dark, no electricity, nobody waiting, nobody anywhere, and then we knew what had hit us. All through these years you had to keep fighting, not to worry, not to think. But now, you realised there is nobody here and nothing, and what do you do now?

The war had ended and with it the mass murder of the Jews. In the immediate aftermath, the Allied powers were faced with the huge challenge of dealing with between seven and eight million people who had been uprooted by the Nazis. These so-called displaced persons (DPs) included former concentration camp inmates, forced labourers and prisoners of war. By September 1945, more than six million had returned to their countries of origin, many of them making their way across the chaos of post-war Europe. During this period there were approximately 50,000 Jews, mostly from eastern Europe, who had been liberated in German and Austrian territory. For many Jewish survivors, liberation did not mean the freedom they had craved for so many years, and many speak of the sense of anticlimax that the end of the Nazi terror brought.

In the main, Jews from western Europe were willing to return to their country of origin and, despite some initial difficulties, were successfully reintegrated into their communities. Conditions in eastern Europe were far less conducive. Before the Nazi onslaught, Poland had the largest Jewish community in Europe. Between 1939 and 1945 at least 90 per cent of Polish Jewry was exterminated, together with the destruction of hundreds of vibrant communities. Although there were many acts of heroic rescue throughout the war, with many Poles risking their lives to save Jews, Polish anti-Semitism, which had been a feature of the war in the east, did not end with liberation. There were many random *pogroms* against surviving Jews; between November 1944 and October 1945 at least 350 Jews were murdered by anti-Communist partisans in Poland.

But it was the *pogrom* against Jews in the city of Kielce on 4 July 1946, in which 42 Jews were murdered, that convinced thousands of Jews of the need to quit Poland. Many entered the DP camps in Germany, others linked up with the *Briha* — flight to Palestine — movement. By the end of 1946 it is estimated that 250,000 Jews lived in Germany, Austria and Italy, mainly in the American occupation zones; the majority were young people in their twenties and thirties.

Michael Etkind
Polish Jewish survivor, Pilsen Czechoslovakia
I walked out of Pilsen, very near was the countryside and I cannot describe the feeling. It was a feeling of weightlessness and happiness. I walked for about half

an hour and then I lay down. The day was absolutely beautiful: the sun was shining, the birds were singing — it was the middle of May, the sky was absolutely blue, the weather couldn't have been more beautiful.

I climbed on to a hill and lay down on the grass; there were a few silver birches and I had a very strange feeling at that moment: I thought I would die, and I was very happy. I don't know how long I was lying there and suddenly a motor bike revved up on the nearby road and that jerked me out of that feeling which I am unable to describe. I have never felt anything like it before or since. My illness must have had something to do with it, but why should exhaustion create that feeling of utter happiness, lightness and euphoria?

Maria Ossowski
Polish survivor, Poland

When I met my husband and got pregnant, it was absolutely marvellous; there was a *life*, I never ever think of our son and his life in conjunction with what had happened during the war — that was the past and it was behind us. This was what was in front of us: new life. It could be my son, it could be other people's children. Now that I am old and wise, I say that was an absolute biological necessity; it was the most normal thing to do.

George Hartman
Czech Jewish survivor, Prague

The main reason that I wanted to survive was that I was a virgin and I couldn't imagine dying before finding out what love and sex were. You survived only if you *wanted* to survive. And you wanted to survive only if there was a goal or some objective for which you wanted to live. For me there were three: number one, I never had sex in my life; number two, I wanted to eat; and number three, I wanted to see my parents — that was number three.

Alicia Adams
Polish Jewish survivor, London
My husband, Adam, was always talking about the Holocaust; he'd read books about it, but I never talked about it. I wanted to *live*: I realised at one stage that life was just passing me by, that I was living with sorrow, suffering terribly and not enjoying life. I read Omar Khayyám (*Rubáiyát*) and realised that every minute counted and time was passing very quickly.

Roman Halter
Polish Jewish survivor, Theresienstadt
One day in liberated Theresienstadt, I was with the group of young survivors who later came to England, known as the "Boys"; I said to the boys that I had learned to swim in the lake of my home town, Chodecz, and that we should go to the Elbe to swim. We broke through the fence guarded by Russians and went where we couldn't be seen. I was the only one who could swim, the others paddled. We had a *wonderful* time: it was sunny and the stream carried me down and I came back. Eventually we had enough, and we dressed again and walked back and came across a field of

strawberries; and we lay in the strawberries and I thought, "Well, this really is liberation," and ate strawberries on all sides. My vision of liberation was really lying in that field of strawberries.

Rena Quint
Polish Jewish child survivor, New York, USA
Nobody really talked about the war. Nobody questioned me, nobody made any references although I'm sure that the whole neighbourhood must have known about the new child coming into it. That was a taboo subject. I don't think I wanted to talk about it. I wanted very much to be accepted. I wanted very much to be liked. Because if they knew, would they want to sit next to me and play with me? So I really didn't want them to know: I wanted to ride a bicycle and play with a doll and run. I remember one day there was a girl, Rita was her name, and she had blonde hair and she was climbing on a monkey-bar and her hair was blowing in the wind. I guess I was about ten and a half then and I remember thinking: Isn't it *wonderful* to be climbing on a monkey-bar and to have your hair blowing in the wind, and being so free!

Leon Greenman
British Jewish survivor, Holland
I went to the Hague and the Red Cross. They produced papers which said that my wife and little son, Barney, had been killed at Auschwitz, in the gas chambers. And when I asked how many had come back from that

transport (of eight hundred) from Westerbork to Auschwitz, he said, "Only two men got back and you are one of them." But I still hoped to see my wife and child, perhaps they'd been liberated by the Russians, perhaps they'd been sent somewhere else and they'd come out, but then as time went on, I realised it was so.

Halina Kahn
Polish Jewish survivor, Berlin
In Berlin my husband went to the hospital because he had broken his ankle. Opposite the hospital was the empty hostel of the *Hitler Jugend* and we got in it. The hostel was near Alexanderplatz and there was fire everywhere. The women were collecting stones to clear the roads. Then every few weeks transports of German survivors from Auschwitz and other camps arrived. They were sitting there in the garden by a fire, they came with shaved heads wearing their striped clothing.

And Germans came and looked and one said to me, "You are Jewish?"

I said, "Yes."

"You have not horns, you have not beards — you are supposed to look like the devil, you know."

They didn't know that Jewish people looked normal. Some of them brought food for us and they said: "We are Jewish, or half-Jewish and we had to hide to survive." They came out to tell us they were pleased to see us, and it was quite moving.

Josef Perl
Czech Jewish survivor, Buchenwald

This Russian had a lorry and he was going to Prague. I asked if I could go with him and he said, in Yiddish, "Jump up." I went to the American Consulate which had been set up in Buchenwald and they gave me a piece of paper and I wrote where I was born, the date, my father's details. This gave me a life-line to have a meal a day from UNRRA (United Nations Relief and Rehabilitation Administration) — they used to have a kitchen on every station. Once I got that piece of paper — how can I explain? — well, it meant the *world* to me. All of a sudden I realised that I was a *human being*. I was born. This was my birth certificate. Seventeen days before my seventeenth birthday and I had a birth certificate! I sat down and sobbed my eyes out that I had been recognised as a human being. When I came to Prague, the people were so kind to the survivors that arrived: they gave us money, they gave us food and clothes, but I had to move on because I was still looking for my parents.

Joseph Harmatz
Lithuanian Jewish survivor, Lublin

The reason for moving out of Lithuania after the liberation was that we did hope to find somebody alive when we came out of the forest; we found *nobody*, which was the greatest shock we could have. Then, when the Zionists left with their dream of reaching the Mediterranean, the friendships created in the underground were so strong that we joined them. That was the beginning of the escape that we called the *Briha*. We reached Lublin in Poland when Warsaw was just liberated. And this was the beginning of what came later: we met people who came from other undergrounds, other forests, from White Russia and the Ukraine, and we started to tell our stories to each other, day and night, and every story was more dramatic than the other one. And we didn't know what to do with ourselves, and we started to speak about vengeance.

It was *then* that we found the people who came out and it was *then* that we listened to what had happened in the camps. Because *we* had finished with the Germans when we left the ghetto, and we didn't know of gassing people, or burning people, of *families*, of *children*, we didn't know about the *volume* of the catastrophe. And then we learnt it and then we started to revolt inside ourselves. But we had an aim, and this was to go south. The more people that came out, the more stories we were told, strengthened our feeling that we should not leave the Continent without having done something.

Jan Hartman
Czech Jewish survivor, Prague

We got to Prague on a street car, still wearing our striped caps. We got out near our home to find out whether our parents had survived. As we got out of the street car in our caps which made it very obvious that we had just come out of a concentration camp, we met a very nice person on the corner of the street who lived in one of our houses.

We asked him, "Could you tell us whether our parents are back?" He said, "No, but it's wonderful to see you, there is a leak in my ceiling."

That was our return home.

Anna Bergman
Czech Jewish survivor, Prague

When we came to the main station in Prague in the evening, it was dark, no electricity, nobody waiting, nobody anywhere, and *then* we knew what had hit us. All through these years you had to keep fighting, not to worry, not to think. But now, you realised there is nobody here and nothing, and what do you do now? We were put up in a hotel near the station and the following morning I got some money for a tram and went to a cousin whom I hoped was still in Prague with his family. And they were there, and they opened the door to me as if I were the queen and I stayed three and a half years with them.

When the summer came, they went on holiday and I went back to my family home in Trebechovice and the people there behaved so dreadfully to me. They had taken all our property, but they had to allocate me somewhere to live, so they gave me a room in my sister's house with no facilities at all. I was very hurt — with the Germans you took it as a fact, but you didn't expect it from the Czechs, the people I had been to school with; it was so inhumane. But my experience with other friends was totally different. I didn't have a clue where my parents had left their goods and people found me and brought them back: valuable jewellery, china and silver cutlery — I got practically all that back.

Josef Perl
Czech Jewish survivor, Veliky Bochkov, Czechoslovakia
Eventually I reached my own town and our house which was near the main road. When I saw the house I felt a flame lighting up in me, I actually thought I was home: home to *safety*, home to the hope of finding some of my family alive. I opened the gate and walked in. Even before I had time to reach the front door, I was confronted by a man I knew all my life, with a shotgun in his hand.

"What!" he said. "You are here! You are still alive! Get off this property!"

I said, "But this is mine."

"No more, this is all mine now."

I begged him to let me sleep in the stables, but he just ordered me off.

I had a gun and said, "What do you think this is — a pea-shooter? If you come for me, you're coming with me."

And he was coming for me. But then I thought, "I'm not going to take my own life over a house," and I turned round and walked out. I sat on the ground outside the gate and had a good cry. Then I locked up my gun and went back to the station and went to Bucharest where I was told there was help.

Jerry Koenig

Polish Jewish survivor, Kosow, Poland

Immediately after our liberation by the Russians one of the men in the bunker, a native of the town of Kosow, was gunned down in the street of his home town when he returned. Of course it was obviously to keep him from claiming his house and properties; so again greed and possibly anti-Semitism caused that. In 1946, on 4 July to be exact, a group of survivors — I think the number was forty-two — who came back to their town of Kielce, were massacred. This was a year after the war ended and it was a signal to dad that there was no future for us in our town of Kosow and our country of Poland and we had to leave; because if those things can happen after the experiences of the Second World War, then our lives were not safe. That was the signal to many other survivors who did the same thing.

The majority simply packed up and left and many of them emigrated to what later became the State of Israel, and many to the United States or Canada or South America. In our case it was a case of simply getting on a train and heading for the border and, eventually after many more experiences, we came to Iowa, in the United States, in February 1951.

Zygmunt Sikora

Polish photographer, Kielce, Poland

Yes, I was in Kielce that day. The Jew who worked for me in the shop came to work — we had a lot of work to finish that day. After some time he said, "Mr Zygmunt, something is going on, there are many people gathering." We heard shots fired. Later it was said that the Jews were accused of keeping a (Christian) boy hostage.

There were some policemen and undercover police walking towards Buczka Street. Later, from the balcony we saw more, and could hear screams, windows being broken and wooden fences destroyed. Someone said that a woman had been thrown out of a window and, after the midday break, more persons arrived from Ludwiks's factory and they were armed with clubs. They were murdering people. This could have been prevented, you needed only two or three policemen to get involved to stop it, but they didn't.

Afterwards, I saw two killed people lying in the street, but many more were murdered. When the Jews came out from the building, they were stoned. There was not one single person responsible for this crime; everyone who participated in it was responsible. It was the mob.

Some of the people that I knew entered my shop and demanded the Jew who worked for me. I refused. I told them that this could only end in another tragedy, that I had survived Auschwitz and no way would I allow anything to happen to him. I told them to go to hell.

Daniella Hausman
Young Polish woman, Warsaw
I felt very sorry about what happened to the Jewish people, but on the other hand it hurts now when you read in the paper that some Jewish people accuse Polish people that they didn't help enough, and try to make

the case that it only happened to the Jewish people, because it isn't true. A lot of nuns and priests helped Jewish people. In Auschwitz and other camps there were thousands and thousands of people of different nationalities. My cousin was imprisoned and ended up in Majdanek, and another cousin died there. So it was thousands and thousands, probably more Jewish people than others, nevertheless others suffered too.

Marsha Segall
Lithuanian Jewish survivor, en route to Munich
On the train to Munich via Hanover, an American came up to the window of this very crowded compartment for displaced persons and told us that we must take along this German. Someone answered that there was no room, not even for a baby to squeeze in. And the American jumped to the window, hit him and said, "You dirty bloody Jew!"

It was a *tremendous* shock — the first "hello" to the American zone in Germany, end of December 1945. Everybody was shocked, and it *hurt*. Some said, "Well, there are all sorts in the army and we shouldn't take it too seriously." But, that was the first shock to my system after the war, gradually I got used to it again.

Nicole David
Jewish hidden child, Belgium
Many Belgians from all walks of life helped Jews: the Belgian railway people tried to sabotage the trains leaving from Mechelen transit camp to Auschwitz. As soon as the Germans realised this, they were replaced

with German guards. Postmen who were suspicious that some letters were denunciations would take the letters, steam them open, go and tell those that were about to be denounced, then re-seal and send them two, three days later.

Jan Imich
Polish Jewish survivor, Nordhausen

I have not the slightest doubt the civilian population around the camp sites knew what was going on. I cannot see any way they *couldn't* have known. And indeed that is the opinion of all the people I spoke to in the camp while we were there, and particularly after the liberation when we discussed that quite a lot. The civilians *must* have known. Perhaps in the middle of nowhere, where there was no camp within a hundred miles of that particular village or so, they probably wouldn't have known, but generally speaking, civilian populations, say in Nordhausen, with Dora and several other sub-camps all around, there was no way they could *not* have known — although it was impossible to find any German civilian after the liberation who admitted that they even suspected anything, never mind known anything.

The authorities did try to keep their activities secret, true; but there was far too much contact with the civilian population one way or another for the latter to avoid realising there was something untoward going on. And of course we looked different: first of all we wore the characteristic clothes of the camps — striped jackets and trousers, striped caps; then, our heads were shaved in the middle — this strip in the middle of one's head, completely shaved right to the skin, so that escapes could be hampered. Also, you could recognise most prisoners because of their emaciated state.

Fritz Moses
German civilian, Munich
We hadn't known about the full extent of the murders; we only knew that something had happened. But this selection, this perfection, I don't think that was known by the mass of the people; only a few knew. But the fact that people knew about it could be concluded from a few things. Like, there was a certain kind of soap, the size of this packet of cigarettes, a terrible grey-green colour and stamped with the initials "R I F" and the meaning most people applied to this was "*Ruhe in Frieden*" — "Rest In Peace", because it was made out of the fat of Jews. I mean, when something like that was spoken, there has to be *something* to it. So now people are supposed to be saying that they didn't know about it — right? That is the proof . . . very macabre.

Hannah Hyde
Young German woman, Hamburg
I had heard of concentration camps even prior to 1938. But neither my mother nor anybody acquainted with us knew of Bergen-Belsen which, as the crow flew, must have been within half an hour or forty minutes from our town in the car. And during all our roamings, ramblings and cycling in the area, we just never knew. (After the liberation of the camp) the local population

411

was made aware of this officially. The people denied it. They said, "No, no, Germany didn't do this." Because that was the first time many people actually heard of concentration camps. They said, "No, this isn't true; and certainly not in our area. Oh no, no, no." So my mother approached the British man who was in charge of the town and she said she would be willing to actually go to Belsen and bring back her impressions to pass on to other people; another lady said she would go with her.

Well, a date was fixed, and a car appeared on the doorstep and they were taken to see the horrors. By then the dead bodies had been removed or dealt with, so mother saw the extent of the site, and the main inhabitants. And she came back looking absolutely horror-stricken. She could hardly speak because of what she had seen. She certainly couldn't take any food. And she duly wrote her report and tried to pass it on to others. But nobody was interested really, and it was certainly never published in the strict sense of the word.

Inga Haag
German woman, member of anti-Hitler resistance
I don't blame people who didn't come forward, but to say they didn't know what was going on is absolute rubbish: in school, in university, you *knew* — not exactly what happened, but that the Jews had disappeared. We thought the worst because my husband said, "If they were still alive we would hear from them." But the fact was they had disappeared, they were just

not there. That, I think, for my family and friends who were against Hitler, was the greatest encouragement (to resist): that citizens can just disappear. As my father said: Germany was a country without law.

Joseph Harmatz
Lithuanian Jewish survivor
In the beginning we were told that we should hit them as painfully as possible and we were looking for means and material. We wanted to do it in five German cities and I was appointed the head of the Nuremberg group — I wanted that because Nuremberg was the cradle of Nazism in Germany. We were very bitter and very tough in those days and very young. We had planned to deal with the whole underground water supply system, cutting off connections where American and other soldiers and those who were not Germans lived. But that fell apart.

The plan we actually followed was to inject "material" — I don't call it by name — into bread. Then we found that the heat of the baking meant the strength disappeared. So we came to the conclusion that we could smear it on the bottom of the loaves of bread, but it had to be mixed with glue and be the same colour, and this chemical engineer, who was one of our people, did his best. The night of 13 April 1946 was chosen — the night from Saturday to Sunday — this was because the American guards of the camp of *Stalag* 13, which was SS, would eat only white bread on a Sunday, and we painted the stuff only on black bread — the Germans only got black bread.

413

It was very well planned but apart from some moral help from a few, without help from Palestine. We prepared about three thousand loaves which were supposed to be eaten by twelve thousand SS, and we know that many SS men were killed by them. The issue is not the number. The issue is, if I may say so, that there was a group of Jewish Underground people during the war, who *fought* the Germans and who wanted to take vengeance, because we went into ghettos, to concentration camps, to bunkers and to old castles where they were keeping Jews, and we saw on the walls there: "Vengeance, vengeance, vengeance!" And some written in *blood*. We felt that this was the last will, the last legacy of what those people wanted from those of us who survived.

Antonie Krokova
Young Czech gypsy woman, Beroun, Czechoslovakia
There was this one German in the camp and what he would do with us children was to ask us to stand around him, to hold our hands like in "ring around the roses", and he would sit on an old pan on a piece of board with a stick held in his hand. And when he liked somebody, he grabbed their necks with the stick and pulled them towards himself and let them sit on his lap. And sometimes he would play with us for half an hour or so. He picked me up several times — he always put me on his lap and stroked me.

Believe it or not, I recognised him after the war from a photograph in the newspaper. He was working in Prague allocating allowances for those of us who had been in concentration camps. They tried him and hanged him. I told them he got too little, that they should have waited for me and my friend. They laughed and said, "Why?" And I said, "I would have really let him have it!" I would have had him tortured like they tortured us; I would have given him harder punishment, knocked his teeth out and other things. The Nazis shot and kicked people in front of us; they shaved their heads and then bashed them over the head and you could see the brains coming out, or the head completely smashed. And they just hanged him. I only got this (medal) and an honourable mention for all that!

POST-WAR REFUGEES TO BRITAIN

Although immigration policies were still in force in Britain as well as the United States and other western European countries, the British Government declared its willingness to take in 1,000 young orphaned survivors. The "Boys", as they are known, 732 young survivors — girls as well as boys — were flown, under the auspices of the Jewish organisation, the Central British Fund, to different parts of Britain in 1945 and 1946 from Prague and Munich. Another operation, organised by Rabbi Dr Solomon Schonfeld in 1946, brought over three boatloads of Jewish children, who had been hidden during the war. Despite frantic searches for enough children to make up the

415

thousand "Boys" approved by the Home Office, not enough surviving children could be found to fill the quota.

Apart from such organised groups, considerable numbers of survivors successfully applied for visas and emigrated to western Europe and the United States. For the majority, years of hardship and struggle were ahead as they faced the challenge of integrating into new societies, often without the language of the host state and during a period of post-war austerity and lack of welfare measures. All this underlined with the tragedy of loss on a momentous scale.

An additional trauma existed for refugee and hidden children when surviving members of their families claimed them, often after separations that had lasted for eight years. Although there were happy reunions, many were reunited with complete strangers, sometimes without a common language to ease the way.

Steven Frank
Dutch Jewish child survivor, London
I remember getting on a plane and flying over the Channel and landing at London's main airport, which was Croydon — just the pilot, my mother, my brothers and myself. It landed, we got out, they closed the door and took off, and there was mother and the three of us standing in the middle of the runway of Britain's premier airport. And let me tell you that everything looks a long, long way away when you're only three feet

high and the runway is very, *very* long. My mother was wondering what to do now, what Immigration was going to say.

Then good fortune was with us again because another aircraft landed and a whole lot of people got off and we just joined these people and walked to a sort of Nissen hut kind of place where a man greeted us, stood on a chair and spoke in a language we didn't understand. Apparently we had joined a group of British citizens who had got caught behind enemy lines when war was declared and they were given a bit of VIP treatment now they were back home. The adults were given cigarettes and the children given some sweets, then we were put on a bus and given a tour of London. It sounds absolutely bizarre, doesn't it? Through south London, over Westminster Bridge: "Here is Westminster Abbey, here is the Houses of Parliament, here is Buckingham Palace . . ." Then we saw quite a lot of buildings had been bombed.

Eventually, we landed up in Canons Park, north-west London and we all got out and went into this building and then they started documenting us. While we were there, this policeman — in retrospect, I can only describe him as a "Dixon of Dock Green" character — a man long in his years of retirement called back to do his duty. And he saw these three scrawny, scruffy little children and he took us to his heart. And from him we learnt our first English which was, "Sundaih, Mondaih, Tuesdaih, Wednesdaih, Thursdaih, Fridaih, Saturdaih." And after that he gave each of us sixpence. I remember two of us got the little silver sixpenny piece and one of

417

us a threepenny bit, two pennies and two halfpennies. I remember it so clearly. It was really the first kindness shown by a total stranger to us personally.

Then we started off this business of being medically examined. So we all went to Great Ormond Street Hospital. We had feet as flat as camels' — we had metal things put into our shoes to rebuild the arches. I was sent off to another hospital because I had this worm infestation. I remember we achieved notoriety in Great Ormond Street hospital because at one time we ran amok in the path lab and were forcibly ejected from the hospital. One must remember that we had no sense whatsoever of manners, behaviour, or anything. We were basically like wild animals that had been brought over in a cage to England.

Kitty Hart-Moxon
Polish Jewish survivor, Birmingham

My uncle met us at Dover and he drove us to London and took us to a hotel. On the way to the hotel we didn't quite know what you could actually say to someone you had nothing in common with, and were very quiet. And when we got to the hotel and he took us down to a meal, he said, "Look, there is something I really would like to talk to you about now before we leave for Birmingham." And he said, "Just remember, in my house I do not wish to hear *one word* of what happened to you during the war. I don't want to hear it. I don't want to know. I don't want my girls upset and I never want you to talk about it in my house."

I looked at my mother, and my mother looked at me in total horror because there was absolutely nothing else that we *could* talk about. So immediately there was a kind of gulf between us almost from the moment we met. And later, whenever I made an attempt to speak about what happened, I felt people either turned away because they were embarrassed or they didn't want to hear; or they even said, "We don't want to hear such horrible things."

So I learnt not to talk about it.

Kurt Klappholz
Polish Jewish survivor, London

Shortly after my arrival in London in 1946, I found a fairly general ignorance of what had happened in Europe, particularly to the Jews. A telling experience came at the London School of Economics (LSE) where I had applied to read Economics. The arrangement at the time was that you could either take an intermediate exam at university, or you could take a Higher School Certificate at school. I did the intermediate exam; in order to specialise in economics you had to get a required grade. I had just missed this and went to see the professor in charge, Professor Lionel Robbins — subsequently Lord Robbins. I said something to the effect that I had missed secondary education as I had been in a concentration camp. He looked me in the face and said, "And what education did you receive in the camps?"

Now here was a man who had spent the war in the economic secretariat of the cabinet and who was pro-Semitic to a simply unbelievable extent; I was genuinely amazed by his question. I gave a brief account of what had happened. When I left he had tears in his eyes. I am sure that I owe my career at LSE to him.

Lili Stern-Pohlmann
Polish Jewish child survivor, London

I left Gdynia on a Swedish boat called the SS *Ragne* with Rabbi Dr Solomon Schonfeld's first transport of over 123 children, on a communal visa. Here was this man, a leader of the ultra-orthodox community, who made no fuss whether we were given kosher food or otherwise. To him it was not the means but the end. I was in a fortunate position because I spoke German — so I became his interpreter and the go-between of him and the other children. He wanted us to learn a little English and so would teach us English songs such as "Daisy, Daisy" and patriotic songs like "Land of Hope and Glory", and by the time we docked in London, we sang it perfectly.

We arrived on my birthday, 29 March 1946. What a birthday present! It was like a fairy-tale; and when Tower Bridge opened up in front of us, what a sight! And when we docked, there was a barrage of photographers and press, and an occasional father who had been in General Anders's Army, waiting for his child; there were also people who had agreed to take a child into their family. It was a labour of love for Dr Schonfeld, an *incredible* feat. This was the end of

420

March and of course the weather was not marvellous, but for us the sun was shining all the time, *all* the time.

Roman Halter
Polish Jewish survivor, Windermere

Well, the group of us known as the "Boys" came to England by plane from Prague airfield. We were loaded up and I saw this very tall officer who was talking from the side of his mouth, emitting these very quick sounds and I thought: I will *never* learn that language, it sounds to me like boiling potatoes. He had a pipe in the corner of his mouth and this moustache and spoke terribly fast, but he was very nice and asked his crew to take off their caps and put them on our heads, and we all felt like pilots. There was a tea reception, not a single slice of black bread, all beautifully *white*. We hadn't seen that before. I thought: we have come to a country of milk and honey. And all these lovely ladies were there who fussed about and gave us bread with jam *and* honey. They all smiled at us and we thought we had landed on another planet, then we were taken to Windermere.

Kitty Hart-Moxon
Polish Jewish survivor, Birmingham

I think I shall always remember Christmas 1947. The rule in the hospital where I worked was that when there was a holiday, you had to move out of your room. Well, of course, I had nowhere to go: my mother was working for this couple who were going to their place in Wales and my uncle and aunt and their family had all gone

421

away over Christmas. And I walked out with nowhere to go and virtually no money. I headed for the station and spent that Christmas just sitting in the waiting room with all the down-and-outs.

I think that I was possibly at my lowest at that point because I felt *totally* abandoned: my relatives had abandoned me, the hospital abandoned me, I had nowhere to go, I couldn't get any food. I had nowhere to sleep. Yet, I was in *England* — what was I worried about? I was *free*! And yet that was the most *desperate* time for me. Much more desperate than all the time during the war, because at least I was with people who understood, and I had friends. I walked around the streets and all lights came on in the houses and people were singing carols, you know, and I just — well, the first time I actually cried was that Christmas.

Bertha Leverton
German Jewish refugee, London

The British Jewish community were not as good as they could have been: they didn't come forward in sufficient numbers to take us in, they didn't in many instances realise what was happening to their brethren abroad until it was too late. Some of them were outstandingly wonderful, but on the whole they could have done more. And in many instances, those who took in Jewish refugees treated them as second class, below their own children. One lady told a brilliant young refugee pianist, "This piano is for my children, it is not for you to play on" — jealousy, you see. But some foster parents became very good to their refugee children and some refugees became like brothers and sisters to the foster parents' own children.

Roman Halter
Polish Jewish survivor, London

Education was a food I was thirsting for. During the war the ghetto and camp experience was a terrible education, because one had to learn the art of reading brutality and sadism on people's faces. There were also a lot of things you had to unlearn. According to religious teaching, we thought goodness, charity and innocence were all rewarded, but this wasn't so. One found that however you behaved, you were earmarked for murder. One felt a terrible fear because every situation was a new situation and one became rather like a little bird, looking behind you to see who's there and looking in front of you thinking, "How are we going to survive this minute, this hour, this day?" So the education of the concentration camp, ghettos, slave labour was such a subnormal thing that it does not relate at all to the life we have now. So to learn afresh here (in Britain) became tremendously exciting for me because although I studied architecture, I had so much energy to read and learn, so really the world became a world of sunshine rather than darkness.

Beate "Bea" Green
Polish Jewish woman, London

When I was living in England, my father came to visit us in London from South America where he and my mother had escaped in 1940. This was long after he had

423

been photographed by the Hearst photographer in 1933 after he'd been beaten and paraded through the streets of Munich with that notice around his neck. During lunch one day our middle son said, "Grandpa, your picture is in my history book."

"Let's have a look at it," my father said.

We were all quite anxious how he would react, but when he looked at the picture, he said, "*Ja Ja, sehr interessant*" — "Yes, yes, very interesting."

My husband then asked him what went on in his mind at the time.

My father said, "Very easy — I can tell you that from the moment they started laying into me I had only one thought in my head and that was: I shall survive you all."

And he did.

Hedy Epstein
German Jewish survivor, London

A myth that I carried with me all these years and never questioned was sort of destroyed for me when I listened to the stories of some of the people who, like me, went to England as children but, unlike me, were later reunited with their families. I always envisioned that my reunion with my parents would be a wonderful thing: that I would tell them that I had always tried to be the good child that they had wanted me to be, and that it would be so lovely. I never questioned that. But these reunions were not always happy: the young people returned to difficult lives and stranger-parents. I was told how the parents looked at them like the small children they had been when they left, and continued treating them as young children. This just shattered my myth: maybe it wouldn't have been as wonderful as I had thought.

Ingeborg Sadan
German Jewish refugee, Oldham, England
The train that they were arriving on was the train that all my friends from Oldham High School were coming back to the village on. I couldn't face meeting my parents after all those years with people watching a reunion that was so important. So when the train was due, Bertha and Theo went down to the station and I said, typically, for now I was thoroughly English, "I'll stay here and put the kettle on." I mean, what do you do in England if there is any sort of crisis? — you put the kettle on. Anyway, they took ages coming, and as they came up the slope towards our house, I ran down the steps and then I realised I couldn't speak to them. I'd forgotten every word of German I'd ever known and they couldn't speak much English. There they were, our parents, but they were strangers.

Margareta Burkill
British civilian, Cambridge
The reunion of these children with their parents was a very heartbreaking thing. The children had been here for six to eight years, they had come approximately between ten and fifteen years old. They had been completely Anglicised. They had passed the war on the British side and they were sent back to their parents in,

say, a completely devastated Vienna with the parents still thinking that their reactions would be like continental children, while they had become completely British and of course their German really wanting. And a great many of those children, as soon as they could, came back to England.

I was terribly against it (their return to Europe) because they did it in 1946, far too early, before there was any contact with the parents, and before Vienna and other cities had got on their feet again. But I couldn't do anything about it. It was also very unhappy for the English people who were taking care of the children. You see, my attitude in life with doing the work I have done (with refugee children) is that water is thicker than blood. I have seen this over and over again: the foster parents were absolutely wonderful, they showed so much love and understanding, while often the parents didn't know how to deal with a closed-up adolescent when they got them back.

Agnes Sassoon
Czech Jewish child survivor
I was so astonished, so overcome that I couldn't move from that bed I was lying in. I loved him so dearly and deeply, and his beautiful blue eyes. He was not a big, tall man — a small man, but a very lovely smiley man, you know. I remembered him despite the fact that I wasn't very much with them. Then I saw him and he was in tears and I just couldn't get out a noise, a word. And after I while I was bursting out, "Daddy, daddy, *daddy!*"

426

Helen Stone
Young Polish Jewish woman, London
I flew to Croydon. I remember I wanted to look pretty for my husband and I put mascara on. And when I saw him I started crying and the mascara ran down my face. I never, never cried in the camp — *never!* Not one tear did I cry until I saw my husband.

Stanley Faull
Polish Jewish survivor, Windermere
When I arrived in England with the "Boys", we were taken to Windermere in the Lake District. In Windermere there were wonderful things: huts with single rooms, our own bed and for the first time we had a blanket and a feather bed, and a table and a bath and other facilities and a central eating area with a kitchen and of course we were given treble rations.

This was the time that, when my brother first met me, he asked, "What have you got in your pocket?"

And I said, "I've got some bread."

"Don't they feed you?"

"Oh yes, we had a lovely breakfast, but say the food dries up? I can sustain myself on what I've got."

He couldn't get over it. That was the mentality — that you had to have provisions on you in order to make sure you'll survive.

It was then that he asked me for the very first time, "Now tell me exactly what happened since I saw you last."

And I started to tell him chronologically what had happened from when I said goodbye to him in 1937:

how I remembered my mother crying and what happened in the two years before war started. Then what happened when war started, how the ghetto began and how most of my family left with tens of thousands to go east, directed to the extermination camps, and how I lost contact with my father and sister. And this went on for two hours. His commanding officer was present, and he walked off. And three-quarters of the way through when I was telling him what I had seen: my mother, the horrors, the disease, the barbaric treatment of human beings by the guards to the extent that I thought this normality — I could see there was this man in uniform, a pilot, my elder brother, who cried hysterically.

And I vowed there and then that I would not discuss this with *anybody*. My own *brother* was so emotionally upset that I said to myself: I will never repeat this or discuss it again. And I have found that we can only discuss these things amongst ourselves because they are not *believable* by normal people — the inhumane, the brutal actions of the guards — who, in the main, were not German — were so barbaric and so sadistic that it's unbelievable. Even now I think it must have been a dream because how a nation like Germany — an educated nation much more than the Poles, a civilised nation — how they could get into that situation to destroy the Jews, a race of people, as well as gypsies, cripples — their *own* people, their own political prisoners — to exterminate them as a matter of law, that to me even to this day is incomprehensible.

Epilogue

There are so many questions that you ask yourself: all the pain of losing your family, your parents, losing everything. It's very hard to bring to my mind my parents' and sisters' faces. When you are older you become more sensitive about things that happened in your early age, it preys on your mind, you have time to think about it, you are not just bent on making your way. I didn't cry at all when I was young, so age must have something to do with my emotion today. The Holocaust was the most impressive part of our lives, it was our youth, our lost youth. We will never get rid of it, we will die with it.

THE LOSS

Hedy Epstein
German Jewish survivor, USA
It was only in 1980 when I stood on the ramp in Auschwitz that all of a sudden I realised that there was just no way my parents could have survived. I knew it then and had to accept it. I'm still having difficulties with it. I know they're no longer alive. It's very important, I think, that we have rituals: we view the dead body, we bury the people, we go to the cemetery and visit the grave. We need to see the deceased and know a place we can visit. I have never seen my parents

431

dead; there's no place where I can visit their grave. There is no one to tell me: I saw your parents when they died, or to tell me where they are buried.

Joseph Harmatz
Lithuanian Jewish survivor, Israel

Take my mother: she was taken during the liquidation of the ghetto to Riga, Latvia, and from there to Kaiserwald. From there she was taken to Stutthof in northern Germany where she worked like everyone else, and from there she was taken on a death march. She ended up escaping from there and she survived. But my mother became an orphan because her parents were killed, and she became a widow because of her husband's death; then she lost two sons, my brothers, she didn't know anything about me, and she survived.

But what kind of survival is it? A woman in her forties? I saw a lot of massacres and it's difficult to come back to it: to see bodies spread out, brains outside the heads of people, young couples embracing each other in death, and young mothers with their babies. These are things you *cannot* forget. It stays with you all your life. You run away from it, you don't want to remember, but it comes like that. What we had to see and experience is impossible to explain. It's *impossible*. Can you imagine what it was like for the *mothers!* It's only when I had my children that I could understand what it meant for my mother to be taken away from her children; and if somebody asks me: do I still hate the Germans? I say I hate them more than ever because now I understand it.

Judith Konrad
Hungarian Jewish survivor, UK

My father had four sisters, they all died in the gas chambers. My grandmother was the only one who cheated the gas chambers, she had a heart attack in the wagon and was dead on arrival in Auschwitz. I had young cousins, all girls. One cousin was only six. Two cousins were sisters, one was fifteen, one fourteen. The fifteen-year-old was separated from the fourteen-year-old because the fourteen-year-old looked more mature. The fifteen-year-old was put in the gas chambers with my aunt, my grandfather and my other aunts. The fourteen-year-old girl, because she looked more mature, was taken away and used by the German soldiers very badly. She'd been experimented on and we know that she actually survived Auschwitz. We don't know what happened to her, we only know through a neighbour of theirs that she said she would never return to Hungary because she couldn't face any of her relatives knowing what had happened to her. She couldn't talk about it.

Alicia Adams
Polish Jewish survivor, UK

Not only my parents, my uncles, aunts and my brother, but also all my childhood friends and all the people I knew in my childhood — the *whole population* of Drobhobycz was wiped out, about thirty thousand people, they were all shot. So it wasn't only my closest family being killed, I watched everybody. I watched somebody being killed *every* day — that was part of my childhood.

Roman Halter
Polish Jewish survivor, UK
Out of our Jewish community of eight hundred in Chodecz, only four survived.

Edith Baneth
Czech Jewish survivor, UK
When we talk together at the Holocaust Centre in Hendon, each story of suffering is different: some shorter times, some longer, some in hiding, some taken away and brought up by Catholic families. I've listened to those stories, each so different. One sorrow we all share: last Sunday we remembered all those we had lost, we lit candles for those who died.

When it comes to the point of thinking of the families which we all lost, it can never be put right. They can't be replaced — the second and the third generation still feel it. When we have weddings and *barmitzvahs*, from other sides there are maybe fifty or sixty people from their family. When my son had his *barmitzvah*, and his wedding, there was no family whatsoever — that's the way the second and third generation feel the Holocaust, they miss their family. My son hasn't *experienced* a family life — having uncles, aunts, grandmothers, grandfathers. There is just that *hole*.

How people can say today that it isn't true, and there haven't been six million killed, is just beyond *belief*. Where *are* all those Jews who lived in those European countries? That's what the survivors have in common: they will all tell you that when it comes to one of those weddings or *barmitzvahs*, the hole is so obvious.

Clare Parker
Hungarian Jewish survivor, UK
My Holocaust experience keeps me a child because I had no childhood — you know, growing-up time, being a *child*. My life stopped when I arrived there. And suddenly I'm grown up, without those years in between in which to grow up. And I have this terrible feeling when I see people who are the same age as my mother: why couldn't *she* still be walking, and talking, and be amongst us — just like these other people of that age? It's very hard. It's not kind to feel as I feel: that this person who is as old as my mother would be now, is a *privileged* person.

Adam Adams
Polish Jewish survivor, UK
Paris was a society in upheaval; it was full of survivors of the war and we found we were all equal there. Here in England, everyone was established, everyone had a family, a place to live. I found it very hard to live, especially without the language as well. Somehow our association was mostly with people in the same situation, all survivors. Those who married English

435

girls, and some in the army during the war, established themselves more quickly. English Jewry was completely strange to us, and they also could not understand us because they were normal people. We are abnormal in a way because all that we had gone through comes back to you.

There are so many questions that you ask yourself: all the pain of losing your family, your parents, losing everything. It's very hard to bring to my mind my parents' and sisters' faces. When you are older you become more sensitive about things that happened in your early age, it preys on your mind, you have time to think about it, you are not just bent on making your way. I didn't cry at all when I was young, so age must have something to do with my emotion today. The Holocaust was the most impressive part of our lives, it was our youth, our lost youth. We will never get rid of it, we will die with it.

FORGOTTEN VOICES

Anne Karpf
British Jewish journalist/writer, daughter of survivors, UK
From talking with my mother, what is clear is that there was no consciousness at all in this country about the Holocaust. It seems extraordinary for us today when there is more awareness, but fifty years ago people didn't want to address the subject. I've heard a lot of survivors say that when they tried to

talk about it, people said, "Oh, don't tell us about that, we had the Blitz." My mother told me that she was at a cocktail party and a woman came up and said to her, "What's that on your arm? Is it your telephone number?" And my mother said, "Yes, the telephone number of Auschwitz."

Jan Imich
Polish Jewish survivor, UK

I never spoke to anybody about my experiences. Jean, my wife, didn't know that I was Jewish for something like four or five years after we got married. It was only through psychoanalysis that I slowly started to come out of the shell as it were. I can see us at that particular moment: we were actually on holiday in the country by the sea, sitting on the grass, and I finally blurted it out. And Jean was wonderful about it. But it wasn't for many, many years after, that anybody else knew. It was only in the last ten years that I've been fairly free and easy, telling my best friends. I suppose I was scared in case people turned against me; maybe I was ashamed of being a Jew. God knows why when I think of it now! It could also have been an outcome of the Nazi anti-Semitism. I know for a fact that, for instance, at this point in time, there are just under two hundred Jews living in Krakow, but there are five or six more times that number of Jews that don't *admit* it, people who might even have changed their names; but they *are* there, I know that for a

437

fact because a lot of friends and acquaintances of my friends in Krakow are Jewish but nobody knows.

George Hartman
Czech Jewish survivor, USA

My brother Jan mentioned to me that he was liberated twice: once in 1945 on 11 April in Buchenwald, and the second time by the Imperial War Museum where for the first time he could open himself and talk about his experiences which he had refused to talk about, for whatever reason — whether he couldn't talk, or because he didn't want to — for him it was a traumatic torture to discuss these things.

Steven Frank
Dutch Jewish survivor, UK

We never spoke about the camps at all. Wasn't spoken about very much in those days: that's something that's left behind you. That's finished. You're now going to start a new, happy, joyful life.

One day I was having dinner with some friends and one of the guests was Czech, who had been brought up in Prague and had escaped during the Dubcek era. She was talking about her childhood and how the Communists indoctrinated all the school children about the wonderful things of Communism and the great evil of fascism. Then she went on, "You won't believe this but they took us as little children to what was a concentration camp near Prague called Terezin and they showed us how brutal the Nazis were against the Jews in this camp." Then she said, "You have no idea what an impression this made on a nine-year-old!" And that was the first time I ever said anything in public; I said, "Yes, I *do* know what impression that makes on a nine-year-old, I was there." Well, that was a real stunner — you can imagine! But it was the first time ever that I publicly admitted that I had been a victim of the Holocaust . . .

I'd been very active in amateur dramatics; money was being raised for a new centre for the local church and I was helping in this task. Through the amateur dramatics I got to know quite a lot of people. The vicar once said to me, "Steve, I want to ask you a great favour. You can shoot me down if you like, but in six weeks, during our eleven o'clock service, we're going to be focusing on and saying prayers for Amnesty International. By the altar we're going to have a candle with a barbed wire around it, their logo, and I would like *you* to light it. And I would like you to tell the congregation briefly about your past. Would you be prepared to do this?"

I thought, "Oh God, in front of all those people!" And then I began to think, "Hell's bells boy, all you're asked to do is to go to a church, stand there and say that you are a survivor of the Holocaust. That's so little compared with the *huge* benefit you've had surviving. All these years and years — 1945 to 1995 — you have lived; you've enjoyed marriage, enjoyed a family — those things denied to so many of my contemporaries in Europe. And all they're asking is for me to do this *little* thing."

I said, "Yes, of course I'll do it."

It was the eleven o'clock service, lots of people I knew turned up. They said, "Hello Steve, what are *you* doing here?" We had the service, I lit the candle and we said a little prayer, and then a cup of tea and a chat. People weren't very gushing, they just said, "Oh, that was nice of you to do that, Steve." And the doors suddenly opened, this private part of me opened and I sort of walked through.

Lili Stern-Pohlmann
Polish Jewish survivor, UK

It is not easy to talk, it takes its toll afterwards; it is a terribly painful subject to talk about, but I feel it is a necessity. If we, the last generation, don't talk about it, then that's it. This is a testimony — although mine is possibly nothing compared with those who went through far more harrowing experiences. But I feel I owe it to posterity to talk of what happened to me and my family; I owe it to the children, to the children's children and to history. This thing *happened*. When one reads about Holocaust denial, isn't it our duty to give witness? After us there are no witnesses, there is only the written word.

Leon Greenman
British Jewish survivor, UK

When I tell you things, I am there again. I'm walking, I'm seeing it, and it's coming out of my mouth. It's always there in my mind. If anyone wants to know, I'll talk about it. I made this promise to God that the world should know about it. I don't want people and children to be killed off just because their beliefs are different.

Kurt Klappholz
Polish Jewish survivor, UK

I have never minded talking about my Holocaust experience. When I got out of the camp I could talk about it quite freely, while I know people who simply do not want to talk about it. At the same time, I always discuss these things in a rather academic manner, as a sociologist would, as an observer. I had that attitude in the camp itself, I looked at things in a distant manner.

Halina Kahn
Polish Jewish survivor, UK

My children know my background but they don't want to talk about it. They feel very sad, they see too much in films and they know I suffered, so it's very painful for them. When I mention it, my son says, "I *grew up* with concentration camps, I know everything, stop it, don't talk about it, talk about something else." My grandchildren also: they know I'm from Poland but they don't know the circumstances because their parents don't talk to them about it. Sometimes they ask me, "You were in a camp, what have you done?" I can't give an answer. How can you describe what it was like dying of hunger and work?

Barbara Stimler
Polish Jewish survivor, UK

I don't think it's possible to understand the Holocaust unless you have been there, even Jewish people cannot.

Anne Karpf
British Jewish journalist/writer, daughter of survivors, UK

We felt we had always to be bright and happy, and of course we often weren't; we were often miserable and horrible and I think we felt very guilty about it. Everything got compared with the Holocaust, so if my sister came back from school and said that one of her friends was depressed — it was never she who was depressed, we couldn't go *that* far — my father said, "Depressed? What's *depressed?* She's not in a concentration camp, she's got enough to eat." That was the yardstick.

And I can see it from their viewpoint: if you've been through something so ghastly, everything does pale into insignificance. But for a child growing up, it means their experience isn't legitimate in its own right, it doesn't have its own authenticity, it's constantly being compared with the worst thing you could ever imagine; and it belittles and undermines that experience and you feel that it doesn't have any validity. I think the range of emotions that I was able to experience was very narrow, because if you're not able to feel the negative emotions, then the positive ones don't have much value. There is a bit of dying in living, you have to do the grieving and

442

the mourning and we couldn't do that, it was too dangerous.

Josef Perl
Polish Jewish survivor, UK

I brought my children up to be normal children. I didn't have any hang-ups and I certainly wasn't going to give them any hang-ups. They knew I was in a concentration camp and they knew about them from books. When my daughter was about twelve and my son about seven, we went to Israel. We went to visit Yad Vashem. I didn't feel inclined to see the dead bodies and the camp again, but the children went in. I said to my wife, "Oh, I was a bloody fool! I didn't prepare the children." When they came out they didn't say a word. They both came, each side of me, caught hold of my hands and we walked silently down the pathway. They didn't say a word and we didn't discuss it. My children have no hang-ups, they're happy and well-adjusted, went to university, did well.

Gertrud "Trude" Levi
Hungarian Jewish survivor, UK

In the last two and a half years I have given fifty-eight talks to schoolchildren and university students. I do it because of what is going on in the world today, I believe it's right to fight racial discrimination in every way. I always mention that others have been affected: the Jehovahs and Communists were also persecuted, but Jews were the lowest category, and we're dying out — we are the last generation that can talk about it. I get a tremendous response from the students, wonderful letters. One girl, for instance, wrote, "I promise you that if anything like this happens where I am, I am not going to be a bystander even if it costs my life."

THE LEGACY

Lili Stern-Pohlmann
Polish Jewish survivor, UK
In some way perhaps our nervous system is impaired, more so in some people than in others. My mother, for instance, she would never cry in a crisis, but she would easily cry about her little boy who perished; there wasn't a day that she wouldn't talk about her lost child, and that was for over sixty years. Maybe because I was younger, I did not experience the same degree of pain — your whole life is in front of you as a child. I never had the feeling — even at the worst, the most dangerous time — that anything could happen to *me*. We children were not so broken by the pride that was taken away from people, from the lack of human dignity — that's what the Germans managed to achieve so well: to make people devoid of their dignity, whereas a child hasn't yet developed that degree of dignity.

Marsha Segall
Lithuanian Jewish survivor, UK
What happened to my hands and feet, due to the frostbite I experienced on the death march, has had a

444

very deep effect on me until today. I am left with three fingers and a thumb on my left hand and just a thumb on my right hand. I had half my toes amputated on the left foot, and on the right foot, everything; also, on the soles of my feet, I have ulcers which are still open today. Some people can get over these things better, some can't. I belong to the second category. I think hands, especially for a woman, are very important — it's *expression*, it's *everything*. I couldn't tell what my husband felt, he never discussed it, neither did my children — I mean they accepted me as I was, they didn't know me any other way, but John did. Some people can't keep it back, and I hear it even now from people who knew me well, who I didn't see for forty years or so, who say, "Good God! What did they *do* to you?" I find it most difficult to meet new people who don't know anything about me.

Rena Quint
Polish Jewish survivor, Israel

There are times when you don't want to think about all the things that happened, and you think that you're properly normal and like everybody else; and then you go to a doctor and the doctor says, "Tell me about your medical history, anybody in your family had heart history?"

"I don't know."

"Anybody die of cancer?"

"I don't know."

"Or diabetes?"

"I don't know."

"What do you mean, 'I don't know'? You look like a woman who *should* know these things."

And you'd like to leave it at that but you realise you can't and you have to say, "Look, I have no history because all these people were killed before they had a chance to get all these diseases." So things like that happen very often and you have to explain it.

Jan Hartman
Czech Jewish survivor, France
Yes, I have suffered physical effects from my experience: my back, from a bad beating and my toes, from frostbite. But I think the psychological effects are worse. They are worse because it reflected upon the education of my children. I felt that they might have to face, some time in their life, a SS man, and that they should get through that business better than I did. So I took the place of a SS man, treating my children very roughly. It was all well meant, but today, looking at it from far away, I see in it a reflection of what the SS and the Germans left with me.

I never spoke to my children about my experiences: first of all it was a shameful thing, it remained with me that way. Whatever they know, they know from my wife, and my wife doesn't know much. I don't think I would be embarrassed to talk to my grandchildren about it, the thing is so diluted in them. My aim throughout was to protect my children. I don't want them to be weakened. I think that my children do suspect that there is a heavy heritage somewhere and it may be better to hear the truth.

This was a trip to Dante's Hell and if there is one thing one could master it was that we *must* survive because no one can *imagine* it. I consider what has happened was an exclusive thing in the sense that for the first time in human history — with the exception of the Armenians — this was done on an industrial scale, not just because it was to Jews because I have seen many gypsies too, but the *unique* thing that happened under the Germans is that it was done on an industrial scale.

Clare Parker
Hungarian Jewish survivor, UK
When I came to England and lived in Birmingham, we lived near a Jewish school which my daughter attended. The children were wearing the Star of David in all shapes and sizes and she wanted one. I bought her one on a little silver chain, but said to her, "Don't wear it anywhere else, on buses or other places." And this poor child, from five years old, couldn't understand what the problem was. Even when she was older, I couldn't explain what had happened to me, and I felt that anyone wearing a Star of David might be in danger; it's only recently that I don't feel that.

Adam Adams
Polish Jewish survivor, UK
Hunger and fear are the most fantastic weapons which Hitler was a master of. To be hungry *slowly* — not just to miss breakfast or to have the day of fast, but to be

447

really hungry, to have less and less, day by day, month by month; so that at the end you only think about one thing: to get something to eat. And the fear is the same: the ultimate thing they can do is to kill you; but the pain, the *fear* is the worst thing. You can get anything out of people if you use these two weapons, and they were torturing a nation.

Taube Biber
Polish Jewish survivor, UK

People read about the Holocaust, but it doesn't have the same impact as what you *experience*. You can only imagine to a certain extent. You lived with fear the whole time. I would say fear is still in my system. I don't like remote places. I can't bear silence.

I always have the radio on. I don't like going to places where I can't see houses and people. I have to be with people. Also food: I can't waste a piece of bread or a potato. Whatever is left over is used the next day.

Helen Stone
Polish Jewish survivor, UK

For me bread is the most important thing, still is. Bread is *Holy*. Do you know, if I drop bread on the floor, I pick it up and kiss it. It is like a religious Jew: if you drop a prayer book you kiss it. For me it is the bread I kiss if I drop it. I will cross the road if I see on the other pavement a piece of bread. I will pick it up and put it on the fence so that birds can have it, so that people can't walk over the bread. Bread is Holy.

Alicia Adams
Polish Jewish survivor, UK

I think my Holocaust experience definitely affected my work (as a painter) especially in the beginning. My pictures were very dark, very blue; they also had a great deal of feeling. I have always painted more with feeling than with the knowledge, although I had a very good training at St Martin's. Art is really about communication and I didn't want to express my feelings in words; it was much easier to paint, to put on canvas what I didn't want to say in words — about parting from my family, about my brother, a wonderful brother for whose loss I can never forgive the Germans.

Marsha Segall
Lithuanian Jewish survivor, UK

That experience changed my life completely. First of all I was very ambitious about education, about degrees, about what I was going to do with my life. I had a very good life, everything in front of me, and everything was *shattered*. Beliefs in life were shattered, everything. To be honest, I never made roots after that. I don't have roots. Sometimes I don't know where I belong. Even now, going to Israel where I feel good, it's all right for a holiday — a month, two months — but to live? I don't know whether I could change like that. You can change so many times and no more, and age doesn't help. I feel

449

now, with age, broken, very much so. The older I get the worse I get.

George Hartman
Czech Jewish survivor, USA

In one way it was fortunate to go to a concentration camp because it changed my life, it changed my outlook. I went through an incredible period of three years when I faced life and death and I emerged a different person. Had that not happened then maybe I would have been an architect in Czechoslovakia. I would probably have been spoiled, and I probably would have been narrow-minded, and I would have lived in another world. And looking back, the price I paid — which was a very dear price — had its rewards in giving me a much richer life today and a perspective on what is important and what is not important. I tried to live as normal a life as I could, which I think was a very healthy attitude, because if you're preoccupied with this horrible past, you really can't live a normal existence. So the only time I would bring it back into my normal existence was as a positive influence saying: this cannot be as bad as a concentration camp.

Alfred Huberman
Polish Jewish survivor, UK

Suffering has taught me that as bad as things are, they are not as bad as they could be. I could sleep *anywhere*. People don't know what discomfort really is, what hunger and insecurity and degradation does to you. You weren't worth *anything*, you were disposable, they could do anything they liked to you.

Bertha Leverton
German Jewish survivor, UK

There were some wonderful people who worked on behalf of those of us who came on the *Kindertransport* to Britain: Jewish, non-Jewish, churches, lots of groups and we are very grateful to them. But I believe that we have also given something to the people who sheltered us. We have given ourselves and made contributions in many fields: education, medicine and many other areas. Also, it must be stressed that many of the boys, as soon as they came of age, joined the British Army, and the girls the Land Army, as well as other services. And after the war, many became interpreters in Germany when the war trials started.

Sir Hans Krebs
German Jewish survivor, UK

I'm thoroughly indebted to Britain for giving me the opportunity of getting here, I feel it every day. At one time I had the opportunity to express my sense of indebtedness. This happened in the 1960s when an organisation of refugees decided to collect a fund and present it to the British Academy for scholarships or other purposes, as a token of gratitude. I was chosen to present the cheque as a very small token of gratitude by refugees — I think it was about ninety thousand pounds. In a brief speech, I expressed the feeling which was shared by many, as they told me afterwards, that it was not merely that we were given shelter, but really given a new *home*. Because a home is not necessarily where one is born or brought up, but where one strikes roots. We had struck roots in Britain and could fulfil ourselves doing the things we wanted to do.

Edith Baneth
Czech Jewish survivor, UK

The Holocaust Centre in Hendon is the only place where I feel I belong and most of the people who go there will tell you exactly the same thing — that although we feel no sense of belonging to those countries we came from, we don't fully belong here. We are not quite English even if we live just like the people here. The *Kindertransport* people who came when they were small and speak English without an accent, they are absolutely English, they just have the bitterness of not growing up in their own homes and of being orphans; but they are completely British. But survivors have accents from our mother language; that doesn't matter at the centre: nobody asks you, "Which country do you come from? When did you come to England?", because we are all alike.

Bertha Leverton
German Jewish survivor, UK

There is a question about who is a victim of the Holocaust. We, the *Kinder* (refugee children), feel that in a way we are not really part of the Survivor Centre (in Hendon), and they also feel that we are not part of them. There is a degree of suffering which they experienced which of course we didn't. They went through the Holocaust itself and those who attend the Centre now were not older than about sixteen or seventeen at the time, and their experiences were so dreadful and traumatic that we cannot share in them. So we feel apart from them because we were blessed with our lives here in England and we're very grateful to the English people.

Nicole David
Polish Jewish survivor, UK

When I would talk about the war, the food, the bombing, whatever, people would say: what do you *mean* about the war, you're lucky, you survived; anyway you were so young, you probably don't remember. We hidden children *were* lucky: we weren't in concentration camps and, of course, how *can* one compare? We can never get into the hierarchy of suffering. But I always say to people: this is not what it's about. It's about understanding how people survived during the war, about the *whole* story of the Holocaust: that besides the camps, there was the fear of having to find hiding places, of how to hide, the separation from parents, of not having a childhood, not having had a youth. It is important for us hidden children to validate our story, to recognise that we have been marked by the war, that we have suffered. It is also important to tell the next generation. We

453

are the youngest survivors of the Holocaust, our story is part of the full story. It's important that this is known as well as the story of the camp survivors. We need to tell future generations in the hope that it will not happen again.

John Richards
Austrian Jewish survivor, UK

The only one that cared for me in England was this kind Quaker lady. I can see now that wherever I went, I was the bad apple in the barrel. Most of the Jewish people who came over had some care given; other boys and girls who went into homes were adopted and kindly treated; but I was a lad on my own, there was nobody to check on me. Until the time I went to London and met this lady later in the war, and who helped me later on in life, I knew nobody. I had no contact with any Jewish or refugee organisation, I missed out on a lot of things.

I have often wished that when I came to England I could have been brought up in the Jewish faith, and been *barmitzvahed*; but the Catholic faith was imposed on me; I was treated like a Catholic and I didn't want this. I have nothing against the faith, but being forced to go to church turned me against it. I still say: if there's a God up there, why did he let my mum and dad, my brother and my sister be persecuted and killed? I do believe in the hereafter and when I die, somewhere out there in this great, vast universe, I'm going to meet my mum and dad, my brother and my sister, my grandfather and grandmother. I believe this.

George Hartman
Czech Jewish survivor, USA

At first my brother and I believed that because of our Jewish ancestry and the way people looked at us and the way we looked at ourselves, we couldn't get away from being Jewish. But we felt that our children must get away from it, that we would never marry a person of Jewish origin — that we'd dilute the Jewishness through the children and the children of the children. We were both willing to sacrifice this tradition and culture to avoid any future persecution which I'm still convinced is going to happen.

Roman Halter
Polish Jewish survivor, UK

As for my sense of being Jewish, the persecution had no effect on this — it's like a blackbird that can't have white feathers — we were *Jewish*. There were other wonderful birds that flew around and we were Jewish, simply that. During the war, the desire to survive came first, the Jewishness was relegated far down. The religious belief was as much as one held within one, but nothing like prayers, no rituals really, no celebrations of certain holidays — every day was the same.

When talking to some orthodox people they said, "Tell me, if it came to renouncing Jewishness and becoming a Gentile, or losing your life, you would rather lose your life wouldn't you?"

I would say, "Oh no, I would choose *life* every time."

And that was the feelings of those around me, although there were a few exceptions: one carried the light of God within one, but discovered that one was powerless against the brutalities.

Jacob Pesate
Romanian Jewish survivor, UK
I heard of the tragedy of what happened to the Jewish people as soon as I got out of the Soviet Union at the end of the war, and what happened to our family and friends. For me, personally, religion meant the following conflict: for my father, it helped him to survive in Transnistria; but I felt that after what happened — that God allowed so many millions to be killed for no reason — this made me think very much about religion and I didn't identify with it any more.

Helen Stone
Polish Jewish survivor, UK
Belief in God? That's a difficult question. It's hard to believe in God if you went to Auschwitz. Why am I alive, and my father, who did so much good for others, didn't have a chance? He went straight to the gas. We used to say, "If we are his chosen people, why didn't he choose somebody else?" But I am very Jewish. I'm proud to be Jewish, but I'm not religious.

Taube Biber
Polish Jewish survivor, UK

My faith was not affected by my experience. I still believe. All I can say is that my survival is destiny. We can ask questions, but we get no answers. Like the late Rabbi Hugo Gryn said, "People were asking, 'Where is God?' But God was asking, where were *you*?" So there are a great many questions but no answers.

Juozas Aleksynas
Lithuania

No, I never spoke about it (killing Jews) after the war. It was a big shame to talk of this. Everything seemed so disgusting. I do not blame anything or anybody except God, if he exists — why he lets such things happen on this earth, why he lets the killing of innocent people happen.

Rena Quint
Polish Jewish survivor, Israel

I went to Poland with my husband on this *March for the Living* — this is a group of young people in the last year of high school who go to the different concentration camps. Majdanek was a very difficult camp. I said, "I'm not going to cry, I'm *not* going to cry," and the two of us hung on to each other. And when we came out, in the field we saw youngsters with Israeli, *Jewish* flags, waving them. And I burst out crying and said, "Hitler thought he was going to wipe us out but look: here is our youth, and they are carrying these flags, and they are proud Jews — and Hitler, you *didn't* win."

Thank God we have an Israel now. We have a place, and if Israel had been born a few years before so that Jews had a place to run to, it would have made such a huge difference for survivors, and what a difference it would have made for victims who possibly *could* have survived. Unfortunately, it wasn't there, that's why I feel so very strongly about making sure that Israel *is* safe and *is* free and is a refuge for anyone who needs it.

Hedy Epstein
German Jewish survivor, USA
It shames me what is going on today in Israel vis-à-vis the Palestinians. Very often people don't see the difference between the Israeli Government and Jews. And I find myself in a very defensive position saying, "I'm not like that." And it's not comfortable being in that position. I'm in an organisation which is called *New Jewish Agenda* which is a progressive Jewish organisation which since its inception in 1980 has been for a two-state solution as the only way to bring about peace in that area.

FORGIVING AND FORGETTING

Roman Halter
Polish Jewish survivor, UK
There was a terrible strain imposed on those Jews running the Lodz Ghetto. It is important not to

accuse Rumkowski and others who were running the ghetto, but to see it now as a totality of what was imposed from Hitler and Himmler down to other SS. They exploited the Jewish people, they robbed them of everything they possessed, and it suited the German hierarchy to keep Lodz Ghetto until the middle of 1944 as a place which gave rich pickings, both in the factories which produced things for the *Wehrmacht*, and also by robbing every Jew who came into the ghetto of all the valuables they had. So I don't really hold it against Rumkowski and the other ghetto leaders. It was terrible when he said voluntarily, "Please give up your children," but these times were abnormal, so horrendous, that one cannot rationalise in the circumstances in which we live today, how people behaved and what they did.

Kurt Klappholz
Polish Jewish survivor, UK
Returning to this episode today, I confront this puzzle: how the policy, the murder of the Jews could have been carried out? That policy could not conceivably have assisted the German war effort, it *couldn't* have done. I'm prepared to believe that the few top Nazis were mad on the subject, simply insane; but one can hardly suppose that *all* those who participated were similarly mad. Also, Hitler did not treat German top people the way Stalin did in Russia; they didn't have the same reason to fear him the way their counterparts in Russia feared Stalin. So I keep asking myself: were

there some people on whose desks memoranda landed, who looked at them horrified? Did they think: have we gone completely mad? We're in the middle of a life and death struggle and we're being asked to divert resources to this insane policy! To me this is a genuinely puzzling question — not on humanitarian, or moral grounds — but if you were a top civil servant or top army person, you surely must have said: this is madness. I'm left with this question.

Michael Lewis
British Jewish NCO, UK

Something had changed for me after I'd seen Belsen camp. Although I'd seen terrible things of war, to have treated ordinary people like this! And there were so many theories and reasons as to who was responsible. And everybody seemed to point a finger around until the finger came round full circle. I had to think hard about it. Why the Germans? They had their own culture, their own civilisation, they produced Beethoven, great scientists, how could it be? Then a sort of revelation came to me, penetrating these terrible scenes, to make me think of all the stories I'd heard about persecutions from my mother and father; here they were, true. But this was a sort of death by administration, impersonal: so many thousands of people, so many cars provided on the trains. And then, were the Germans alone to blame? Why were not the railway lines to the camps bombed? Where were the religious institutions of the world? They knew what was going on. We had heard rumours, we had known. And surely these people would have known better than us ordinary people. And they had been silent.

Hedy Epstein
German Jewish survivor, USA

I continued to hate the Germans across the board with the exception of those who would have been too young at the time. I didn't buy products made in Germany, if I met somebody who was of an age and German, I would very aggressively ask them, "Where were *you*? What did you do?" But in early May 1970, it became public knowledge that as part of the Vietnam war — which I had opposed from the start — the US was carpet-bombing Cambodia. I became very angry that we were doing this and protested against it.

Suddenly this triggered something across the oceans and across the years and I thought: if the Germans had done the kinds of things I'm doing here, marching and sending telegrams of protest to my President and congressional representatives, if the Germans had done that, they would have ended up in a concentration camp, been severely punished, lost their lives; so, how can I condemn a whole nation for not being heroes? Would I have been a hero if my life were at stake, my family's lives at stake? So all of a sudden this hatred that I had carried far too long disappeared.

461

Aliza Shapiro
German Jewish survivor, UK

I feel it is very important for us Jews to understand the children, the new generation in Germany and what their shame is about; what they need to work out of their system because *they* are not guilty, but they carry the guilt like a second generation of Holocaust survivors carry the shame.

Warren Mitchell
British Jewish actor, UK

How could a country that produced Beethoven, Schiller, Heine, Goethe — some of the greatest artists in the world — produce that kind of horror! It is one of the greatest mysteries to me. I went to Germany only once since the war to see a play and I was uncomfortable because I was automatically putting a SS or *Gestapo* hat on anyone of my age. But there is a new generation, several new generations since the war. We hope the Holocaust will never be forgotten and we hope that the European Union will overcome these problems.

Michael Etkind
Polish Jewish survivor, UK

I read about the Nuremberg Trials in the papers and followed what was going on. But I felt there were *millions* of Austrians and Germans that took part in the murders, not thousands, but millions, and here were a few dozen on trial, and because of this I felt the futility of it all: what was the sense of punishing not even one thousandth of the guilty. It wasn't justice, it was just making a gesture and because of this I didn't pay much attention to it. But I remember in the *Picture Post* there was correspondence going on for weeks. The letters were saying, "Well, we're Christians, we should forgive the crimes," and so on and so on. There was one letter written by a teacher which said, "What right do we have to forgive, only God and the dead have the right to forgive." Somehow that expressed what I would have liked to have said.

Bertha Leverton
German Jewish survivor, UK
I must stress one point though: everybody in the whole world closed their doors. Germany was going to let us go until October 1941 and the world closed its doors. If they had opened their doors, they could have saved European Jewry; after all there are so many parts of America and Brazil and Australia and Canada that had plenty of room for Jewish communities to be established. That is a guilt that the whole world has to bear, as well as Germany. And if Britain had done what it could have done: opened the gates of what was then Palestine, they could have saved European Jewry. But they did more than any other country in the world in saving Jews, and that record stands.

Sir Hans Krebs
German Jewish survivor, UK
Many people in Britain were extremely helpful when refugees arrived in the 1930s. The Home Office in the earlier stages put on many restrictions which I think

were unduly severe. They were prompted by unemployment in this country as many members of the general public, especially in the working class population where unemployment was greatest, objected that people should be coming in and taking jobs away. But I think on the whole this was a very narrow viewpoint because quite a few of the refugees in fact created jobs, they introduced new industries.

Kurt Klappholz
Polish Jewish survivor, UK

As regards blaming onlookers, it depends who one is talking about: political leaders such as Roosevelt and Churchill I think deserve blame and I'm prepared to blame them. That is not to say that acts of omission deserve the same moral censure as acts of commission, but nevertheless that happened. As regards individuals, that's a different story. What, for example, did I do to help people during the genocide in Cambodia? What did I do to help people in Biafra? Individuals who act individually can't contribute to the amelioration of such situations, it just isn't within their power. So far as individual Germans are concerned, apart from the sadists, it seems pointless to blame such people; that is why I regard collective guilt as a morally misguided notion.

Josef Perl
Polish Jewish survivor, UK

When I look back on my life it's always from the periphery — from the outside looking in. I have witnessed the world unhinge itself momentarily, and when I wake up from my nightmares, I ask myself: am I really that little boy that saw all this? I wake up and I'm wet through. Subconsciously, I know I'm safe, but the older I get, the worse it gets, it eats me up. Sometimes I don't want to go to sleep — it's something that will never go away, this is how you live. But I count my blessings every day: be positive, be happy, share your life. Never in my wildest dreams did I think that I would have children and grandchildren to love and to love me.

Steven Frank
Dutch Jewish survivor, UK
One of the things I'm often asked by the children when I give talks in schools is, "What's the worst thing that happened to you in the camps?" I always tell them that the worst thing that happened was that I learnt to hate.

Ignacz Rüb
Hungarian Jewish survivor, UK
An assistant professor at the university was also in the camps; he wasn't Jewish, but a social democrat. One day he called us together and said, "Look, I know what it means to you to study in the German language. I know about the camps, I was there too. I know how you feel, but you know if you hate someone, the one you hate isn't hurt, he doesn't know about it, he doesn't care. But when you hate it hurts you. And if you hate, you cannot judge things correctly; try not to hate, don't forget, you cannot forget, but don't hate." You know,

465

I've never forgotten that fellow. Later in my business, I had machines from Germany and friends in Germany. I don't hate. The only thing that makes me very uncomfortable is when I see an old German and I think: what did you do in the war?

Magdelena Kusserow Reuter
German Jehovah's Witness survivor, Spain
We forgave, yes. We never hate people, just the bad things, the bad actions. After the war I married a man who had been in the *Hitler Jugend* and had served in the German army. I met him after he had become a Jehovah's Witness.

Max Dessau
Polish Jewish survivor, UK
You can forgive, but you cannot forget. I get nightmares even today which my wife can vouch for. In the middle of the night she will wake me up. I get *terrible* nightmares. So how can you forget? You just can't forget. It is impossible to forget.

Kurt Klappholz
Polish Jewish survivor, UK
What I would like to stress with all the emphasis at my command is, even though I was deprived of liberty — which on any reckoning was in a monstrous way — my personal experience, looking back, doesn't really bother me very much. It wasn't a pleasant two years and ten months (interned in fourteen different concentration camps), it would be silly to say it was;

466

but what I *can't* get over is what happened to my parents and the rest of my family. That is a nagging wound which doesn't seem to get better with the passage of time; in fact to this very day I can't really bring myself to think about the way in which they died. It seems to have been a pathological policy, and the effects on the victims — well, they don't bear thinking about.

John Richards
Austrian Jewish survivor, UK

No money on earth is going to compensate me for the loss of my family, the loss of my home. No, I will *never* come to terms with the loss of my family. I have sleepless nights; I then get to a period of calm. Then suddenly you read an article in the paper about how when they opened up between east and west, the neo-Nazis were burning people out of their homes and desecrating Jewish cemeteries; and you wake up in the night and think: are they going to be stupid enough to let it happen again? Then the past comes over you and you lie in bed and you think about your family and all you lost, and you start to cry. You think: I've had six children, what would my father say if he saw my family now? How would he react? What would my grandson say to his great-grandfather? How would life have been different to what it is now? Then you grow calm again. Then you suddenly hear of the ethnic cleansing in Bosnia and the whole process starts again. You lie there and think: what can I do as an individual? I wish I were well up in politics, or that I were a younger man so that

467

I could go out and help people. You think of these things the whole time — the ugly past rears its head.

Anne Karpf
British Jewish journalist/writer, daughter of survivors, UK

Krakow is the most beautiful place, I fell in love with it — the main square and all the cafés, I just adored that. I felt that my family had lost all this, this was part of my family's history and culture and it was all lost. I'd never felt English, I've spoken to countless children of survivors and refugees and they all feel the same. We have such a strong sense of our culture of origin; in terms of food, in terms of music, of language — we spoke Polish before we spoke English. So going to Poland for me was astonishing in that respect. I started to speak Polish there, it just felt very familiar; there was something so rich about the culture and one has to mourn this sense of rupture I feel so acutely. That's what the loss is: the loss of continuity. Maybe it would all have died out, but it was murdered along with the people: the culture was murdered.

Kurt Klappholz
Polish Jewish survivor, UK

There is a very strange sensation going back to a town and finding there is no one you knew. I broke down on one occasion — that is when I visited the Jewish cemetery. The Jews who had returned to Bielsko Biala from Russia engraved the names of those family members, who had been killed by the Germans, on the

468

gravestones of those who had died in the normal way, before the war. You would see gravestones with — God knows how many — names on them. It's not that I didn't know this, but somehow the sight of looking at gravestone after gravestone with this series of names on each is why I suddenly went aside and wept.

The other thing that impressed me was that not a single building which had been a Jewish community place had been marked as such; there was no public sign that there had been a Jewish community there. The temple had been burned down on 4 September 1939, the day after the Germans arrived; now there was a little paved garden, but no plaque which said the Jewish Temple had stood there. I was saddened that there should have been such a complete erasure of our Jewish community.

Halina Kahn
Polish Jewish survivor, UK
We are the last survivors, we are no longer young, who after us will tell? This is why we make testimony. This was something that was not supposed to happen in the twentieth century: it was absolutely systematic murder.

Ruth Foster
German Jewish survivor, UK
I have been asked many times when I tell my story, "Could you ever forget?" Then I tell them, "It is as when you stand on a lake and you throw a stone into the lake. First you have large ripples, then the ripples get smaller and smaller still, then the surface is calm,

469

but the stone is still on the bottom. That is the same with me and that sums me up. I appear like an ordinary human being, but the stone of my experience is still lying in my heart."

Sound Archive,
Imperial War Museum

List of Contributors

18275 Adam Adams
18670 Alicia Adams
16672 Wolf Albert
15441 Norna Alexander
22065 Dennis Avey
18582 Else Baker
16595 Andrew Bakowski
19779 Rudi Bamber
17474 Edith Baneth
16506 Ludwig Baruch
26752 Anna Bergman
17514 Taube Biber
14863 Christabel
        Bielenberg
15367 Peter Bielenberg
9122 Esther Brunstein
4532 Dr Edith Bulbring
15745 Abram 'Adam' Bulwa
4588 Margareta Burkill
19586 John Chillag
9182 Leslie Clarke
14582 Stephen Dale

9538 Janina David
15431 Nicole David
9236 Max Dessau
8996 John Dixey
17291 John Dobai
10623 Premysl Dobias
8942 Zdenka Ehrlich
14763 Gisela Eisner
16484 Herbert Elliott
12397 Hedy Epstein
21610 Bill Essex
10406 Michael Etkind
19783 Danny Faulkner
18272 Stanley Faull
16594 John Fink
19782 Ruth Foster
22600 Steven Frank
10589 F Gilliard
10348 Szmulek Gontarz
16784 Beate 'Bea' Green
9274 Leon Greenman
9280 Hugo Gryn (Rabbi)

4644	Sergei Hackel	17558	Gertrud 'Trude' Levi
16632	Kitty Hart-Moxon	15626	Jane Levy
17183	Roman Halter	4833	Michael Lewis
17636	Leslie Hardman		Margot (anon)
18221	Joseph Harmatz	16785	Harry Lowit
19984	George Hartman	18682	Harry Miller
18557	Jan Hartman	16636	Eva Mitchell
18488	Daniella Hausman	19856	Warren Mitchell
9091	Martin Hoffman	17184	Preben Munch Nielson
16825	Michael Honey		
18050	Alfred Huberman	17559	Margie Oppenheimer
10380	Hannah Hyde	19795	Albin 'Alex' Ossowski
16821	Jan Imich	19794	Maria Ossowski
18671	Janine Ingram	14864	Clare Parker
18437	Daniel 'Danko' Ivin	12597	Martin Parker
16838	Ezra Jurmann	2049	Helen Pelc
19857	Halina Kahn	17883	Josef Perl
17428	Anne Karpf	19025	Jacob Pesate
13913	Jorgen Von Führen Keiler	16703	Rena Quint
		17355	John Richards
9425	Kurt Klappholz	17974	Ignacz Rüb
17602	Edyta Klein-Smith	17290	Ingeborg Sadan
9092	Freddie Knoller	15623	Charles Salt
22577	Jerry Koenig	15622	Ryvka Salt
4498	Hans Krebs (Sir)	12526	Halina Sand
19946	Peter Kronberg	9093	Agnes Sassoon
19793	Magdelena Kusserow Reuter	9164	Marsha Segall
		18222	Aliza Shapiro
11914	Anita Lasker-Wallfisch	17885	Jack Shepsman
20998	John Lawrence	18672	John Silberman
17310	Bertha Leverton	17177	Susan Sinclair

17340 Lili Stern-Pohlmann   15442 Jim Wheeler
17475 Barbara Stimler   10110 Gerda Williams
19675 Helen Stone   9192 Abraham Zwirek
3839 Clive Teddern

United States Holocaust Memorial Museum, Department of Oral History

List of Contributors

RG-50-444-011	ANTONIE KROKOVA
RG-50-444-022	ANTONIN DANIEL
RG-50-473-010	JUOZAS ALEKSYNAS
RG-50-486-0009	GUDRUN KÜBLER
RG-50-486-0010	Dr HELMUT KÜBLER
RG-50-486-0011	FRITZ MOSES
RG-50-486-0013	Dr FRIEDRICH CARL SCHEIBE
RG-50-488-006	STEFAN KUCHAREK
RG-50-488-017	ALEKSANDRA NIZIE
RG-50-488-0068	ZYGMUNT SIKORA

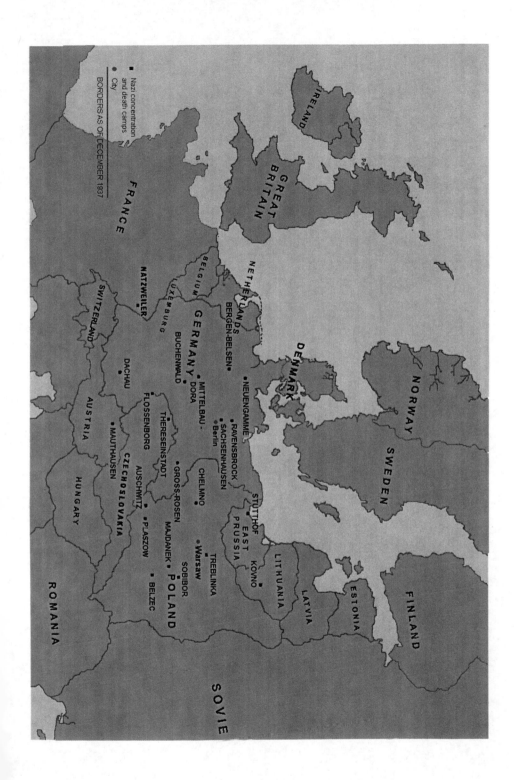

BORDERS AS OF DECEMBER 1937

■ Nazi concentration
and death camps
● City

IRELAND

GREAT
BRITAIN

FRANCE

BELGIUM
LUXEMBURG
NETHERLANDS

SWITZERLAND

NATZWEILER ■

DACHAU
■

BERGEN-BELSEN ■

BUCHENWALD
■

GERMANY

● NEUENGAMME

● RAVENSBROCK
● SACHSENHAUSEN
● Berlin

● MITTELBAU -
DORA

FLOSSENBORG
■

AUSTRIA

MAUTHAUSEN
■

THERESEINSTADT
■

CZECHOSLOVAKIA

AUSCHWITZ
■

HUNGARY

ROMANIA

DENMARK

NORWAY

SWEDEN

FINLAND

ESTONIA

LATVIA

LITHUANIA

KOVNO
●

EAST
PRUSSIA

STUTTHOF
■

GROSS-ROSEN
■

CHELMNO
■

PLASZOW
■

MAJDANEK ■

SOBIBOR
■

BELZEC
■

TREBLINKA
■

● Warsaw

POLAND

SOVIE

Operation Millennium

Eric Taylor

"Operation Millennium" was the terrible culmination of months of pressure from "Bomber" Harris to get this new and deadly strategy accepted. It was an extraordinary feat of organisation involving 1048 bombers, over 6000 aircrew and 53 British airfields. To ensure success, "maximum effect" was the order. The Royal Air Force waged a campaign against any airmen who showed faltering commitment, ruthlessly trying them by court martial.

The atmosphere of night bomber stations is vividly recalled — the comradeship, the pity and the fear. The raid on Cologne is remembered by the crews of Bomber Command and the unlucky citizens of Cologne who endured the night raids. Eric Taylor has interviewed Britons and Germans, whose eye-witness accounts testify to the horror and heroism on both sides.

ISBN 978-0-7531-5665-0 (hb)
ISBN 978-0-7531-5666-7 (pb)

My Life as a Spy

Leslie Woodhead

In the spring of 1956, 18-year-old Leslie Woodhead received a summons to serve Her Majesty. National Service signalled the end of boyhood. But it was the beginning of his "life as a spy".

An only child, living above a shop in post-war Halifax, Woodhead grew up with austerity and secrets. But nothing prepared him for the comically bleak RAF training camps he now found himself in, nor the isolated Joint Services School for Linguistics on the east coast of Scotland. Here he was trained by a colourful staff of émigrés, who taught a course of total immersion in Russian for purposes not always clear to their pupils. A posting to an ex-Luftwaffe base in a war-scarred Berlin provided only partial explanations. In the ruins of a city gripped by espionage and paranoia, he discovers adulthood and his vocation as an observer and documenter of people.

ISBN 978-0-7531-9366-2 (hb)
ISBN 978-0-7531-9367-9 (pb)